The Will of the People

THE WILL

of the

PEOPLE

The Revolutionary Birth
of
America

T. H. BREEN

The Belknap Press of Harvard University Press
CAMBRIDGE, MASSACHUSETTS
LONDON, ENGLAND
2019

Design by Dean Bornstein

Library of Congress Cataloging-in-Publication Data

Names: Breen, T. H., author.
Title: The will of the people : the revolutionary birth of America / T. H. Breen.
Description: Cambridge, Massachusetts : The Belknap Press of Harvard University
Press, 2019. | Includes bibliographical references and index.
Identifiers: LCCN 2019007162 | ISBN 9780674971790 (alk. paper)
Subjects: LCSH: United States—History—Revolution, 1775–1783—Social aspects. |
United States—History—Revolution, 1775–1783—Committees of safety. | Middle
class—Political activity—United States—History—18th century. | Working class—
Political activity—United States—History—18th century.
Classification: LCC E209 .B775 2019 | DDC 973.3/11—dc23 LC record available at
https://lccn.loc.gov/2019007162

For Lady Susan, once again

CONTENTS

The Will of the People

INTRODUCTION
Revolutionary Voices

We encounter them daily, if we care to look. We identify them not by their clothes, which range from battle fatigues to jacket and tie, or by their settings, which vary from urban streets to rural mountain hideouts and everything in between. Instead, we know them by their faces. On television or in magazines, they demand attention, their countenances etched with vivid emotions, often little more than wordless expressions of fear, anger, determination, sacrifice, and hope. These are the revolutionaries of our own times, mostly nameless individuals, brought to our attention because they appealed for personal security and social justice and have become caught up in political whirlwinds that now transform their lives. Revolutionary movements of this sort always give us leaders—some famous, others less so, the names come and go—but the enduring face of resistance is a revolutionary people.

When we bother to think about it, we sense that over two centuries ago revolutionary Americans must have looked like these ordinary men and women. But curiously, they have largely gone missing from the stories we tell ourselves about our nation's origins. Like their contemporary counterparts, we do not know their names or, indeed, very much about them. The fault is ours; the consequences significant. Their absence from our shared historical memory impoverishes our understanding of how they turned a colonial rebellion into a genuine revolution and in the process constructed a new political culture. Without their participation in organizing effective resistance to Great Britain on the ground and then sustaining the cause over eight difficult years of war, the Revolution would surely have failed.

If we listen carefully, we can still recover these revolutionary voices.[1] It is essential that we do so. They speak of original meanings, of our nation's founding values that now more than ever must be reclaimed. As we shall discover, the passage of time has not silenced Americans who made the Revolution work and who during moments of great personal peril insisted that the best government was a government based on the will of the ordinary people. Surviving records from the period recapture their ideas and experiences: A Maryland farmer in a fit of rage tells a local committee of revolutionaries "they might kiss his ass." A minister witnessing the outbreak of internecine violence in his community writes that "parents and children, brothers and sisters, wife and husband, were enemies to one another." A contributor to a Pennsylvania newspaper condemns war profiteers on the ground that "every right or power claimed by any man or set of men should be in subordination to the common good." Wives in New York State publicly protest that since they do not share the political beliefs of their Tory husbands, they should be allowed to keep their farms. A Connecticut minister to a tiny congregation strives to inculcate "in the minds of the people, a just sense of their rights." Thousands of ordinary Americans from Georgia to New Hampshire spontaneously create a huge, unprecedented charity to relieve the people of Boston—perfect strangers—during the British occupation. This is the human face of our revolution.

Such people are not familiar figures in the revolution that Americans celebrate. They should be. They hold the key to explaining why our revolution ended differently from most other revolutions that have shaped the modern world. Facing revolution's anger, fear, and passion—crucial elements in mounting effective political resistance—ordinary Americans repeatedly preserved a rule of law. They avoided violent and destructive excesses. Political liberation went hand in hand with restraint. Throughout the war this commitment sustained a powerful sense of shared purpose—which in fact energized a new spirit of nationalism—that brought forth the kind of political stability that has eluded so many other revolutionary nations. It was an impressive accomplishment, one that we should not take for granted. They promoted and secured a political culture that endures even as waves of partisan anger threaten to negate their achievement.

I

The American Revolution still speaks to us, although not so clearly as it once did. Over the years the message has become so estranged from us that we no longer quite comprehend what insights into a shared political culture we should now be trying to recover. This is especially challenging at a moment in our country's history when there is so little agreement about how the past might speak to an uncertain future. The solution may require an entirely new perspective on the country's political origins. To restart the conversation, we might ask: *Where* exactly did the American Revolution take place? The question may seem strange, largely because we usually recount the history of national independence in terms of heroic personalities and major military events.

A different story of the Revolution—one that addresses more persuasively many concerns of our own generation—offers immediate and striking rewards. Indeed, merely posing a question about the *where* of revolution invites a telling of the Revolution that shifts attention away from a familiar narrative of the nation's political origins. That approach builds upon a well-established, largely intellectual interpretation of the founding. About the importance of ideas about rights and liberty in securing independence there is no doubt.[2] The more pressing interpretive issue—one addressed here—is how those fundamental rights and liberty were actually achieved, and who did what in achieving them.

As we shall discover, a recounting of abstract constitutional principles is not sufficient. A revised perspective must weave these political assumptions with the day-to-day experience of resistance on the ground. This is a crucial element in explaining how revolutions work.[3] Demonstrating the complex ways that ideas and experience interacted alerts us to something generally ignored in the American story of revolution: human passion. Unless we acknowledge how such basic emotions—chronic fear, desire for revenge, or suspicion of betrayal, for example—profoundly affected how people adjusted to the shifting demands of revolution, we cannot fully understand what the revolutionaries were trying to tell us, not only about their rejection of monarchy and aristocracy, but also about the creation of a new political order.

The initial question about the *where* of the Revolution, of course, sparks obvious responses. We could direct our attention—as many historians have done—to the battlefields where George Washington and the Continental Army defied all odds and emerged victorious after a long struggle. Or we could center our revolutionary narrative on the Continental Congress, where the key debates about nationhood occurred, and in the process come to a fuller appreciation of the extraordinary achievements of the country's political leaders. The Founders not only managed to finance the war and preserve a sense of union, but also drafted documents such as the Declaration of Independence that to this day affirm our shared commitment to rights, liberty, and freedom.[4]

No one would fault either strategy. Americans certainly could not have succeeded in their struggle with Great Britain without the perseverance of the army or the contributions of the Founders. As I shall argue, however, we could just as persuasively locate the Revolution in the thousands of small communities and port towns where men and women from Georgia to New Hampshire sustained the war effort and established a political regime that remains central to our own beliefs about power and its abuses.

Although many communities contributing to the success of the Revolution took no direct part in the major military campaigns, we should not allow their distance from organized combat to conceal their fundamental importance in mobilizing resistance to Great Britain and continuing the war effort when battlefield reverses and internal disputes eroded public morale. It was in these settlements—in towns, county seats, or crossroads marked only by a courthouse, church, or tavern—where people swept up by political passion made choices that changed their lives: decisions about political allegiance, about policing domestic enemies, about supplying scarce funds and resources to advance what became known as the country's common cause, about maintaining solidarity during a period of hyperinflation, and about other Americans who had aided the British during the war and after the peace wanted to return. The challenge of sustaining a revolution within these intimate personal networks over eight years was more difficult than most of us fully comprehend. The history of these networks, of the Americans who sustained them, is the missing piece we must recover. Simply put, without the continuing support of the people on the local level in their own fight for independence, the entire conflict would have amounted to little more than a failed colonial rebellion.

II

The testimony of ordinary Americans is quite different from that produced by the celebrated national leaders of the Revolution. Indeed, a revised history of the period focuses on men and women living in small, largely agricultural centers and in larger ports as well, where the crucial moments that defined the Revolution occurred among people they already knew. These sites of revolutionary discovery were often meetings of local committees of safety and observation. Many Americans with little or no previous political experience served on these committees or joined other groups where they were asked to assess the patriotism of neighbors, collect money and supplies for the war, and recruit reluctant soldiers.

A community perspective restores to the revolutionary story a largely unappreciated cast of characters who often wanted no more than simply to survive the war. As they soon learned, however, turning their backs on unprecedented political demands seldom worked. Revolutionary committees forced their hand, compelling them to declare their allegiance and to make commitments that exposed them to immense personal danger. Surviving records recount their brief appearances before the committees of safety, boards of selectmen, or justices of the peace where they accommodated to the revolutionary challenge in different ways: begging for understanding, justifying their actions, confessing political errors, and not infrequently defying authority. The range of appeals was huge. Tens of thousands of people had to negotiate with neighbors about the character of a new regime. These were difficult local conversations. As one man confessed during the Revolution, because "my comfort does so much depend on the regard and good will of those among whom I live[, I promise not to act in political matters] contrary to the minds of the people in general."[5] After a number of townsmen in Milton, Massachusetts, fell under suspicion of being too friendly to royal appointees, they expressed sorrow that they had "displeased our Neighbors." They hoped that their apology would restore them to "the inestimable blessing, the good Will of our Neighbors, and the whole Community."[6]

Such exchanges bring into sharper relief the everyday face of the American Revolution. They alert us to a huge group of people caught up in chaotic political change that included not only members of the committees, but also, more importantly, thousands of spectators. This massive participation is key to understanding how the American people managed to sustain resistance over eight years of war. Their experience restores to the story of independence men and women whose sacrifice we so often ignore, people who simply watched enforcement proceedings, often as silent witnesses to history, lending legitimacy to the representatives of the new regime, reacting on their own terms to the demands of revolution, and moving inexorably forward with neighbors toward the creation of a new political culture even when they were not too sure where the larger flow of national events was carrying them.

III

For Americans, revolution always involved a process of discovery. It constantly opened up new conversations on new ground. One remarkable example of this process comes from a small New Jersey community. It reminds us how revolutionary action progressed incrementally from discussion to resistance. At the center of the story was Matthew Potter, an immigrant from Ulster, Ireland, who had been forced in 1740 to leave home because of English commercial restrictions that nearly destroyed the linen trade. Potter made his way south from Connecticut, trying his hand at blacksmithing and logging. He settled at last in Bridgeton, New Jersey, where he established a popular tavern.

Late in 1775, as the constitutional controversy with Parliament seemed increasingly intractable, a notice appeared in Bridgeton and other communities in Cumberland County—named ironically for George III's uncle who had brutally put down a rising in Scotland. A group of townspeople concerned about "the circumstances of the times" announced that "the most Important Service that they can render Society, will be to communicate—Weekly, to their neighbors the result of their inquiries and speculations on political occurrences and other important Subjects particularly calculated to suit this place."

The declaration signaled the launch of a newspaper known as the *Plain Dealer*. The only problem with the proposal was the inability of organizers to obtain a printing press. Improvising with the resources at hand, they urged authors of opinion pieces to attach handwritten texts to a board in Potter's Tavern where anyone could read them. A new essay was posted every Thursday. The *Plain Dealer* protected the anonymity of its contributors, noting in its original appeal for commentary that, "the Secretary being under obligation to keep the names of the persons who write the pieces secret, those that desire it, may communicate their sentiments to the public without the inconvenience of being known or personally criticized." Patrons of Potter's Tavern were encouraged to discuss the essays, even to copy them, but the rules prohibited them from taking the original statements home.

Only a few numbers of the *Plain Dealer* survive, something of a miracle considering their fragile composition. The first essay appeared in late December 1775, fully six months after the Battle of Bunker Hill. The author showed no interest in American resistance, advocating instead a campaign to raise the general level of public education. The writer invited everyone "both male and female who have ability or inclination to serve in this way" to help improve Bridgeton's intellectual life. Over the next several Thursdays only one essay directly addressed the political situation. It excoriated "*rank Tories*" and "Turn-Coats," and praised the "True Whigs," who believed that "all power is derived from the people and not from any imaginary divine right." This attempt to distinguish friends from enemies did not generate as much discussion as did the next week's contribution, a somewhat prurient analysis of bundling, a practice encouraging courting couples in Cumberland County to spend the night together in bed.

Little more than a month later, by the end of January 1776, it became increasingly difficult to ignore the imperial crisis. Local writers struggled to comprehend how armed resistance in distant cities such as Boston might play out in Bridgeton. Public discussion exposed differences of opinion. The growing intensity of the tavern exchanges certainly annoyed one writer, who insisted that he was a "true Son of Liberty." He declared that Lord North and his allies in Parliament "are a pack of rascals, & deserve to have their brains beat out." The author also thought that many locals who loudly proclaimed support for the American cause were hypocrites who "would Immediately change sides if a good opportunity offer'd." In his opinion, most of the townsmen who pontificated about politics were ignorant fools. "I believe," he informed readers at Potter's Tavern, "many people who talk about politics know about as much of the matter as a hog does Latin, or a Horse of divinity." These know-it-alls reminded him of a monkey climbing a maypole. "The higher an ignorant man gets," the author insisted, "the more he will show his A___."

However irritating it may have been to listen to half-baked assertions, the people of Bridgeton gradually found that they could no longer escape the revolutionary ferment. In their small, rural town everyday political conversation over drinks became more heated, more partisan. People increasingly found that they had to declare where they stood; neutrality was no longer a public option. The flow of events persuaded the writers of the final surviving issues of the *Plain Dealer* to explain to the readers at Potter's

Tavern how Britain's rulers were responsible for the political situation. One person prepared a pro-American history of Parliament's senseless attack on colonial liberty. Another essay recounted the death of Richard Montgomery, a Continental Army general, during an ill-fated American attack on British fortifications at Quebec City. The local conversation was no longer about pompous neighbors pretending to know more about the imperial crisis than did their friends. One essay called for courage and sacrifice: "Arouse my Countrymen. . . . let us draw our swords, and never return them into their scabbards [sic], till we have rescued our Country, from the Iron hand of Tyranny, and secured the pure enjoyment of Liberty, to generations yet unborn!"

The results of the political discussion in Bridgeton were not much different from those occurring in other settlements throughout America. The point is that the people who read the handwritten postings, arguing points and making concessions, came to an understanding of organized resistance to imperial power that was not only fundamentally local, but also similar to the kinds of conversations taking place in other communities. Potter's Tavern was the site where men and women crafted their own stories of revolution, a narrative of pigs, horses, and monkeys, of the death of generals and drawn swords, and not of great political philosophers. It was around the posted essays of the *Plain Dealer* where folksy observations about misrule energized mobilization for war.

Captain Joseph Bloomfield, then a local lawyer who later became governor of New Jersey, appreciated how his friends and neighbors in Cumberland County had transformed the discussion of political grievance into a commitment for military service that might cost them their lives. Facing a newly recruited company of Continental soldiers on March 26, 1776—almost three months before Congress proclaimed national independence—Bloomfield recognized young men in the group who had grown up in this community. They were his neighbors, the sons of friends. "As most of you were born and brought up in this place with me," he observed, "I feel myself greatly interested in your welfare & success."

Bloomfield then spoke to the men about why the confrontation with Britain now required armed resistance. It was an eloquent speech. "The American states [have] entered a new *era* of politics," he explained. At such a moment the soldiers must stand together, avoiding faction and confusion that could promote anarchy and lead to the rise of an "aspiring *Demagogue*, possessed of popular talents and shining qualities, a *Julius Caesar*, or an *Oliver Cromwell* ... [who] will lay violent hands on the government, and sacrifice the liberties of his country to his own ambitions and dominating humor." It would be a hard fight. "Some of you will lose your lives in battle," and should that happen they should know "you will die gloriously; you will expire in the defense of your country, and suffer martyrdom in the cause of liberty."

The audience probably appreciated Bloomfield's stirring words. He spoke the language of an educated gentleman. But for the local men going off to war, political conversion to the American cause had occurred earlier. As one writer of an earthy essay commented in the *Plain Dealer*, "I believe the best method to frighten hogs out of mischief is to lug them well by the ears."[7]

IV

An effort to restore lost revolutionary voices is not intended to romanticize the ordinary people who supported independence and brought forth a new government. They were products of an eighteenth-century culture quite different from our own. To be sure, they often sacrificed personal comfort and security in the name of rights and liberty. For that accomplishment they deserve praise. At the same time, we must also acknowledge that many revolutionaries held disturbingly negative beliefs about African Americans and Native Americans. Few of them openly condemned the slave trade, much less the enslavement of a large portion of the country's total population at the time of the Declaration of Independence. They condoned the wanton killing of Indians along the frontier, justifying massacre of Native Americans as the just revenge for their allegiance to Great Britain.[8]

While such actions should not be excused, one might note that for time immemorial revolutionary change has been an extremely messy business in which the kinds of violence that few people would normally condemn become sadly commonplace, reflexive responses to real or imagined dangers.[9] In this way Americans who sustained the war against Great Britain—and this group included many African Americans and Indians who also responded to the liberating rhetoric of revolution—were little different from those people who participated in the French, Haitian, or

Russian Revolutions.[10] The list continues into our own time. Self-proclaimed liberators did terrible things in the name of pragmatism and survival and in the defense of ideological or theological purity, developments frequently overlooked when later generations circulated heroic accounts of revolutionary events.

However, observing that people swept up in violent political change often act in ways that they later come to regret is not in itself a sufficient explanation for public behavior—at least, not in the American case. While taking a broad comparative perspective on how Americans organized and sustained a revolution—making it work over eight years—we must also accept a fundamental element that distinguished the character of American resistance to perceived imperial oppression from that of many other countries throughout the world. The key difference was race—or more accurately, perceptions of race.[11] Other nations may have allowed religious or ethnic identities to excuse domestic violence. In America the issue was almost always race. After all, about 20 percent of the nation's population in 1776 was African American and enslaved. It is perhaps not surprising to discover, therefore, that deep-seated anxieties borne of racism served powerfully to reinforce a conviction among the revolutionary majority that the common cause for which they were fighting was their cause and not the cause of slaves or Indians.

Although derogatory assumptions about these two groups certainly pre-dated the conflict with Great Britain, there can be no doubt that the war itself amplified long-standing racial prejudice. The intensification of fear was especially manifest in the South. But hostility against people of color shaped revolutionary experience in other places throughout America. Even as committees of safety moved to control loyalists in their own communities, they worried about the possibility of slave risings and Indian attacks along the frontier. It was in the context of imagined insecurity—a product of New World demography—that Americans managed to sustain resistance against Great Britain.

Something more needs to be said on this topic. However central racism may have been to the experience of revolution, it did not reduce African Americans or Native Americans to the status of hapless victims. Like other Americans—those of European heritage—they discovered that the political crisis presented personal choices—unexpected, often life changing, but for them particularly difficult. Some slaves managed to escape to British lines; others fought for American independence. Their opportunities were limited. At a moment in history when revolutionary leaders spoke in a strictly political sense of England's desire to enslave Americans, men and women who endured real slavery were seldom liberated from bondage. The majority of Native Americans allied themselves with the British—a strategic decision—but some such as the Oneida did not. There was no single revolutionary story. Appeals for national unity and acceptance of racial exclusion went hand in hand.

V

By shifting our perspective from national congresses and crucial battles to the affairs of small communities, we expose what has long been a nettlesome question about the character of the American Revolution. What, we may ask, made it revolutionary? In other words, what made it an event that amounted to more than a colonial rebellion? After all, achieving independence was not in itself revolutionary.

The argument put forward here is that the Revolution transformed American political culture by allowing large numbers of people who had previously been excluded from politics to come forward, to speak up, and to shape the flow of events. They rejected without second thought aristocratic privilege. Within an eighteenth-century context in which political power revolved around figures claiming authority simply as a result of bloodlines, this was a radical development.

The war did more than dismiss the pretentions of lords and ladies. Managing the imperial conflict opened new opportunities for local men who suddenly found themselves in charge of organizing and policing resistance. They did not come from the same social background as that of George Washington, Thomas Jefferson, or John Adams—just to cite three celebrated figures. The newly empowered actors were neither owners of large plantations nor prosperous merchants. In comparison with their neighbors—usually farmers like themselves—they perhaps had enjoyed a greater measure of economic success, but most people who served on committees of safety or accepted demanding posts in local government would have remained obscure individuals in a colonial society had not the Revolution intervened, presenting unanticipated challenges and responsibilities.

David Ramsay, a Continental officer who wrote a brilliant history of the Revolution, understood as well as any contemporary what was happening. He marveled how the war transformed traditional social relations. According to Ramsay, the conflict with Great Britain "called forth many virtues, and gave occasion for the display of abilities which, but for that event, would have been lost to the world. When the war began, the Americans were a mass of husbandmen, merchants, mechanics and fishermen; but the necessities of the country gave a spring to the active powers of the inhabitants, and set them to thinking, speaking and acting in a line far beyond that to which they had been accustomed."[12]

What we call the American Revolution cannot be linked to a single moment such as the signing of the Declaration of Independence. Rather, it was a gradual shift in popular thinking about the relation between ordinary people and government power. The revolution was a process, contingent and open-ended, a complex move from revolution to Revolution. The new men took charge of community affairs before they became revolutionaries, before most of them even openly advocated national independence. They were caught up by the sudden collapse of British authority outside a few major port cities. They learned on the job, gaining a measure of self-confidence through the daily challenge of policing politically suspicious neighbors, recruiting Continental soldiers, overseeing the local militia, collecting taxes, and supplying soldiers with food and blankets. It was this common experience that allows us to generalize about revolutionary voices. To be sure, we recognize profound regional differences, some greater than others. South Carolina was not Massachusetts. Moreover, records in the South are not as full as those surviving in the Middle States and New England. We might note religious and economic variations or contrasting racial statistics. But such distinctions and uneven records should not discourage us from looking at the Revolution as a whole. After all, one can examine resistance in local communities, while at the same time making broad generalizations about a revolutionary people at war.

The revolutionary journey of the American people occurred in stages, discrete moments, each in its own way threatening and demanding. It involved a series of adjustments to a constantly changing political situation. Almost no one in 1775 called either for independence from Great Britain or for the rejection of monarchy. They wanted in the first instance only to persuade the British Parliament to repeal acts that demanded colonial tax-ation without representation—in a word, to reform an imperial system that suddenly seemed oppressive.

A second, entirely separate moment occurred after the British refused to back down. Parliamentary intransigence created a situation in which petitioning and nonviolent protest gave way to armed resistance. Once the war began, communities throughout America faced an entirely different set of problems—funding, recruiting, and policing. Later in the controversy—certainly after 1778—severe financial strains triggered by inflation raised the possibility that the enemies of political liberation were in fact other Americans, war profiteers and speculators who betrayed the common good.

During the course of this evolving political crisis, a colonial rebellion gave birth to a genuine revolution. Although the precise moment varied from region to region, there can be no doubt that the transformation brought forth a new political culture. The driving force behind the creation of a regime based on the will of the people can be found in the quotidian experiences of managing local affairs, of actually participating in a political system in which ordinary Americans found that they had to negotiate power with other ordinary Americans, people who insisted that they were as good as any other member of civil society, in essence discovering a powerful sense of mutual equality that remains the rhetorical foundation of our political culture. A government by the people was not something that the revolutionaries could take for granted; it had to be discovered and then reaffirmed by living through a challenging period of political change.

Throughout the war the people we shall encounter explained and justi-fied their actions in strikingly different ways from how the celebrated Founders did so. While the nation's leaders—members of the Continental Congress, for example—framed the controversy with Great Britain largely in an abstract language of constitutional law and political theory, revolu-tionaries (a term we shall use instead of patriots) in small communities and seaports seldom linked their support of the Revolution to leading po-litical thinkers of the Italian Renaissance or English Civil Wars. Largely absent from their statements were references to political philosophers such as Montesquieu or Harrington. Ordinary revolutionaries may have read these texts, but when called upon to declare what they believed and why they believed it, they rarely drew upon the same intellectual traditions as the men who drafted the pamphlets that shape our modern understanding of revolution and nationhood.

The assumptions and beliefs that energized the Revolution on the local level can be recovered in the records of town meetings—forums in which people worked out ideas about political power—in weekly newspapers, and in countless sermons that schooled communities throughout America about the character of just wars, the moral obligation to resist tyranny, and the responsibility of a covenanted people to preserve God-given rights from despots. The declarations were simple and direct. Old Testament stories about the punishments visited on the Jews when they failed to heed the Lord's admonitions complemented examples of betrayal and heroism encountered in secular histories. As David Ramsay explained in 1789, the revolutionaries closely studied the Old Testament. Here, they learned that the Jews had made a terrible mistake when they appealed to the Lord for a king. As Americans interpreted biblical lessons, "even the name of a king was rendered odious" and "Hereditary succession was turned into ridicule."[13]

These popular ideas helped turn complaints about taxes and representation into armed resistance against Great Britain. That is a key distinction. We are exploring the fundamentals for revolutionary mobilization, retrieving explanations for personal sacrifice. The central element in justifying violence was the deeply personal conviction that if one did not take an active stand against tyranny, one thereby offended God. Accepting despotism was not simply an act of cowardice; it was sin. This religiously driven sense of political responsibility was not the perspective of the Founders, students of the Enlightenment. But in the larger revolutionary society a scriptural message resonated persuasively with the American soldiers and with the communities that sent them to war. As respected members of small communities, ministers provided guidance in spiritual matters. They also spoke to parishioners about political concerns. Did God condone rebellion? What did the Bible say about neutrality in the fight against oppression? Should one forgive an enemy who has inflicted pain on the community? Unless we grasp the revolutionary challenge as congregations throughout America would have interpreted them, we will fail to understand why these revolutionaries took oaths on the Bible so seriously or why they frequently offered domestic political enemies a chance of redemption and reconciliation through public confession.

Restoring the voices of ordinary people to the story of the Revolution requires an additional element. After all, abstract and highly intellectualized ideas about public virtue and vigilance—sometimes seen as the driving force of revolution—were not sufficient to trigger or sustain resistance. Something more was needed, an additional catalyst. Revolutions require passion. What we often forget—although any contemporary news report about insurgencies throughout the world would clarify our historical understanding—is that during our own revolution assumptions and beliefs about the exercise of political power were amplified by raw emotions such as anger and hate. Accepting the emotional base of revolutionary resistance does not lessen the achievements of the founding generation. To the contrary, it makes them more human. As the Reverend Henry Cumings explained in a sermon delivered in Lexington, Massachusetts—to a congregation that included families who had recently lost sons and fathers in the battle of April 19, 1775—"Though rage, and inflamed wrath, are no essential properties of patriotism; yet patriotism, without feeling or sensibility, is a mere name."[14]

By restoring passions to the narrative of the Revolution, we gain a strikingly different perspective on the origins of American political culture. Instead of an event-driven story, one that sweeps us smoothly along from the Stamp Act crisis of 1765 to the Declaration of Independence and to the peace treaty of 1783, we will recover shifting emotional environments that were characterized in turns by a sense of rejection, a search for assurance, a climate of fear, a demand for revolutionary justice, a discovery of betrayal, a desire for revenge, and finally, an acceptance of reconciliation.[15]

We start with *rejection* (1774–1775), a humiliating sense that the American colonists were second-class subjects in the British Empire. During the early months of the imperial crisis ordinary people expressed optimism that the rulers of Great Britain would come to their senses and avoid more serious confrontation. That did not happen. British obstinacy fueled American resolve. As it became apparent that parliamentary leaders would not retreat, Americans troubled by doubt—Can we win a war? Is it a just war?—sought *assurance* from local ministers who justified resistance (1775–1776).

After actual fighting began and a large number of people openly supported the British, strategies for responding to *rejection* gave way to the most dangerous emotion, *fear* (1776–1778). As the histories of many modern nations reveal, a people who are terrified, who are continuously anxious about their own security, often demonize their enemies and entertain actions that they later come to regret. During the early years of war, fear gave credibility to rumors of conspiracy; it promoted hate. And yet, however crudely they demonized "domestic enemies," the Americans who enforced revolution, who administered revolutionary *justice* on the ground, exercised remarkable restraint when dealing with domestic political enemies.

Although the surrender of General John Burgoyne and his British troops at the end of 1777 and the French recognition of the United States convinced revolutionaries that they might actually win the war, they found themselves facing a huge threat to national unity. Hyperinflation—a phenomenon that has undermined the stability of many modern countries—tested patriotic commitment. As Americans living in small communities struggled to enforce wage and price controls, they accused speculators and profiteers of *betrayal* (1779–1781). At the end of the war when thousands of Tories proposed returning to their original homes, creating the country's first great refugee crisis, the dominant popular emotion was a desire for *revenge* (1781–1783). Why, the revolutionaries asked, should those who sacrificed so much for independence welcome back into their communities those who had fled, or worse, actively aided the British? Despite the calls for punishment and rejection, the American Revolution—unlike so many revolutions throughout history—ended relatively peacefully. That achievement alone is something worthy of note. People got on with their lives, choosing at the end of the day to ignore past wrongs. Their example invites modern Americans to reflect on how a founding people overcame partisan divisions that could have destroyed the country at the moment of birth (1783–1784).

VI

As we move through the different stages of revolution, we encounter a controversy about the fundamental character of a society founded on the will of the people, one that echoes in the political debates of our own times. Convenient labels such as conservative and liberal do not adequately reflect the nature of the dispute. Such terms carry too many modern, ahistorical associations. By whatever name we adopt, we discover in revolutionary communities how expectations about the future of republican society became a source of division, occasionally taking on a hyperbolic quality.

Americans who supported independence convinced themselves that other Americans—revolutionary allies—harbored dangerously extreme ideas about political authority in the new nation. One side worried that revolutionary unrest might seriously erode the fabric of civil society, encouraging anarchy in the process of overthrowing monarchy. We encounter such sentiments in Joseph Bloomfield's warnings about the rise of an American Oliver Cromwell or Julius Caesar. It seemed possible to people such as Bloomfield that the breakdown of a rule of law—something they observed had happened in other revolutions—would threaten the security of property and persuade ordinary people that they did not have to pay contractually negotiated debts. These revolutionaries wanted to preserve a traditional social order, a system of relations that permitted the wealthy and wellborn to exercise political power in the name of the people.

Such fears were greatly overblown. Even the most radical revolutionaries condemned anarchy. No one wanted mob rule. The charge, however, provided a rhetorical device by which some Americans warned other Americans of the perils of popular excess. Their opponents engaged in a similar practice, charging that the real threat to revolution was a concentration of political authority in the hands of a few. People who feared the return of despotic authority did not, in fact, advocate a radical economic or political agenda. But throughout the war, they argued for the creation of a social system that guaranteed a rough sense of economic equality—fair play in the marketplace and censure of special privilege in any form.[16] Such issues arose whenever ordinary people suspected that elite national leaders intended to curtail the activities of popularly elected committees, which were often self-constituted bodies that punished domestic enemies, enforced wage and price controls, and attempted to banish loyalists from their communities after the war ended.

Peace failed to resolve the political tensions that had divided revolutionaries throughout the war. The debate over how much power the people should have in their own government continued through the ratification of the Constitution. Over time it became the hallmark of an untested political culture founded on the assertion that all political power derives from the people and that they hold certain rights that government cannot compromise. Even Americans who have despised political rivals—calling them too conservative or too liberal—have subscribed to these basic beliefs. The unresolved question that has energized our society from the very beginning, therefore, is not whether Americans possess rights, but rather, which Americans do so. Who can be excluded in the conversations we have with ourselves over conflicting rights claims? What is the justification for constraining the rights of some people, but not of others?

A conversation begun in revolutionary communities continues. Those outside the circle of rights—women and African Americans, for example—have demanded the same rights as other people. After long struggles that sometimes turned violent, they have generally succeeded. The Civil War shredded the fabric of civil society, but following that disaster the political discussion returned to issues that the revolutionaries in small communities would have understood. What, we still ask, is the proper balance between freedom and authority, privilege and equality, unbridled liberty and the rule of law? During the fight for independence, ordinary Americans explored these fundamental questions. They often stumbled. They sometimes gave into excess. But for all that, they remind us of the need to balance passions and constraints in our own political culture.

CHAPTER ONE

REJECTION

What conditions transform sporadic discontent into effective political resistance against the state? As we all know, popular mobilization is a confusing, often messy process. Participants are often not honest about their own original motivation. Almost always, uncertainty about goals and strategies mark the moment of decision. But however they evaluate the situation, people enjoying the comforts of everyday life suddenly find themselves confronting the possibility that their political choices may involve great personal sacrifice, even death itself. Understanding better the burden of decision provides insight into why the American Revolution succeeded while others have not.

The challenge of organizing protest is especially hard for colonial subjects grown weary of imperial rule. One thinks of India and Algeria, perhaps even of Ireland. In these places a deep sense of resentment has contended with traditional loyalties. It is common for restive colonists living under the authority of powerful imperial regimes to express profound ambivalence about terminating their dependent status. On the one hand, they often identify with the culture of the mother country, reproducing as best they can the customs of the imperial center. The desire to be accepted by ruling elites—seen as the arbiters of good taste—encourages colonial passivity. A yearning for approval can also inflame ambition among provincials who dream of achieving social equality with their cosmopolitan masters. On the other hand, rejection by imperial authorities—the humiliating discovery that the colonists' efforts to win approval have failed—can trigger violent reaction. Haunting suspicion of second-class status is one thing, policies that openly affirm inferiority quite another.[1]

It was precisely a sudden awareness of their own perceived inferiority within the empire that initially persuaded many Americans to challenge king and Parliament. An emotional response to marginalization energized popular demands for imperial reform, and later, somewhat reluctantly, for armed resistance. But the breakdown of the old order brought little joy—at least, not at first. Rejection sparked profound regret, a sense of loss every bit as strong as the anger sparked by taxation without representation. Even as the colonists passionately defended their rights and appealed for liberty, they hoped that the imperial connection that had long been a source of pride as well as prosperity would somehow be restored on terms that would make them feel genuinely British. It was not easy. Even after the final crisis sparked widespread violence—the arrival of a military force in Boston intended to punish the city for the destruction of tea in December 1773—they struggled to reimagine their social and political identity; such tensions reflected sentiment as much as reason. Thomas Jefferson tried to include his own sense of cultural loss in the Declaration of Independence. In an initial draft he lamented what seemed to have been Britain's unfeeling rejection of its own colonies. The use of armed force to subdue the American rebellion, he wrote, has "given the last stab to agonizing affection, and manly spirit bids us to renounce for ever these unfeeling brethren. We must endeavor to forget our former love for them . . . we might have been a free & great people together; but a communication of grandeur & of freedom it seems is below their dignity."[2] Congress wisely concluded that such expressions of nostalgia had no place in the final document.

Parliament, of course, gave no ground. In fact, Lord North and his allies doubled down in their efforts to force the Americans to accept the sovereignty of Parliament in "all cases whatsoever," an infamous phrase that appeared in the Declaratory Act of 1766. For the colonists these words repeated frequently in protest documents became a badge of their own inferiority within the empire. The claim of superiority by a legislature in which they had no representation effectively denied the colonists a voice in taxation.[3] For ordinary people the triggering event in the imperial crisis—the painful discovery of rejection—was not the Boston Tea Party, but rather Parliament's unexpectedly harsh response to the destruction of the tea.[4] In a series of punitive statutes known collectively as the Coercive Acts, Britain's rulers closed the port of Boston to all commerce. An army of occupation was dispatched to bring order to Massachusetts Bay, and the king appointed a general to serve as the colony's governor. These developments shocked Americans. Suddenly, throughout the colonies—but especially throughout New England—local committees of correspondence sprang up, each one a spontaneous expression of popular anger about how Britain's rulers had treated the Americans as lesser subjects.

The establishment of so many committees transformed dramatically an entire colonial political culture.[5] It happened quickly. Resistance at the community level introduced a popular dynamic to a volatile situation. New men came forward to assume authority in small communities that had expressed only passing interest in previous British regulations. During the summer of 1774 and continuing through 1775 one can almost feel a surge of energy that coursed through the entire population in the documents they left behind. Fast-moving events demanded declarations of allegiance—signs of personal commitment to a cause that remained ill defined. In this radically altered environment ordinary people began discussing in earnest strategies of resistance. They devised local justifications for rebellion. Their goals were modest. No one mentioned independence. Indeed, even as the imperial regime toppled in the countryside, townsmen still pledged their steadfast loyalty to George III. They were not being disingenuous. Unhappy colonists simply wanted the members of Parliament to come to their senses and restore an imperial relationship that had worked relatively well for almost two centuries.

The significance of these committees was not, therefore, the specific content of their resolves. More important for understanding the development of a powerful revolutionary mentality—responses on the grounds that would later provide the essential infrastructure required to sustain the revolution—was the actual experience of taking charge and making decisions in the name of the people. Moreover, the power of the committees was greatly amplified by communication through newspapers. As communities learned that other communities were calling for the boycott of British imported goods and collecting arms, for example, they gained a comforting assurance of being part of a larger mobilization. They could imagine a vast network of strangers cooperating in unprecedented ways.[6] The experience of reaching out to other Americans—many of them at the time strangers—reaffirmed shared political values and in the fullness of time gave rise to a new spirit of popular nationalism.

I

In politics, as in life, resentment is a close cousin of rejection. We encounter this emotional shift in an incident that occurred on the road between Hopkinton and Boston, Massachusetts, in May 1775, just weeks after the battles at Lexington and Concord. It reveals the depth of alienation that energized the reactions of ordinary militiamen to representatives of the imperial ruling class. That latter was composed of prominent men who owed much of their prosperity and social standing to British patronage. Some Crown appointees came from leading colonial families; others had traveled from England in search of opportunity. Whatever their personal histories, they carved out privileged lives on the edge of empire. Not surprisingly, when the Americans rebelled, these royal officials abandoned their country estates and sought the protection of the British army in Boston.

A few barely escaped with their lives. During the summer of 1774, a *posse comitatus* chased Benjamin Hallowell, the Crown's commissioner of customs, on horseback from Cambridge to the edge of Boston. Hallowell rightly feared for his life. His arrogance made him an especially despised figure within the royal establishment.[7] Thomas Hutchinson, a royal governor who had spent his entire life in Massachusetts, fared little better. Almost overnight he became the most hated officeholder in New England.[8] The animosity toward Hutchinson resulted not only from his defense of Parliament's right to tax Americans, but also from a conviction that patrons in the mother country had helped him gain an array of lucrative provincial appointments. His success in feathering his family's nest nearly drove James Otis to distraction. John Adams was only slightly more restrained. Calling Hutchinson a "courtier," Adams complained that the royal governor's career bore witness to the "amazing ascendancy of one family, [that created a] foundation sufficient on which to erect Tyranny."[9]

These complaints expose a raw nerve. Modern histories of the run-up to national independence usually concentrate on the constitutional arguments found in the pamphlets of the day. But closely reasoned statements of this kind were not sufficient to spark actual resistance. That required an emotional component—a volatile mixture of contempt and jealousy— capable of fueling attacks on the leading representatives of the imperial establishment. One such spark was struck at a checkpoint on the Hopkinton road.

In May 1775 members of the new provincial government, hastily constituted in Massachusetts to organize military resistance after the bloodshed at Lexington, ordered a small unit of militiamen to set up the checkpoint. They were under the command of Captain Abner Craft, who lived in Watertown and was an officer in Colonel Thomas Gardner's recently formed regiment. No doubt, the men were a bit anxious. British forces in Boston were capable at a moment's notice of dispatching troops to the Massachusetts countryside. Craft's soldiers were expected to monitor traffic to and from the port city. People intent on escaping rebel-held areas required special passes signed by a member of the provincial council. American authorities adopted a fairly liberal policy on the flow of people, arguing that if the militiamen stopped too many loyalists the British might respond by prohibiting the colonists who supported resistance from reaching American lines.

On May 17 Craft's soldiers defied a specific command issued in writing by the Provincial Congress then meeting in Watertown. They detained a small number of wagons carrying Lady Frankland and her personal possessions to Boston. She showed them a pass signed by Dr. Benjamin Church. Though Church would later be convicted for providing General Thomas Gage with vital intelligence about American military preparation, at the time the soldiers had no reason to question his authority. The militiamen ignored the document for their own reasons. Although they probably had not met Lady Frankland before this moment, they surely had heard stories about her extraordinary rise from extreme poverty in Marblehead to a privileged position as the companion of one of the few English gentry to reside in the American colonies. The ordinary people knew her as Agnes Surriage.

Many years earlier Sir Charles Henry Frankland had arrived in Boston, where he took up a highly remunerative appointive post as collector of customs revenue. The job carried a good salary, but Sir Charles made far more money from the perks of office. He was also something of a rake. In 1742 he journeyed to Marblehead on business, and there at the Fountain Inn he encountered a young woman who happened to be scrubbing the floor on her hands and knees. The sight so moved the visitor that he offered to take Agnes—then only sixteen—to Boston, where he promised that he would educate her to become a proper lady. Her parents were so poor that they immediately accepted this unusual arrangement.

Within two years, it was clear to the members of polite society in Massachusetts that Agnes had become Frankland's mistress. True to his word, however, he taught her about music and how to speak and write as if she had been born to privilege. People in Boston knew better. They regarded her as a parvenu, as did Sir Charles's family when he later took Agnes to England. Over the following years, Frankland's luck took a turn for the better. He became a baronet, and thanks to powerful friends in the mother country, he received a highly desirable post in Portugal. In 1755 he was almost killed during the great Lisbon earthquake, but Agnes dug him out of the rubble, an act of love that so moved Frankland that he immediately asked a Catholic priest to join them in marriage. Later he had second thoughts about the Catholic ceremony and remarried Agnes in an Episcopal service. The couple eventually returned to Massachusetts, residing in Frankland's large estate in Hopkinton. He owned a dozen or more slaves. Indeed, Sir Charles and Lady Frankland enjoyed a highly visible life of privilege in rural Massachusetts.

Frankland died in 1768. Even in death he refused to remain in America. He was later buried near an English church in the small village of Weston, not far from Bath. Agnes maintained appearances, and she would have probably remained in Hopkinton had the colonists not demanded an end to parliamentary oppression. In this context she came to symbolize much that the people of her community found objectionable about the *ancien regime*. During the spring of 1775 Agnes decided to move to England, and armed with an official pass, she gathered the personal goods she would take with her. The slaves remained in Hopkinton. Soon after she departed, her neighbors plundered the estate. None of this deterred her. She was determined to escape.

Provincial officials demanded that Lady Frankland provide an inventory of all items she thought essential for her journey. Considering her rush to reach the security of Boston, she does not seem to have left much behind. According to a document submitted to a committee of safety in Massachusetts, she carried "6 trunks: 1 chest: 3 beds and bedding: 6 wethers [gelded male sheep]: 2 pigs: 1 small keg of pickled tongues: some hay: 3 bags of corn: and such other goods as she thinks proper." We will never know the contents of the six chests, but it is doubtful that the militiamen who stopped her could have afforded such an assortment of goods.

However much Captain Craft and his men may have resented Lady Frankland's social pretentions, they had no authority to stop her. The next day the Provincial Congress ordered Colonel Bond and six guards "to escort Lady Frankland" to Boston. It then rebuked Craft for disobedience. The punishment was light. The leaders of the rebellion wanted to teach him a lesson, not to humiliate a good officer. After a committee heard the allegations against Craft, it resolved "he should be *gently* admonished ... and be assured that the [Massachusetts] Congress were determined to preserve their dignity and power over the military." During a second session, the head of the provincial committee "politely admonished" Craft for his actions. At issue was the civilian control of the military, a key condition for stable republican government. The committee swiftly brought the incident to a close, ordering that people who had taken Frankland's "goods or chattels" to return them to Hopkinton. Whether they did so is not known. Agnes recouped her losses in England. Colonel Gardiner, Craft's commanding officer, was killed a few weeks later on Bunker Hill.[10]

The politics of rejection played out differently in other colonies. But wherever they resided, the royal governors created small courts populated by speculators, sycophants, minor Crown officials, and diehard believers in the empire. Some governors won the respect of local people; others thought that a show of force would impress unruly Americans. In the end, it did not matter much how the king's representatives went about their business. John Wentworth, who came from a long-established New Hampshire family, fled when the crisis broke. Josiah Martin threatened recalcitrant people in North Carolina. John Murray, fourth Earl of Dunmore, adopted the same strategy in Virginia. In neither case did coercion work. Both men tried to govern from British naval vessels anchored offshore, a pathetic reminder that they were no longer welcome on land. Sir Robert Eden's easygoing ways and cosmopolitan tastes earned the affection of some of Maryland's wealthy planters. But he too was forced to leave. What is so striking about this record is how rapidly British authority broke down outside a few major port cities. As appeals for reform turned violent, the royal governors and their followers found that they had little political capital on which to draw.[11] Their departure created a sudden vacuum in the countryside, quickly filled by people nursing injury even as they swore undying loyalty to George III.

II

How can we explain such an unprecedented burst of popular political activity, not only in Massachusetts, but in the other colonies as well? As we shall see, answering the question may not be as difficult as it might at first appear. The problem is that a large and impressive interpretive literature stands in our way. For more than two centuries historians have confidently asserted that the American Revolution began in 1760 with the coronation of George III. The traditional interpretation traces rising colonial discontent from one parliamentary act to another, and it often relies on organic metaphors involving children growing to maturity and demanding independence from a dominating mother country.

The litany of British regulations that allegedly connected initial protests to armed resistance is familiar to most of us. The narrative is teleological in character—it knows where history is going, even though the participants did not. The account usually starts with a young king and incompetent counselors who abruptly decide to reorganize administration of the empire. Intent on collecting additional revenue from the American colonies, the Parliament, dominated by the king's supporters, passes the Sugar Act (1764). The revolutionary story races forward to the Stamp Act crisis (1765) before jumping to the Townshend Acts, which led to a dramatic confrontation with British troops known as the Boston Massacre (1770). The narrative picks up again with the Boston Tea Party (1773), Lexington and Concord, and finally—almost inevitably—the Declaration of Independence. We might note that this tale of a slow ratcheting up of popular resistance largely centers on the street violence that occurred in Boston. More to the point is the assumption that a mere listing of parliamentary regulations enacted over more than a decade provides a sufficient causal explanation for a widespread eruption of popular political energy during the summer of 1774.

A skeptic might observe that these separate moments did not, in fact, flow smoothly toward a predestined event—the independence of the United States. From the perspective of ordinary Americans, a radical break—a rending of the flow of time—occurred in the revolutionary story that transforms our understanding of the sudden and massive mobilization of the American people. We recognize, of course, that there were long-term developments that figured into the revolutionary calculus. Many colonists—especially those in New England—had come to take local self-government for granted. For a century identification with Great Britain had bred a sense of complacency. Imperial commerce brought widespread prosperity. These bonds of political identity were not easily eroded.

It is not surprising, therefore, to discover that urban protests against the Stamp Act and Townshend Acts—temporarily annoying to be sure—did not create a shared revolutionary mentality. They were one-off affairs. For complaint to become something more required the introduction of provocative elements entirely different in character.[12] As we learn from other revolutions throughout the world, a radical shift in political consciousness—a willingness to employ violence against the state—requires a direct assault on the people, in this case, an imperial policy impacting lives in a much more threatening manner than the possible imposition of a new tax. That tipping point came with the passage of the Coercive Acts of 1774 and the arrival in Boston of a large British army of occupation, thousands of regular troops policing the streets of a major port. These unprecedented events sparked a public reaction that no one anticipated.

To be fair, a familiar revolutionary story that has endured for so long deserves serious review. Those who claim to see in provincial protests of the 1760s signs of revolutionary aspirations in the colonies fail to take into account how British politics at the time actually worked. Throughout the eighteenth century, British bureaucrats showed a remarkable ability to maintain order in England, Scotland, and Ireland. They were masters at putting out local fires. Negotiations with unhappy subjects usually involved a pragmatic mixture of carrots and sticks, limited punishments and a generous distribution of patronage. At the end of the day, even when lethal violence had to be employed, the episodes of local unrest were almost always contained or rechanneled. For example, the bloody conclusion of the Massacre of St. George's Fields in London on May 10, 1768—at least seven protesters were shot by government troops—was not an indication that ordinary British people were conspiring to launch a revolution. Like the Boston Massacre, it did not spark a crisis for the imperial regime.[13]

Conditions in the North American colonies were much like those in Ireland, Scotland, and England. Resistance to the Stamp Act stirred little enthusiasm outside a few port cities, and in any case, many colonists condemned mob violence in Boston. The Boston Massacre certainly did not lead inevitably to Bunker Hill or the Declaration of Independence. Instead, this particular event that figures so centrally in the traditional revolutionary chronology—the shooting of several people by British Regulars—introduced three years of extraordinary peace within the empire. The failure to generate ongoing momentum for protest drove Samuel Adams, a leading Boston agitator, to despair. Lamenting the lack of revolutionary fervor, he feared that he and his friends would never be able to sustain popular resistance to parliamentary regulations. He may have lamented the lack of revolutionary fervor. But as he could see for himself, ordinary Americans between 1771 and 1773 thought that the imperial crisis was over. During this period efforts to prohibit the importation of items such as tea came to nothing.[14]

In recognition of the return of political normalcy after 1770, Americans raced to the stores, purchasing record amounts of imported British manufactures.[15] They celebrated their association with an empire of goods. From this perspective, we can view the incidents of mob protest in Boston as only small perturbations within an imperial regime embroiled in other, more pressing concerns. Moreover, these relatively minor flare-ups were not uniquely American. For comparison, we might consider the Irish situation, where eighteenth-century British authorities were able to deal easily with the likes of William Wood (author of an extremely unpopular scheme throughout Ireland to produce a new coinage) or Charles Lucas (a radical Dublin apothecary whose political ideas led to exile but not to revolution).[16]

No doubt, Parliament's attempts to raise revenue from stamps, sugar, and other consumer goods irritated colonial Americans, especially those who resided in port cities. Moreover, it is true that the members of the British cabinet found the destruction of private property in Boston alarming. But the fact of the matter is that the organizers of the various Boston protests—even at the height of the Stamp Act crisis—did not receive much support from ordinary people living in other parts of British America. Leading members of the colonial assemblies wrote to their counterparts in other colonies; highly localized threats of coercion persuaded the collectors of stamp fees to resign their posts . . . that was about it.[17] Even in Massachusetts—the alleged hotbed of discontent—residents of smaller towns expressed little enthusiasm for the agenda of the Boston radicals. Indeed, community records contain far more discussion about the need to fence pigs and supply ministers with firewood than about parliamentary regulations on commerce. Attempts to organize boycotts of British manufactures sputtered, and American merchants seemed more worried that other American merchants were cheating than about the threat of parliamentary oppression.

The empire's success at controlling occasional provincial risings should be unsurprising. After all, colonists viewed their contribution to the victory of Great Britain over the French during the Seven Years' War (1756–1763) as incontrovertible evidence of their loyalty to the empire. By their own lights, they were now full partners in a powerful, expanding imperial regime. Ties with the mother country represented opportunity, not oppression. Inasmuch as the Americans experienced a growing sense of nationalism after the war, they expressed an almost reflexive emotional attachment with Great Britain, a bond sometimes described as colonial nationalism. Like other subjects throughout the empire, they believed that their relationship with Britain preserved fundamental constitutional rights, stimulated Atlantic commerce, and advanced the Protestant faith against Catholic rivals.[18] An ambitious London press carried cultural and commercial information from the center of the empire to the Atlantic periphery, providing yet another mechanism for affirming a shared British identity. The historical irony here is that a strong new sense of American political identity—what we know as American nationalism—resulted in the first instance not from a century or more of local tradition, but rather from the experience of rejection within a political and economic system that seemed to have worked so well. It was a sudden awareness of marginalization within the empire that gave rise to a new revolutionary solidarity.

The argument that the 1760s played only a tangential role in the coming of the American Revolution gains yet another measure of plausibility when we consider the celebrated colonists—John Adams, Benjamin Franklin, and John Dickinson, for example—who published impressive statements defending colonial rights against parliamentary oppression. These writers, whose works figure centrally in modern collections of revolutionary pamphlets, were not heralds of the creation of an independent republic. Like the so-called Irish patriots of the late seventeenth and early eighteenth centuries—John Toland and William Molyneux, to name just two—the colonists who chronicled the American grievances were members of a creole elite. Wealthy, privileged, and well-educated, these men felt like second-class subjects within an imperial structure centered in London.[19]

With a few notable exceptions such as Dickinson's *Letters from a Farmer in Pennsylvania* (1767–1768), their essays on constitutional rights within the empire did not enjoy broad readership, certainly nothing even remotely comparable to the vitriolic collection in *The Crisis* (1775) or Thomas Paine's *Common Sense* (1776).[20]

What these ambitious provincials most desired was the respect of leading British figures. They wished to be considered as fully British and not as lesser beings inhabiting the distant marchlands of empire. George Washington sulked when he was not given a proper commission in the British army. John Adams, looking to make a legal career in Massachusetts, complained bitterly about local Crown favorites who he thought received an unfair amount of imperial patronage. Protesting his imagined inferiority in British eyes, Adams announced, "I say we are as handsome as old English folks, and so should be free." James Otis agreed. Benjamin Franklin held on to the hope of British acceptance to the very eve of revolution, and it was only after Alexander Wedderburn, the British solicitor-general under Lord North, humiliated Franklin during a public hearing in London that the American felt the full sting of rejection.[21] Other creole leaders expressed similar resentment at what they perceived as their inferior status within the empire.

The point of these observations is not that men such as Adams and Otis were hypocrites mouthing the language of colonial rights when they were really scheming for office and honor. They wrote nobly about freedom and liberty within the context of what they regarded as a very appealing imperial bureaucracy. They demanded acceptance, not separation. Francis Bernard, royal governor of Massachusetts during the 1760s, understood how easy it would have been to accommodate these ambitious colonials. On 4 February 1769 he advised the Earl of Hillsborough that if Parliament created an upper house in each colony—a sort of provincial House of Lords—filled with wealthy Americans appointed by the king, it would "go a great way to remedy the disorders which the Governments of America are subject to." Bernard predicted, no doubt correctly, that eager Americans would fall all over themselves to have "Baron prefixed to their Name." The beauty of the change would be that the addition of so "many royal honors in the new form of Government, will assist the establishment of it, by engaging men who are ripe for honors to reconciling the people to the System which introduces them."[22] The Reverend Jeremy Belknap claimed that the members of privileged families were entirely receptive to such notions. Writing at the time, Belknap claimed, "We had, among ourselves, a set of men, who, ambitious of perpetuating the rank of their families, were privately seeking the establishment of an *American* Nobility; out of which, an intermediate branch of legislation, between the royal and democratic powers, should be appointed."[23] How ordinary Americans would have reacted to the creation of a colonial aristocracy is not known. They never warmed to doffing their caps in deference to social betters. In any case, nothing came of the proposal, since parliamentary leaders did in fact look at the Americans, as well as the Irish and Scots, as lesser subjects of the king.

The traditional narrative of the coming of the Revolution confronts one other curious anomaly. During the early 1770s, tens of thousands of Irish migrants flooded into the middle colonies. Most of them were Protestants, driven from their homes in part by British regulations restricting the export of linen from Ireland to England. These regulations compromised an industry on which the income of many Irish families depended. Even as the First Continental Congress was meeting in Philadelphia in September 1774, boatloads of Irish men and women arrived almost daily in the city. They marched in huge numbers past Carpenters' Hall on their way to western Pennsylvania.

What is significant about this migration is that a very large percentage of the Continental Lines that fought with distinction during the American Revolution were Irish. These men had no personal memory of the Stamp Act protests of 1765 or the Boston Massacre of 1770. They were not part of the story we tell ourselves about the decade-long series of grievances that led inevitably to independence. They brought their own histories to the New World. One observer at the time noted that the Irish emigrants had "dispositions which savors too much of rebellion." A British merchant warned Lord Dartmouth, "These rebellious sentiments were especially prevalent in the back settlements particularly in Pennsylvania."[24] We might also consider that many of the American soldiers during the Revolution were but small children at the time of the Stamp Act. It is hard to comprehend their commitment to independence outside the context of the British army's occupation of Boston and its use of armed force against the ordinary people in the Massachusetts countryside. They certainly did not have personal memories of earlier moments of protest.

III

When, we might ask, did the American Revolution begin? Most Americans believed that the effective start occurred soon after the destruction of the tea in Boston Harbor. David Ramsay, a gifted historian, declared confidently that this moment marked the commencement of "a new era of the American controversy." Ramsay continued:

> The Revolution was not forced on the people by ambitious leaders grasping at supreme power, but every measure of it was forced on Congress, by the necessity of the case, and the voice of the people. The change of the public mind of America respecting the connection with Great-Britain, is without parallel. In a short span of two years, nearly three millions of people passed from love and duty of loyal subjects, to the hatred and resentment of enemies.[25]

The Reverend Jonas Clark, who had witnessed the killing of members of his congregation by British Regulars at Lexington, put the point even more forcefully. He argued that it was the events of April 19, 1775, that triggered a surge of popular resistance to the imperial regime. "It is not by us alone, that this day is to be noticed," he explained. "This *ever memorial day* is full of importance to all around—to this whole land and nation; and big with the fate of *Great-Britain* and *America.*—From this *remarkable day* will an important *era* begin for both *America* and *Britain*. And from the *nineteenth of April, 1775,* we may venture to predict, will be dated, in future history, THE LIBERTY or SLAVERY of the AMERICAN WORLD."[26]

Although the exact dates may vary from commentator to commentator, there can be no doubt that the political landscape of colonial America changed radically. Suddenly, almost spontaneously, thousands of ordinary people—most of them living in small farming communities—resisted British authority as they had never done before. In terms of numbers alone, their participation in rebellion had no precedent. As one would expect, the confrontation with British officials occurred for the most part in Massachusetts. Groups of armed colonists drove members of the governor's council—men appointed to the post by the king—from their country homes. They demanded that these representatives of the Crown resign. They forced local militia officers who bore royal commissions to step down.

Although no one died as a result of the mobilization of so many people, the threat of violence hung in the air. General Gage, the newly appointed royal governor of Massachusetts, was not prepared for this huge wave of unrest. Writing to his superior in London, Gage reported "popular fury was never greater in this province than at present."[27] He did not exaggerate. Hundreds of angry Americans appeared in Cambridge, where they confronted Lieutenant Governor Thomas Oliver. At such moments it was always tempting to blame the disruption on a few malcontents, troublemakers and rabble. But these insurgents were ordinary Americans, property holders and not the dregs of society. As Oliver observed with obvious surprise, "I perceived they were the land-holders of the neighboring towns." He later reaffirmed that the people demanding their rights were "no mob, but sober, orderly people."[28]

Each passing day throughout the summer of 1774 it became increasingly clear that those who had previously remained silent or expressed indifference about the state of imperial politics were coming forward. Newspapers carried stories of communities where a newly empowered public demanded that British leaders retreat from their insistence on parliamentary sovereignty. A newspaper reported, for example, how a relatively obscure village dealt with the crisis. One can almost imagine how a group of ordinary people, perhaps a little uncomfortably, debated issues that had only recently intruded on their lives. The "inhabitants of the 5th parish in Gloucester" described themselves as "being few in number, and chiefly poor fishermen, [who] have not time nor skill in the studies of politicks." But whatever their education may have been, they deemed it time to speak up. In an essay appearing under the title "The Fish Hook and Fowling Piece," they announced, "we have in our colonies, many stupid villains endeavouring to aid in fastening on our necks and that of our posterity the yoke of bondage . . . How warm we feel; good God, our trust in thee. Our fowling pieces are ready while our fishing lines are in hand."[29] Most towns passed resolves declaring their loyalty to the king and enforcing a boycott on tea, the symbol of British tyranny in America.

We can attribute this whirlwind of activity to two elements that greatly exacerbated the sting of rejection. First, as we have noted, people living in the countryside who had not experienced serious inconvenience as a result of earlier parliamentary regulations viewed the Coercive Acts—significantly, known in America as the Intolerable Acts—as an unwarranted and highly personal attack on their economic and political lives. In general, New England farmers did quite well. They purchased imported British goods in ever-increasing volume. They may not have liked the introduction of new taxes on favorite items such as tea, but they certainly could have paid higher prices for consumer satisfaction.

The Coercive Acts passed early in 1774 were entirely different in character. They were punitive. The members of Parliament made it abundantly clear that they intended to make an example of Boston throughout the empire. According to Lord North, the town would either compensate the owners of the lost tea or suffer dire consequences. Some of his allies could hardly contain their sense of vindictive pleasure at the prospect of teaching the unruly colonists a lesson. One representative insisted that "the flagitiousness of the offense"—dumping the tea into Boston Harbor—fully justified the belief that "the town of Boston ought to be knocked about their ears, and destroyed."[30]

Such jingoistic declarations played well in England. More to the point, they circulated in the London newspapers that eventually reached America, fueling even greater popular discontent. A few members of Parliament remained skeptical of the punitive policy—a show of toughness in the absence of constructive remedy—and confronting North they warned that the Coercive Acts will "soon inflame all America, and stir up a contention you will not be able to pacify." Another speaker warned that no good could come from ill-conceived vindictiveness. He observed with the kind of regret that comes from knowing that a government has charted a path that can only make matters worse: "I now venture to predict to this House, that the effect of the present Bill must be productive of a General Confederacy, to resist the power of this country."[31] He was correct. The ruling majority, hell-bent on teaching the colonists a lesson, never gave his warning a second thought.

The Coercive Acts were the name given to what was in fact a bundle of four separate statutes.[32] The two most inflammatory pieces of legislation were the Boston Port Act and the Massachusetts Government Act, both of which impinged directly on the lives of ordinary people throughout the colony. The Port Act closed Boston to all commerce. The British navy enforced the law, cutting off not only long-distance Atlantic trade, but also local markets for such basic necessities of urban life as firewood and fresh meat. Goods destined for Boston had to be off-loaded in other ports—

Salem being the most suitable—and then at considerable additional expense transported overland to Boston. The disruption of the local economy
affected the labor market almost immediately. A large number of workers
associated with maritime trade—sail makers, caulkers, and coopers, for
example—lost their source of income. These men were vulnerable in the
best of times; the Port Act reduced them and their families to poverty.

A second highly irritating component of the Coercive Acts was the
Massachusetts Government Act, which was designed to curtail popular
participation in normal political affairs. It annulled key sections of the
Massachusetts Bay Charter that had served for almost a century as the
colony's *de facto* constitution. Under the new regulations, the king appointed the members of the governor's council. Voters had previously participated in open elections for local representatives and those who served
in the Lower House of Representatives. The House of Representatives
and the council had elected members of the council. By the standards of
the times the franchise in Massachusetts was quite large, certainly larger
than that found in many towns and boroughs in England, and so the
change severely impacted representation that was independent of Crown
influence. The legislation also limited town meetings to one a year. It is
tempting to romanticize local government in Massachusetts as a democratic forum in which colonial farmers felt empowered to speak freely
about a variety of topics. Even if this nostalgic depiction exaggerates the
level of popular participation, we should recognize that Parliament's punitive legislation hugely upset the governance of local communities. Lord
North may have believed that this change would dampen dissent. As with
so many imperial policies that only make sense thousands of miles from
the places where they are implemented, this one interrupted routine business while inflaming universal anger.

Both acts had a palpable impact on people who had played absolutely
no part in the destruction of the tea. This is a fundamental point in understanding the politics of rejection. No doubt, many colonists saw the implementation of the Coercive Acts as another distressing indication that what
passed for constitutional law in England did not do so in Massachusetts.
But the depth of popular rage reflected more than indignation over abstract principles. The fact that the hated acts directly touched the lives of
urban workers and rural farmers served to exacerbate the emotional reaction. It was one thing to read essays discussing whether the common law

extended to the New World or the applicability of ancient statutes to America, and quite another to lose one's job or be prohibited from holding town meetings.

Earlier confrontations with Parliament had led to compromise, adjustments, and strategic retreats in the face of resistance. Those possibilities were not on offer in 1774. George III and Lord North dug in their heels, loudly proclaiming that this time the uppity colonists would not get off so lightly. It is no wonder that in this radically changed political environment Americans concluded that they had become second-class subjects of the king, indeed were being marginalized in an empire long associated with prosperity and freedom. As the author of a 1775 "Letter to the Inhabitants of Massachusetts Bay" explained, the colonists were entitled to "*all* the liberties of Englishmen." But the fact of the matter was that "because you are colonists, you can pretend no claim to them."[33] Another writer in a piece specifically directed "to the PUBLIC" observed, "If the Parliament of Great Britain are allowed to bring their Laws upon your Farms and your soil, to regulate your internal Policy, and snatch from the honest Proprietor his peaceable and well earned Possessions ... [then] adieu to Liberty and all the Train of Blessings that attend her." After all, the summer of 1774 had brought forth "Men who think it laudable, and their Duty, to die in the Defense of their Liberties."[34]

Hostility to the Coercive Acts might have been sufficient to ignite organized rejection to British authority throughout Massachusetts. But there was another element in this volatile mix that intensified popular discontent. On May 13, 1774, General Thomas Gage arrived in Boston to assume his duties as the colony's governor. A large number of regular troops accompanied him. Employing the military to police civil society is almost always bound to increase tensions. Boston proved no exception. Only a few months earlier Gage had charmed George III by observing that the Americans "will be Lions, whilst we are Lambs, but if we take the resolute part they will undoubtedly prove very meek."[35]

For all of his bravado, Gage quickly discovered that the colonial lions were more formidable animals than he had anticipated. To be sure, Americans were not prepared to confront the British soldiers in pitched battle. But they controlled the immediate countryside, so that Gage was extremely reluctant to send troops outside of Boston. Before the action at Lexington and Concord almost a year later, he authorized only a few raids beyond the city center. More significant for our purposes is how ordinary people reacted to military occupation. Some writers raised constitutional issues about how a standing army endangered civilian liberty.[36] However persuasive such legal arguments may have been, they did not fully capture the emotional response of residents who had to deal daily with soldiers on the streets. As anyone knows who has followed more recent events throughout the world, military occupation is not a theoretical matter. It involves real people, most often poorer residents and underpaid soldiers who miss the comforts of home.

There was certainly no love lost between the British troops and the colonials who lived in Boston. The Regulars who camped out on the Commons competed with ordinary people for increasingly scarce resources such as food and firewood. Residents resented the humiliation of being stopped at military checkpoints, where sentries demanded formal passwords. The soldiers harassed men and women conducting normal business.[37] A writer in the *Boston Gazette* reported, "The inhabitants now receive that insult and damage which was never experienced in the hottest wars we have been engaged in with France and Spain, and their allies." He added, "What further cruelties we are to suffer, we know not, but whether America, or even this single Town, is in this way to be brought to the feet of Lord North, with the full surrender of their inestimable rights and liberties, time only can determine."[38] Considering the extent to which leading members of the king's cabinet had underestimated American resolve, it is not surprising that Gage was soon begging superiors in London for as many as 20,000 additional troops.

It is important not to get too far ahead of the story. The traditional narrative of independence usually jumps from the arrival of British troops and the passage of the Coercive Acts in 1774 all the way to Lexington and Concord in 1775. The Battle of Bunker Hill looms on the horizon. The problem with this perspective on the flow of events is that it deflects attention away from two developments fundamental to the transition from scattered, isolated incidents of resistance to large-scale mobilization possessing genuine revolutionary potential. The first element was the creation of a huge charity designed to assist the people of Boston who had been thrown out of work by the Port Act. The second was an order issued in September 1774 by the Continental Congress authorizing the formation of local committees in all thirteen colonies. With this decision, Congress effectively ceded responsibility for policing political resistance to the small communities of America.

Throughout their long history Americans have frequently shown compassion for others who have suffered from flood, fire, or famine. The extraordinary outpouring of aid and sympathy that occurred in 1774 may have been the first example of such a display of public generosity. It certainly had no precedent in the colonies.[39] The appeal was electric. As "A Friend to American Liberties" announced in June 1774, "There are thousands . . . which depend wholly on their daily work for their bread, and are now reduced to distress for want of employment, and are not able to support their families." The question that colonists could not ignore was whether they would "enjoy plenty and see our brethren suffer in *our own* cause, and we not relieve them when it is in our power? The love of ourselves, the love of our country, and the love of GOD and religion calls for our assistance!"[40]

Without prodding from a central government, communities and individuals provided support for distant strangers whose lives had been disrupted by political oppression. It was not constitutional concerns about parliamentary sovereignty that triggered this outpouring of generosity. People living in places as far away as South Carolina imagined men and women like themselves as the innocent victims of oppression. A sense of shared humanity inspired a spontaneous wave of giving, which among other things served to heighten awareness of common grievances and interests. Charity fed into politics, helping to create the emotional capital necessary to sustain revolution. As one respected political figure in Philadelphia observed, "What can be done to relieve them [the people of Boston] and serve the cause of the liberties of America is the great Question which agitates the minds of the People."[41]

Even by modern standards the size and complexity of the relief network was impressive. Although several colonial assemblies urged Americans to contribute to the cause, the donations were entirely voluntary. Gifts large and small poured into Massachusetts. Many communities raised money through local subscriptions. Transferring these funds to Boston's Committee of Donations proved extremely difficult in an age before checking accounts and credit cards. More common were shipments of food and other household supplies. Surviving records acknowledged the arrival of rice, sheep, rye, corn, codfish, firewood, flour, peas, and butter. One man provided a load of cabbage; a person in New York dispatched "the best pipe of Brandy in his distillery." When someone asked whether the laboring poor of Boston really needed strong drink, he responded, "The generosity of the Virginians & Carolinians &c. was great and honorable with respect to food," but he believed that the "glorious sufferers for the common good ought to drink as well as eat."[42] The desire to help extended to "the Aboriginal Natives of Christian-Town on Martha's Vineyard." The Native Americans collected two pounds sterling, a large amount coming from a group that understood the meaning of oppression.[43]

Without prodding from prominent colonial leaders, people in small communities connected their own generosity to an imperial crisis that had engulfed Americans about whom they knew very little. The suffering of others invited local discussion about imperial policy that the king and the members of his cabinet surely did not welcome. Ordinary people were forging links, thinking about a shared political identity quite different from that binding them to the mother country.[44] These were nascent glimmerings, to be sure, but insomuch as public opinion shapes policy decisions, the American people were adding something more than the fencing of hogs and the mending of roads to their conversations about power and its abuses. In June 1775 residents in Savannah, Georgia, informed the Boston Committee of Donations, "There are many among us, who sincerely espouse the great cause contended for by you; & who ardently wish that the noble stand you have made in defense of these rights, which as men, and as British subjects we are entitled to, may be crowned with success."[45] Like their imagined brothers and sisters in Massachusetts, they felt slighted, rejected without justification. The inhabitants of Stonington, Connecticut, celebrated the prospect of participating in a larger cause. "We rejoice to see so many of the neighboring Colonies, and even Towns," they declared, "vying with each other in the liberal Benefactions to the distressed, injured Town of Boston."[46]

Two villages in Connecticut reveal dramatically how reports about the suffering of Boston's impoverished workers sparked a political awakening. Neither town was the scene of battle; at this time military occupation was not a serious threat. And yet despite their relative isolation, these communities turned a general call for donations into seminars about resistance to the British Empire. Such examples of local mobilization alert us to the power of sympathy in generating broad, even national political engagement.

Lebanon is located in eastern Connecticut, north of New London. Participants in an emergency town meeting held on July 18, 1774, conducted a kind of teach-in that encouraged members of the community to explore, as they had not done before, their full commitment to the needs of other Americans at a moment of crisis. The turnout was unusually large. At least "three Hundred respectable Freeholders" took part in a discussion sparked initially by "the most alarming and dangerous Situation of American Liberties . . . and to consider what we ought to do for the Relief of Boston."

After the inhabitants had carefully reviewed the issues at stake, they concluded that "the Controversy now subsisting between the Parliament of Great Britain and the English American Colonies, respecting the Rights and Liberties of the latter, is a Matter and Cause of the most important and interesting Nature, that can affect our Minds, next to our own everlasting Welfare." For a political issue even to come close to concerns about eternal salvation highlighted its extraordinary significance. The closing of Boston forced them to question ideas about their relationship to a wider imperial world. They praised their ancestors for leaving seventeenth-century England, where they had been persecuted for their religious beliefs, "to explore and settle a new World." Townspeople in Lebanon asserted that as colonists in America they possessed the same rights as did the king's subjects living in the mother country, and therefore, they felt justified in condemning the Coercive Acts, which clearly compromised those very same rights. These Connecticut farmers were not about to accept political rejection without a fight.

As the discussion grew more animated, a crucial shift occurred. The residents of Lebanon suddenly realized that they had not come together simply to talk of abstractions. They focused their anger on the practical issues at hand. After all, the rights and liberties that needed defending belonged to the suffering poor of Boston, real men and women with whom they identified. The people in this village reaffirmed an active belief that Boston's cause was in fact their cause. What we encounter on the local level is the fabrication of a powerful commitment to cooperation. Without intending to do so, Lebanon farmers found themselves thinking about their political responsibilities within the empire from a radically new perspective. For them, it seemed entirely reasonable to declare that innocent people in Boston were victims of "unparalleled Hardship and Distress ... for their having been ever forward and resolute in Defense of their and the common rights of the Colonies." Within this emotionally charged context, the community recognized a duty to contribute "to the Relief of those poor and distressed Inhabitants of said Boston." Donations raised in the town served as the tangible seal of political solidarity. Aware of the importance of communication in promoting a sense of shared purpose, the people of Lebanon not only entered their resolves into the official "Records of the Town"—a message of determination for future generations—but also inserted them in the *Connecticut Gazette*.[47]

Stonington, a small Connecticut community located on the Long Island Sound, also linked the need to help the suffering poor of Boston with a general threat of British tyranny. As in many other villages during this period, the people who attended an official town meeting on July 11, 1774, began by reaffirming their loyalty to the Crown. By their own lights they did not condone rebellion and most surely did not support independence. They insisted that the imperial crisis could still be defused. But the danger to all Americans was very real. The North administration had clearly violated the Magna Carta as well as the British constitution. Suddenly finding themselves thrust into a larger colonial debate about an uncertain political future shared with distant strangers, the Stonington meeting declared that is was "Deeply impressed with the alarming and critical situation of our Publick Affairs, by the many repeated attacks upon the liberties of the English American Colonies, by sundry acts of parliament, both for the purpose of raising a revenue in America, as well as the late most extraordinary act for blocking up the port of Boston." What could these people do? How could they demonstrate their resolve though actions rather than words? The answer was charity. Announcing that they "heartily sympathize with our distressed brethren, the Bostonians, who we view as victims sacrificed to the shrine of arbitrary power, and more immediately suffering in the common cause," the townspeople created a committee charged specifically with gathering donations for Boston. The meaning of "common cause" was left ambiguous.[48] By imagining solidarity at this moment, they were in effect creating it.

A second major development that brought huge numbers of ordinary Americans into the resistance movement happened almost by accident.

The First Continental Congress met in Philadelphia in September 1774. The mood of the delegates was somber. Some representatives wanted to make a strong defense of colonial rights. Others urged Congress to move more slowly, fearing that voicing firm opposition to British policies might compromise ongoing negotiations. No one advocated independence—at least, not openly. Whatever their intentions, events on the ground radically changed the political climate. No sooner had the delegates gathered than they learned that the people of New England had organized a large insurgent force, and that even as the debates were taking place in Philadelphia, some twenty thousand armed men were marching on Boston. As it turned out, a bizarre rumor had sparked this spontaneous rising. Misinformation about the deployment of British troops in Boston persuaded people in small towns from Connecticut to New Hampshire that the British navy was planning to bombard the city. The justification for this attack was apparently revenge for past disobedience. It did not occur to the New Englanders until much later that the destruction of Boston made little sense while so many British Regulars were stationed there.[49]

Congress almost panicked when it heard the news. It appeared that the ordinary people were getting ahead of their leaders. If the delegates lost control of the situation, then all hope for a united front opposing Great Britain would be destroyed. In their effort to keep the protest movement from fragmenting, Congress endorsed what was known as the Association. The goal of this scheme was to strengthen and coordinate an effective boycott of British goods. Bringing pressure on Parliament through an interruption of the marketplace had been tried before, but competing economic interests in the colonies had undermined the plan's impact. With the imperial crisis deteriorating, Congress decided to enforce a boycott more rigorously.[50] In a statement of October 20, 1774, it announced, "To obtain redress of these grievances which threaten destruction to the lives, liberty, and property of his Majesty's subjects, in North America, we are of opinion that a non-importation, non-consumption, and non-exportation agreement, faithfully adhered to, will prove the most speedy, effectual, and peaceable measure."[51]

The Association contained fourteen separate articles, most of them addressing the precise dates that various parts of the system would go into effect. Section eleven stands out, since its implementation altered the entire character of the American Revolution. Perhaps because the boycott did not force Parliament to back down, historians have minimized the Association's extraordinary significance. That is unfortunate. The agreement gave ordinary people throughout the British colonies direct and personal responsibility for executing congressional mandates. It made certain that the "where" of revolution would be in thousands of small American communities.

The Association reflected profoundly pragmatic reasoning. In 1774 Congress did not possess constitutional legitimacy. It was an extralegal body whose members were sensitive about the source of their own authority. Because of its tenuous standing, Congress desperately needed to demonstrate that it did in fact represent the interests of all thirteen colonies. The Association addressed the problem by establishing a brilliantly innovative power-sharing agreement. The plan linked small communities throughout America to a nascent central government, an act that served to affirm Congress's right to legislate for a country that was not yet a country. The Association encouraged large-scale mobilization by creating a huge network of local committees possessing the power to police the boycott. That certainly represented a crucial step forward in establishing a viable central government. By the same token, however, it awarded the people a voice in the revolutionary process. In a marvelous exercise of circular logic the men who served on the committees could now plausibly claim that their own legitimacy derived from Congress.

Key passages in the Association invited local communities to expand the base of resistance. The eleventh article authorized that "a committee be chosen in every county, city, and town by those who are qualified to vote for representatives in the legislature, whose business it shall be attentively to observe the conduct of all persons touching this Association." The resolution charged ordinary people with the task of monitoring the flow of goods—in other words, with responsibility for overseeing their neighbors' commercial activities. Local bodies were given the power to define the size and character of the committees. The resolution called for elections. Since most colonies allowed a majority of adult white males to vote in assembly elections, Congress opened the door for broad popular participation in the enforcement of revolutionary edicts.

Moreover, Congress gave the committees unambiguous police powers over political transgressions. The eleventh article authorized "a majority" of any committee to investigate possible violations of the general boycott—

drinking tea, for example—and if it concluded that a breach had occurred, it should "forthwith cause the truth of the case to be published in the Gazette; to the end that all such foes to the rights of British America may be publicly known, and universally condemned as the enemies of American liberty." People who ignored the Association risked becoming nonpersons, individuals literally excluded from society. Supporters of the agreement pledged to "break off all dealings with him or her." Enduring public shame may not sound particularly menacing in more modern times. But in the late eighteenth century the threat of being shunned by neighbors was sufficient to discourage the purchase of British goods. And the identification of political wrongdoers in a newspaper meant that for ordinary people there was no escaping public condemnation.

These two developments—the creation of a huge voluntary charity and the Association—did not in themselves turn rebellion into revolution. But for ordinary Americas these changes in the political landscape prepared the ground by involving people living outside New England in coordinated resistance. The widespread belief that the poor of Boston were the innocent victims of oppressive imperial policies transformed theoretical complaints about undermining the British constitution into blame. For people to ask in highly personal terms "Who has done this to us?" is a harbinger of regime instability.[52] The Association helped channel this emotional response. The network of enforcement committees may at first have focused attention on local commercial transactions, but once a structure had been established, the committees did a lot more than exposing tea drinkers.

IV

In the popular mind, reports about revolutionary committees throughout the world conjure up frightening images of undisciplined mobs, kangaroo courts, and gruesome executions. In these stories menacing vigilantes appear on the streets of capital cities demanding reform, or more often, the overthrow of what they see as an oppressive and corrupt government. Such groups played a major role in advancing the French and Russian Revolutions, just to cite two major examples. As the ancien regime in France lost legitimacy after 1789, sans-culottes claimed authority, enforcing ideological purity on the populace as it struggled to comprehend radical political change. In 1917 Russian committees of workers and soldiers sprung up almost overnight.[53] These were extralegal bodies that justified their actions, however violent, in the name of the people.

We do not often think of the period immediately before American independence in these terms. We should. At minimum, to do so would be instructive. In 1774 and 1775 local committees performed many of the same functions as did those found in France or Russia. They mobilized opposition, ferreting out counterrevolutionary elements from New Hampshire to Georgia. These revolutionary cells sustained resistance to Great Britain during periods when it seemed that the colonists had little chance of victory.

But for all that, the American experience differed greatly from that of other revolutionary regimes. From a comparative perspective, we should observe two aspects of the American committee system that distinguished it from those of countries such as France and Russia. First, the American committees seldom sanctioned popular violence, however extreme their rhetoric may have sounded. Even when they identified domestic enemies, they expressed fear that popularly selected, extralegal committees might inadvertently promote anarchy. They saw mob rule—or perhaps more accurately, the threat to private property—as a threat equally as great as British tyranny. American committees meted out punishments, but tellingly, they generally endeavored to reconcile neighbors who had failed to support resistance. They encouraged public confession; they urged those caught aiding the British to take oaths promising not to engage in loyalist activities in the future.

There are several ways to interpret this behavior. Warnings about the dangers of anarchy may have revealed deep-seated fears among wealthier revolutionaries—those who served in Congress, for example—that political resistance against Britain might encourage ordinary Americans to think of oppression in terms of economic class. People who enjoy privileged lives seldom welcome the notion that less privileged people might actually be their social equals. Calls to maintain order in a time of political crisis not only promoted unity in the fight against Britain, but also served to discourage domestic divisions that might have upset the social structure. Another possibility was present. In a racially divided society the committees—especially in the South—may have concluded that white revolutionaries in the name of solidarity should encourage pardons and forgiveness of other whites lest slaves conclude that their masters had lost control of the political situation. The committees certainly had no interest in including real slaves in their complaints about slavery to king and Parliament. Appeals for liberty in the new nation always strained against the institutions of unfreedom.

Whatever the case may have been, implementation of the Association meant that ordinary people gained a voice in public affairs that they doggedly preserved throughout the war. The committees sustained resistance to Britain and provided a forum in which revolutionaries could air grievances—against imperial rule as well as against other Americans who wanted to limit popular participation in public life. Although the committees figured prominently during the early years of the rebellion—1774–1775—they continued to operate throughout the country long after the war had begun. They became part of the nation's political culture. If they were not, as some might argue, a reflection of the growth of democracy, then they were at least a latent force in American politics known as public opinion. As we shall discover, throughout the war the people in local communities repeatedly revived the committee system whenever they thought that the government—even their own—had gone astray.

Americans called their revolutionary committees by several different names. The most common, especially before the creation of the Association, was simply Committee of Correspondence. By 1775 some committees identified themselves as Committees of Safety or Committees of Safety and Observation. To add to the confusion, after British authority collapsed throughout the countryside, some colonies—now states—formed centralized committees of safety, which were tasked with responsibility to coordinate community or county committees. Whatever they were called, these various bodies took on similar duties, the chief being implementation of the articles of the Association.

Although Congress thought that free and open elections should determine membership on the committees, the actual selection process varied greatly from region to region. In North Carolina "mass meetings" chose the committees, which Josiah Martin, the last royal governor, described as "extraordinary tribunals."[54] In the middle colonies and New England, committees were usually subject to annual election. Local governments determined the size of these groups, and some had more than fifty members.

The Committee of Safety in Wilmington, North Carolina, was a rarity in that it kept detailed records of all its activities. It held its first meeting on November 23, 1774. The "Freeholders" of the town assembled at the courthouse to select persons "to carry more effectually into Execution the resolves of the late congress held at Philadelphia." Nine names were put forward and without much discussion were "universally assented to." Within a few months, however, the townsmen had second thoughts about the initial selection. Perhaps because of complaints, Wilmington ordered an entirely new election based on an expanded franchise. The community justified the change on the basis of its strong belief that "the people [should] have an opportunity of confirming or annulling their former choice." By March 6, 1775, Wilmington increased membership on the committee to twenty-five, more than double the original number. The men who served may have felt a larger committee would provide them with a measure of security. After all, if resistance to the Crown failed, they could find themselves subject to arrest. Whatever their reasoning, this large body resolved "that all Members of the Committee now present go in a body & wait on all Housekeepers in Town with the Association . . . & request their signing it, or declare their reasons for refusing, [so] that such Enemies to their Country may be set forth to public View & treated with the Contempt they merit."[55] One can only imagine the shock residents of Wilmington felt when they confronted such a large committee standing in the street in front of their homes. Under such conditions only a very brave or foolish person would have refused to sign the Association.

The people serving on these committees seem to have had little previous experience in local affairs. According to the eighteenth-century historian Jeremy Belknap, protest against Great Britain helped advance men "who knew nothing of the theory of government, and had never before been concerned in public business."[56] Although they were certainly respected property owners, the newcomers were by no means wealthy. We know that they were in general younger, less socially prominent than those men who they pushed aside. The most significant point about this sudden shift in personnel is the magnitude of the transition. Thousands of separate committees recruited huge numbers of *new* men into the political forum. Because so many records have been lost, it would be impossible to give a precise figure for the surge of committee participation. But there is no doubt that the total was very large. In Philadelphia, for example, several hundred new men took leading roles in the resistance movement. In rural Pennsylvania the number was many times larger. In New Jersey the committees attracted at least 450 who had never before held positions of leadership.[57] The story in the other colonies was much the same. Probably few congressmen who voted for the Association anticipated the radical consequences of their decision.

A plan to enforce a continental boycott had brought forth by 1775 a formidable infrastructure of revolutionary leadership. The Reverend Isaac Mansfield fully appreciated what had happened. Preaching to a body of new army recruits in Roxbury, Massachusetts, Mansfield praised the spirit of union that energized resistance. How had such cooperation come about?

> The means of forming this union deserve some notice. Distinct Committees were appointed in most of the towns of this province, and through the continent for the management of special matters, particularly such as were of a commercial nature. These Committees were large, and composed of persons that had not before been honor'd with the confidence of the public; the public eye stimulated them to exertion ... each one acquired a degree of importance which was new to him; and by that means, whole communities and societies were Cemented together.[58]

In this unstable political environment the committees soon expanded their political agenda. That was to be expected. No doubt, they were responding to swiftly moving events that by April 1775 had sparked military confrontation. After Lexington most Americans who had supported resistance—boycotts and petitions to king and Parliament—knew there was no turning back, and following the battles in Massachusetts, the committees spent a lot of time attending to military matters: supplying local militia units with gunpower and firearms, overseeing drilling, and communicating with other committees about troop movements.

They did much more. In a wide range of political matters the committees aggressively filled the vacuum left by the collapse of imperial authority. Almost all of them pressured neighbors to sign the Association. Such efforts served to identify friends and foes. Even if some people misrepresented their allegiance—perhaps out of fear—the gathering of names proved to be an effective device for solidifying resistance to Great Britain. In New Hampshire local committees were impressively thorough, supplying the provisional state government with detailed lists of everyone willing publicly to support the American cause.[59] Most local committees disarmed suspicious people.

Political activities of this sort revealed a curiously unsettled situation. Throughout the country, the local committees insisted that they were carrying out the orders of Congress. At the same time, however, they responded to parochial concerns—in other words, to the people who had elected the members of these committees. Trying to comprehend events that were occurring in distant places, these local bodies found themselves forced to strike a delicate balance between order and insurgency, between resistance and reconciliation. A committee in Bergen County, New Jersey, attempted as best it could to negotiate the political tensions. It obtained 368 signatures from people pledging to enforce the Association, which the committee seems to have defined as an obligation to stand up to British troops. But even as it promoted armed rebellion the Bergen Committee worried about the "Anarchy and Confusion which will necessarily attend the present struggle for our Liberty unless the proper Steps are taken to preserve Regularity and Unanimity among us." Perhaps the committee members worried that an appeal for order might sound too tepid. In any case, they immediately added that they would "not submit to those Acts of Parliament which impose taxes on us Without our Consent and deprive us of our Constitutional Rights and Privileges."[60]

By attending to events in places such as Roxbury, Massachusetts, and Bergen County, New Jersey, we illuminate how the people worked out the meaning of resistance within their own communities. Each precinct, town, and county—wherever there was a committee—developed its own understanding of the imperial challenge. It was here that allegiances were forged and tested. The small town of New Windsor, New York—located a few miles north of West Point on the Hudson River—provides insight into these local conversations. Town residents met in May 1775, and in a moving statement of purpose they resolved:

> Persuaded that the salvation of the rights and liberties of America
> depend, under God, on the firm union of its inhabitants in a vigorous
> prosecution of the measures necessary for its safety; and convinced

of the necessity of preventing anarchy and confusion, which attend the dissolution of government, we, the freemen, freeholders, and inhabitants of New Windsor, being greatly alarmed at the avowed design of the Ministry to raise revenue in America, and shocked by the bloody scenes now acting in Massachusetts Bay, do, in the most solemn manner resolve never to become slaves.

The men attending this meeting then pledged to follow the orders from the Continental Congress and the Provincial Congress of New York, and "in all things follow the advice of our General Committee respecting the purposes aforesaid, the preservation of peace and good order, and the safety of individuals and property." Scores of people signed their names to this document, an agreement that at once affirmed a desire to maintain order in New Windsor—a conservative goal—and to resist parliamentary acts that they deemed oppressive—a radical proposition.[61]

Local committees soon found that maintaining order during a time of upheaval required more than collecting signatures pledging support for the Association. Many groups began more aggressively to identify potential enemies in their midst. As most authorities eager to suppress political dissent have learned throughout history, the committees discovered that it was very difficult to reveal exactly where their neighbors stood on political matters. If those who harbored deep reservations about organized resistance to Great Britain kept their opinions to themselves, no one could be certain whether or not they posed a real danger to the community. Exposure required public actions that betrayed secret allegiance or perhaps just profound doubts about the course of resistance. Of course, refusal to sign the Association broadcast a clear indication of reservations about defending America's "rights and liberties." Anyone who rejected the invitation to join the rebellion invited punishment. Failure to appear for militia practice triggered investigation. In this environment, it was not a good idea to express one's opposition in print or in speech. A committee in Middlesex, New Jersey, declared its "contempt and detestation of those insidious scribblers, who, with the vilest views, enlist themselves in the cause of the Ministry, and by the vilest means endeavor to affect a disunion among the good people of the Colonies . . . [as well as those who] persist in retailing the rotten, exploded, and ten thousand times confuted doctrines of passive acquiescence in the measures of Government, however distempered and tyrannical."[62]

Other examples reveal just how far the committees had come from the initial goal of boycotting British imports. In June 1775 the First Provincial Congress of South Carolina declared that "any person having violated or refused obedience to the authority of the Provincial Congress, shall, by the Committee of the district or parish in which such offender resides, be questioned relative thereto, and upon due conviction ... and continuing contumacious, such person shall, by the Committee, be declared and advertised, as an enemy to the Liberties of America, and an object for the resentment of the public." For good measure the Provincial Congress added that however the local committees went about the business of enforcement, they would "be supported in so doing."[63] The Provincial Congress of New Jersey announced a similar guideline. It voted to accept the decisions of the local committees, noting at the same time that civil officials were to be obeyed only "as far as shall be consistent with the measures adopted for the preservation of American freedom." The Somerset County Committee hardly needed encouragement. It ordered all committees throughout the county to institute immediately proceedings against those "who shall, either by word or deed, endeavor to destroy our unanimity in opposing the arbitrary and cruel measures of the British Ministry." In August 1775 a committee in Sussex County declared that anyone who "Shall hereafter Asperse any of the friends of Liberty in this County on Account of their Political Sentiments, or Shall Speak Contemptuously or Disrespectfully of the Continental and Provincial Congress or any of any in this County or in any Measures Adopted, or Appointed to be pursued by the Congress or Committees for the Public good & Safety" should be brought before a committee with the assistance of the local militia acting as a political police force and "dealt with according to his or their Deserts."[64]

Even at this early stage of rebellion—it did not yet merit being called a revolution—the committees' bark was more intimidating than their bite. Other revolutions throughout the world have experienced horrific bloodshed as groups of laborers or soldiers seized control of government in the name of the people. By comparison the actions of the American committees seem surprisingly tame. One might not have anticipated that local bodies would pass up the opportunity to use violence against suspected political enemies. Vigilantes did not roam the countryside burning estates; militia units did not summarily execute suspicious persons. How do we explain such constraint, especially when the committees spent so much time trying to ferret out neighbors who had not shown themselves to be "the friends of Liberty?"

The answer appears to have been a pragmatic realization that there were a lot more supporters of king and Parliament than the committees bargained for, and if small communities were to avoid outright civil war, they would be well advised not to alienate permanently other Americans who expressed loyalty to the mother country. In any case, people who criticized the committees—perhaps after too many strong drinks—often confessed publicly to their misconduct, took an oath not to do so again, and returned to the community. In a typical exchange the Rowan County Committee in North Carolina recorded that "Mr. Cook the Baptist Preacher" had appeared "and in the most explicit and humiliating Terms [professed] his Sorrow for signing the protest against the Cause of Liberty, which lately circulated in the fork of Yadkin—and other parts of his conduct in opposing the just Rights and Liberty of the Nation in general and American Liberties in particular."[65] Reverend Cook had been caught out; he learned his political lesson. The committee may not have converted him to the American cause, but it probably persuaded him that silence in the future was wiser than open opposition. Another man in Philadelphia apologized "in the presence of a great concourse of people" for an essay that contained "political sentiments . . . founded in the grossest error."[66]

No doubt, the entire episode embarrassed the author, but he was not physically punished. Perhaps even more to the point the spectators who watched the committees go about their work may have had second thoughts about openly praising the monarchy. African Americans played almost no part in these local affairs. They existed—except for those who fought for the new nation—outside an emerging revolutionary culture. Committees worried about bringing the likes of Reverend Cook back into the fold, but the slaves remained property, not future citizens of the republic.

V

Although the committees exercised unexpected restraint in dealing with their opponents, they did achieve their goal. They effectively outmaneuvered the loyalists before they became a serious counterrevolutionary force. Committee interrogations, the circulation of the Association, the disarming of suspicious people, and the publication of the names of those who violated the boycott served to maintain public order as well as to discourage potential enemies. As Joseph Reed, a Philadelphia leader, noted well before the Declaration of Independence, "I know of no power in this country ... that can protect an opposer of the public voice and conduct."[67] Another man in New Jersey echoed that opinion, adding that "unless you Join the Generall Cry you are deemed an Enemy to your Country."[68]

In local communities throughout the colonies, the people had taken control of the resistance movement. Some of their supporters worried that they had gone too far and had even promoted anarchy, for as Elbridge Gerry, a respected figure in Massachusetts politics, observed, "the people are fully possessed of their dignity from the frequent delineation of their rights, which have been published to defeat the ministerial party ... They now feel rather too much of their own importance, and it requires great skill to produce such subordination as is necessary."[69] He might have added more charitably that ordinary people had gained experience in organizing local affairs. They had tasted a measure of political equality.

An incident at the home of Thomas Mann Randolph, a great Virginia planter, revealed just how uppity the ordinary people had become. An English visitor noted that some Virginia "peasants" upon entering the house "took themselves chairs, drew near the fire, began spitting, pulling off their country boots all over mud, and then opened their business." When one of Randolph's friends complained of such rude behavior, the planter explained "it was unavoidable, the spirit of independency was converted into equality, and everyone who bore arms, esteemed himself upon a footing with his neighbor, and concluded with saying, 'No doubt, each of these men conceives himself, in every respect, my equal.'"[70] On this point he was absolutely correct. A robust sense of white equality was really not a problem. As Mercy Otis Warren, one of the first historians of the American Revolution, noted, the committees "produced unanimity and energy throughout the continent." As she explained, "thus, as despotism frequently springs from anarchy, a regular democracy sometimes arises from the severe encroachments of despotism."[71]

For all their enthusiasm, the American people did not know where resistance would take them or how long the conflict might last. The real test of popular participation in revolutionary activities would come later when the initial surge of popular defiance triggered by a sense of rejection gave way to a contagion of fear—the most dangerous political emotion.

CHAPTER TWO

ASSURANCE

Almost all revolutions face the ordeal of the second day. At the start of popular unrest, people take to the streets, excited, surprised at their own courage and audacity. Expressing confidence in their ability to effect genuine reform, they convince themselves—perhaps naively—that they will succeed. It soon becomes clear, however, that revolutionary goals are harder to achieve than the eager participants imagined. Doubt tempers enthusiasm; commitments to family and work fuel second thoughts. Most of all, they want assurance that they are justified in employing violence in a political cause. Like other revolutionaries throughout the world, ordinary Americans at the beginning of the contest with Great Britain wanted to be certain that they had not made a huge mistake.

As we have seen, during the two years before the Declaration of Independence, the humiliation of feeling treated as second-class subjects in the empire sparked resistance. But it soon became apparent that an additional element was required to move forward. After all, sustaining commitment to a political cause over time—the key to effective mobilization—required providing the American people with confidence that resistance did in fact possess intellectual and moral legitimacy. Otherwise, there was a possibility that taking up arms against the British state would be seen as no more than lashing out against objectionable government policies, an insupportable and short-lived phenomenon. Americans fiercely denied that they were rebels or rioters, or worse, common criminals. They insisted that they had a larger purpose, a vision of a new civil society worthy of personal sacrifice, even death.

At the moment of decision—when protests and petitions were no longer sufficient to carry the rebellion forward—Americans sought to justify resistance to British authority in ways that resonated persuasively within their own communities. Hard political choices were local and personal matters. Both emotion and reason came into play. How, they asked, could they defend taking up arms against king and Parliament? Were their actions justified in the eyes of God? Indeed, what responsibilities did ordinary Americans who seized power in the name of the people have to each other and to the state?

One might immediately insist that the answers to these questions about the legitimacy of revolution were self-evident. We have long subscribed to the belief that during the Revolution, Americans sacrificed the comforts of daily life in the name of noble principles such as rights and liberty. That claim is true to a point. But the assumption that such abstract principles—however worthy they may be—persuaded large numbers of colonists to sustain a political cause over a long war in which their lives and property were in peril raises nettlesome problems. One has to do with the character of human memory. After all, someone who had supported independence might look back after the war was over and explain his or her participation as an expression of an uncompromising love of liberty when in fact other beliefs and assumptions had been involved in making the actual decision to support revolution.

Many leading scholars have insisted that we should see the American Revolution as a transformative moment in the history of political ideas.[1] To be sure, these historians have recognized the importance of military operations and foreign negotiations, but for them, the crucial defining element during the run-up to independence was an extraordinary burst of intellectual creativity. Leaders reviewed classic political theory and developed powerful new arguments for a government based on the will of the people. This narrative of the origins of the American Revolution focuses on the writings of a small group of men who achieved national prominence during the war. One can easily understand why the country's most educated, cosmopolitan statesmen have received so much attention. Their lives were well documented, their correspondence collected, so we know not only what they read, but also how they interpreted these texts. Although their thinking was not secular, they generally adopted what were regarded at the time as enlightened, even deistic views on religion.

There is a lot more to the story. It is not that intellectual explanations for revolution are wrong. Rather, the challenge is connecting local experience to the writings of national figures such as Jefferson and Adams. When we turn to the ordinary people who experienced the day-to-day realities of revolution, we encounter a different interpretation of revolutionary events. For them, broadly shared religious assumptions about political responsibility explained why they should support the struggle for independence. Their understanding of revolutionary politics did not involve a rejection of the values of their leaders. The people's defense of rights and liberty—of sacrifice and responsibility—complemented that advanced by the Founders. Although the two languages of resistance promoted the same political goals—national unity and the establishment of a genuinely representative form of government—they sprang from quite different sources. Unless we fully appreciate how both groups—celebrated statesmen and ordinary people—gave meaning to revolution, we will not understand why it succeeded.

I

How the American revolutionaries explained the Revolution to themselves is a topic of fundamental importance in understanding how ordinary people created a new political culture. There has been no shortage of answers. Like other major political upheavals that have transformed the modern world, the American Revolution provoked a thorough examination of the foundations of political authority. One familiar approach concentrates on highly educated figures who warned that unless the people maintained constant vigilance, corrupt rulers would compromise inalienable rights Americans held dear. The danger could be reduced, they insisted, if citizens maintained their virtue in the political forum. In this scheme, virtue involved personal independence, an ability to stand above the political fray and avoid even a hint of corruption that would compromise honest judgment. Without active participation in public affairs by virtuous gentlemen, liberty would die and with it, the last best hope for the republic.

Revolutionary pamphlets often contained another significant defense of rights and liberty. American writers with legal training encouraged resistance to George III on the basis of a searching analysis of English statutes and the British constitution. A correct reading of English legal history, they insisted, validated independence and the creation of a new nation.[2] Whether these assumptions and beliefs qualified as a genuine ideology—in the sense that Communism did during the Russian Revolution, for example—remains a matter of debate, but there is no doubt that within this interpretive framework socially prominent American authors who are still honored today made a persuasive case for national independence and a new form of government.

At this point it would be fair to ask whether formal arguments about law and power advanced by the country's leading statesmen resonated persuasively among other Americans. Were these the ideas that mobilized an entire population? That brought them to battle or gave meaning to personal sacrifice? That justified the rejection of monarchy and the establishment of a new government founded solely on the will of the people? That explained why the people could never surrender their fundamental political rights? The answer involves what Sherlock Holmes might have described as the mystery of the dog that did not bark in the night. An interpretive piece is missing. Something is not present in the commonly accepted analysis of American revolutionary ideas that ought to be there.

The difficulty with a defense of revolution based on civic humanism, classical republican theory, or English constitutional law is that Americans living in rural communities seldom depicted political resistance or personal sacrifice in these terms. It is not that they rejected the language of rights and liberty. Throughout the conflict with Great Britain these revered concepts figured centrally in how Americans perceived independence, and after that the challenge of establishing a constitutional republic. They hated tyranny and oppression. They complained that Parliament intended to turn them into slaves. What was generally absent from their discussions, however, were references to the famed political commentators of the Renaissance, to ancient Common Law statutes, to theorists who had defended republican government during the English Civil Wars, or to the obscure eighteenth-century London essayists who warned readers about the decline of civic virtue.[3]

Why the people did not speak about rights and liberty in the same ways as the authors of the major revolutionary pamphlets of the period has seldom generated much curiosity. It should have. Perhaps the explanation seemed painfully obvious. We might posit, for example, that since most Americans at the time were ignorant of formal political theory and constitutional law, we should concentrate attention on elite writers schooled in the relevant sources. Or, we might state that investigating popular views on political allegiance and good government is not worth the effort, since ordinary people merely parroted ideas put forward by their leaders. Both conclusions deserve swift rejection. If nothing else, they are extraordinarily condescending. Moreover, judging from the experience of other revolutions, it would be very strange indeed to discover that the American people were unable to explain to themselves in their own terms why they supported a cause that required the use of arms and seemed at first to have little chance of success.

The contrast between elite and popular ideas about revolution most likely resulted from the need to communicate effectively to very different audiences. The national leaders of resistance aimed their arguments at other highly educated men, trained lawyers, wealthy merchants, and well-read planters, some of whom harbored serious reservations about independence. The goal of these essays was to persuade such individuals that a break with the British Empire had intellectual and legal legitimacy. The pamphlets were also intended for English contemporaries who at least before 1776 wondered whether Lord North and his allies in Parliament were pursuing punitive policies that might only make matters worse.[4] But at this critical moment, certainly before 1776, thoughtful writers on both sides of the Atlantic struggled to find ways to avoid armed conflict.

What has gone missing from discussions of the intellectual origins of revolution is a set of parallel arguments about rights and liberty that spoke directly—one might say passionately—to the concerns of a majority of Americans. One might characterize this defense of resistance as more self-consciously religious than that of the Founders. It spoke to the deepest values of a highly Protestant culture. The goal was foremost to provide assurance—an amalgam of hope and comfort—to an uncertain, frightened public at a moment of profound crisis. Unlike the discussions of abstract political and legal theory, this more popular discourse was intended to enflame emotions, overcome doubts, encourage commitment, and provide certitude that Americans liberated from British oppression would in fact establish a more equitable society. It reminded ordinary men and women that all political power came from the people. To be sure, many different Protestant sects flourished during the Revolution, and these groups often regarded religious competitors with contempt. But at the end of the day, most Americans subscribed to a general religious culture, a bundle of basic assumptions about morality and responsibility that energized political purpose.[5]

In almost every community, the task of explicating and motivating commitment to the Revolution fell primarily on the clergy. Ministers delivered thousands of sermons during this period. Many of them, of course, did not directly address the fighting, and many others have been lost.[6] Some clergymen questioned independence. Episcopalians and Methodists voiced strong objections. But among the sermons published by representatives of other leading Protestant denominations, we encounter a coherent explanation for organized resistance to political oppression that deserves more attention than it has received. With only rare exception, ordinary Americans did not see their ministers as enemies of revolution. That is a significant point within a broadly comparative context since in other revolutions, such as the French, the clergy seemed to obstruct political reform, and as a result, many thousands of priests were murdered.[7]

The centrality of the American ministers in calming their parishioner's doubts and providing assurance should come as no surprise. These men knew that their standing within small communities depended on their ability to address not only the mysteries of salvation, but also the actual experience of violent political transformation. In this capacity they relied on Scripture—mostly on the Old Testament—to help ordinary people understand the nature of civil government and the responsibilities that men and women had to other members of their communities.[8] This was the social and political environment in which they spoke of rights and liberty. As one minister declared in 1775, "In the church the people are taught their duty to God and the king, and there the most powerful arguments and motives are presented to their minds, to prevail with and persuade them to a suitable conduct towards both."[9] The religious rhetoric was not restricted to the sermons. It permeated the general culture, influencing newspaper essays and reports of town meetings.[10]

American clergymen reached a far larger audience than did the authors of the revolutionary pamphlets we so often quote today.[11] Week after week, they broadcast a persuasive narrative that made sense of allegiance, neutrality, and justice in a changing world. Most important for our purposes, they explained—often to the soldiers who would actually do the fighting—that God expected ordinary Americans to rebel against tyrants. The people had no choice. Compromise with tyranny was not a political failing; it was sin.

II

Recovery of popular religious explanations for the American Revolution might best begin with the Reverend Dan Foster, who spent the war years as the pastor for a small Connecticut congregation. Like so many other ministers of the period, Foster viewed his religious responsibilities through the lens of the Great Awakening. At midcentury a charismatic English clergyman, George Whitefield, had toured the American colonies, and everywhere he traveled he radically transformed how ordinary people experienced religion. He had little use for formal theology. Spidery arguments about obscure points of interpretation, he insisted, only deflected attention away from the attainment of a new birth in Christ. Whitefield addressed the people directly, often in open fields. The new evangelical religion spoke to the concerns of the heart, to intimate feelings about the divine. Over time religious enthusiasm spread, overcoming opposition and redefining traditional expectations between ministers and congregations. The Great Awakening empowered ordinary people to voice their opinions about church matters and to challenge clergymen who failed to serve their spiritual needs.[12]

Foster transferred much of this popular religious energy to political affairs. Even his name communicated a break with formality, with tradition, for one would have expected him to identify himself as Daniel, not Dan. He had been ordained in 1771 in Poquonock, the Second Church of Windsor, Connecticut, and when he accepted the post, the congregation boasted only twenty-four members. Perhaps because his ministerial duties were not too demanding, Foster turned his attention to the conflict with Great Britain. What, he wondered, had gone wrong with America's relationship with the mother country? In his study, far removed from college libraries, Foster developed an elaborate justification not only for independence, but also for a government of the people. Although not written with the stylistic polish of Thomas Paine's *Common Sense*, Foster's sermons shared Paine's emotional intensity. In the context of the times, Foster's ideas were politically subversive, and although his attack on kingship did not have the extraordinary impact of Paine's, Foster presented his views to the public many months before Paine called for independence.

Foster published his reflections in Hartford in 1775 as *A Short Essay on Civil Government*. Short, it was not. Foster worked out his thoughts in seventy-four densely argued pages. According to the title page, he first developed his ideas in six sermons delivered in Windsor in October 1774. What the members of his church made of the performance, we can only guess. But the fact that it was printed at all—an expensive undertaking that discouraged many authors from turning manuscript drafts into print—suggests that his audience found his essay persuasive.

Foster's *Short Essay* has never appeared in modern collections of revolutionary pamphlets. Perhaps it was too long for inclusion. A more likely explanation is that it did not pay sufficient attention to major figures in the history of political thought or to lawyer-like reviews of British law. Just as folk art creations are generally treated as less worthy of investigation than are classical paintings and statues, Foster's analysis of political responsibility does not fit comfortably into how we usually think about the intellectual defense of revolution.

Foster also had a chip on his shoulder. He dreamed of reaching a larger audience, but unlike Paine, who enjoyed the patronage of Benjamin Franklin, Foster lacked an influential sponsor who could have recommended the *Short Essay* to a broad readership. Foster tried to turn social obscurity into a virtue. In the preface, he observed that because "I have no Maecenas [famed patron to Roman poets]," his discourses on politics had to "recommend themselves." But he knew it was an uphill battle. Foster did not fear stirring controversy or experiencing rejection so much as he anticipated that other commentators on the imperial crisis would simply ignore what he had to say. "I am not so vain as to imagine that what I have written," Foster announced, "will be very entertaining or profitable to my intelligent readers, if I should have any, who have perused large volumes, studied much and are thoroughly acquainted with the laws of nature and nations."

Foster insisted that the possibility of being dismissed by "intelligent readers" was not a great concern. After all, he had a much larger goal. He announced that he wrote only "for the advantages of the people, to whose natural and justly acquired rights and privileges, I am firmly & inviolably attached." Writing two and a half years before the Declaration of Independence, Foster desired to cultivate "in the minds of the people, a just sense of those rights." And perhaps we should take him at his word. If his ideas lacked sophistication, if he was unable to season his text with quotations from major political theorists, he relied upon his own unadorned reason and knowledge of the Old Testament to buttress his case.

The matter of sources, however, raises another question. Although Foster distanced himself from scholarly tradition, we should note that his ideas are remarkably similar those put forward originally by John Locke in his *Two Treatises of Government* (1689). Foster worked within a theoretical framework associated primarily with Locke that viewed both the formation of human society and the establishment of government as voluntary compacts. The issue is not that Foster plagiarized Locke's justification for rebellion against tyrants. Rather, by 1775 Locke's arguments about fundamental natural rights and the creation of political society had become so common in colonial America that it may not have occurred to Foster to cite Locke in his sermons.[13]

Foster opened with the Old Testament account of the aging patriarch Samuel. This biblical figure had allowed his two sons to become the judges of Israel, but their maladministration angered the Jews, who begged Samuel to let them have a king. Samuel feared that the people might be making a mistake, but he eventually endorsed the appeal. The Jews would have the king they desired. For Foster this was a moment of profound importance for subsequent political history. The point was not whether the Jews did in fact obtain a king who would rule according to God's law. Rather, the key lesson from Scripture was that the "people have a natural and inherent right to appoint and constitute a king supreme, and all subordinate officers." Indeed, the Bible left not the slightest doubt that the people were the source of "all civil powers."

Foster's insistence on demonstrating the popular foundation of kingship may initially seem excessive, since most subjects of the eighteenth-century British Crown believed that they lived under a constitutional monarch whose authority had been precisely defined by Parliament during the Glorious Revolution of 1688. What energized Foster's argument was a conviction that older assumptions about the divinity of kings persisted still, even in colonial America. These authoritarian notions had been originally championed by the English political theorist Robert Filmer (1588–1653), who in the face of gross incompetence by Stuart monarchs proclaimed the divine right of kings. Locke spent most of his *Two Treatises* shredding Filmer's arguments, which among other things had advised the people who suffered tyranny to exercise passive obedience—in other words, to accommodate to the political situation whatever the provocations.

Although Foster never mentioned Filmer by name, he sensed that many Americans harbored lingering beliefs about the divinity of kings. Consequently, they were reluctant to show open resistance to a monarch who failed to preserve popular rights. Foster countered those who accepted the divine right of kings by showing that while God authorized civil government—be it a monarchy, aristocracy, or republic—he let the people select their own rulers. The Lord, Foster maintained, "always allowed the people a voice in all elections of their civil and military officers and rulers."

God did not care one way or another if the people deposed a corrupt monarch. That was their business. Foster did not reject the idea of kingship, but by aggressively showing that the office of the king was little different from any other position dependent on the judgment of the people, he effectively stripped away much of the wonder associated with the king's person. Foster explained that "Those men who plead that Kings derive their authority and right to reign over the people from God only are either grossly ignorant . . . or they can plead for any thing, just as it shall coincide with their particular humours, or their despotic principles; and so are not worthy to be heard, tho' they say ever so much."

Having demonstrated to his own satisfaction that kings derive their powers solely from the people, Foster described how an elective monarch should behave in office. One has the impression in this section that Foster is racing forward, eager to reach his conclusion but obliged to cover well-traveled ground. He provides readers with a list of responsibilities so self-evident that they required only minimal discussion. A good king would, of course, guarantee the physical security of his subjects. He would protect their property. Why else, Foster asked, would rational beings surrender some of their natural rights to the state? On such matters even kings chosen by the people had limited authority. They could not simply declare law. Foster expected them to work closely with properly constituted assemblies, thus assuring that the people always "have a voice in the making of all such laws."

Kings also defended religion, not by forcing people to belong to this or that denomination, but by openly recognizing the importance of religion—and here Foster meant only Christian religion—in maintaining public order. After all, he observed, "If all preachers of religion should be discountenanced, and all public assemblies for the worship of the Deity cease, in any Christian country, there would be no such thing as holding the people together in civil society." Unlike many contemporaries, Foster did not put much faith in the Magna Carta. If one had an honest king, one did not need formal legal agreements between ruler and people. These documents were redundant, since "every King is bound to make the people's good his Magna Carta, in all his administrations."

Foster passed quickly over the people's responsibilities to their rulers. When kings upheld the original contract by insuring social justice and tranquility, the people owed them obedience. Good rulers deserved honor and respect. They were the proper objects of the people's prayers. Foster also counseled the people to reward their political leaders. In a well-governed polity, he thought that there should be no quibbling over salaries. Even on this relatively minor topic Foster's feisty populist beliefs came to the fore. When establishing a fair rate of compensation for political officials, the people should carefully weigh a leader's personal abilities and social background, for in practice some civil servants deserved more support than did others. "I ask," Foster declared, "whether a king is made such for himself, for his own ease and pleasure, that he may spend his days in luxury, wantonness and debauchery? Or is he made such for his wisdom, probity and benevolence?"

Foster saved his most radical comments for a final section demonstrating—he believed with as much certainty "as any proposition in Euclid"—that "the people have a right and authority to dethrone their king, and put down all other civil officers and rulers ... whenever they shall counteract their obligations." This was dangerous intellectual territory. In England the topic could lead to arrest if the authorities could locate the author of such revolutionary ideas. Foster asserted that the people retained basic natural rights no matter the character of their government. In no case did they surrender "their rights to the enjoyment of their persons and properties," their "right to have a voice in all public decisions concerning peace and war," or their "right of judging and determining in matters of religion."

What, then, could the people do when a king and his officers violated these rights? This was the essence of the matter. Resistance required prudence. First, the people had to judge for themselves whether the monarch really acted on the basis of "tyrannic and despotic principles." Even good kings made mistakes. A single bad law or objectionable policy did not provide sufficient reason to encourage rebellion. One needed irrefutable evidence of a king obstinately proceeding "to prosecute such measures of administration, to make and execute such laws as are detrimental to the state, and destructive of the liberties, peace, happiness and tranquility of the people."

Even if such betrayal of the public trust could be demonstrated, the people had no call to take up arms against the evil prince. There was another step. Foster advised those who complained of oppression to appeal for reform, to urge their kings to abandon "despotic and destructive procedure." And if they were turned away, mocked and rejected, then and only then were they justified "to exert themselves more rigorously, and dethrone their king, and take all such corrupt rulers out of those places of power and trust." In surprisingly strong language, Foster described the people as a kind of popular jury capable of punishing the agents of misrule. They had a right to appraise the king's performance, and more, "if the states of parliament are also corrupted, and have drank so deep, with the king, of the spirit of absoluteness and despotism, that the people are deprived of their natural rights and privileges so that they can no longer endure; then both the legislative and executive powers are reverted to the people, and they have a right in the sight of God, the king of kings and lord over all, to convict, judge and condemn the king and the states of parliament."

It is precisely at this point in the *Short Essay* that Foster seems to acknowledge in full the subversive character of his own argument. There was no denying that he had encouraged the people to "exert" themselves against corrupt rulers who refused to disown autocratic principles. But if the people actually rose up and reasserted their voice in political affairs, would they not invite social chaos? Would it not be wiser to suffer despotism than to risk undermining the entire foundation of civil society? What exactly did it mean for the people to "exert" themselves?

Foster knew such concerns kept ordinary Americans from unequivocally rejecting king and Parliament. They worried that resistance "will introduce anarchy and confusion, club-laws, &c. to the inevitable destruction of the liberties, peace and happiness of the whole community." Foster admitted that lawlessness and disorder presented a problem, since the exertion of the popular will could have "bad tendencies, unless great care, wisdom and prudence be exercised." But it could be done. In a stunningly radical attempt to remove doubt—to promote assurance that the people's cause was just—Foster drew upon English history to demonstrate that the effort to establish popular government outweighed the danger of anarchy. "England," Foster observed, "was never more happy before, nor much more since, than after the head of the first Stuart was severed from his body, and while it was under the Protectorship of Oliver Cromwell." These words took Foster well beyond the pale of polite political discourse. Few contemporaries awarded Cromwell—the man who overthrew monarchical rule in England—honorary status. Some would have regarded the reference as treasonable.

After such incendiary rhetoric, Foster ended the *Short Essay* with a whimper. A reader who expected him to issue a general call to arms was sure to be disappointed. He refused to spell out the practical meaning of political exertion. "I have said little or nothing," Foster confessed, "about the method in which the people ought to proceed, in treating with civil magistrates, who do not use their power and authority for the good and interest of the people." The burden of judging king and Parliament, he thought, fell "to the politicians and statesmen." As for Foster, he described himself as a "liege subject to my rightful sovereign." Coming after a passage celebrating the execution of Charles I, we must assume that Foster's retreat from radical resistance was a self-protective move, a tongue-in-cheek stepping back that only forced his audience to reflect more deeply on the challenge of exertion.

We might search Foster's text for echoes of Renaissance and early modern political theorists. No doubt, such an analysis would reveal names other than Locke's. But the effort would yield little insight into the wellspring of revolutionary mobilization. The Windsor parishioners who heard Foster's original sermons would have cared little about identifying intellectual references. They recognized Oliver Cromwell, of course. But within their small community they had to deal with more pressing matters. As they listened to Foster, they surely sensed that a gathering imperial storm would soon force them to affirm the people's voice.

III

Dan Foster's sermons invite us to consider how ordinary Americans made sense of their participation in the Revolution from a fresh perspective. He reminds us that justification for violence is never easy. It is certainly not a process that we should take for granted, as if simply hearing the words *freedom* and *liberty* were sufficient to transform decades of obedience into determined resistance. After all, as revolutionary histories throughout the world demonstrate, people find it very hard to give up the security of everyday family life and take up arms against the state. What triggers the decision? What calms doubts about resistance?

Foster suggested answers. But he was by no means an isolated or idiosyncratic voice. He tapped into a popular intellectual current that encouraged ordinary colonists to interpret an unfolding imperial controversy within a coherent religious framework. Within this body of ideas and assumptions, Scripture provided inspiration and explanation. American clergymen did not ask people to reject enlightened common sense. Whatever their theological persuasions may have been, they were not fundamentalists. They did, however, unite religion and reason in an accessible language that helped to mobilize a people at a moment of profound political crisis. In small communities throughout America they urged ordinary men and women to make *an appeal to heaven.*

This phrase resonated powerfully throughout the colonies on the eve of independence. One incident in particular reveals its popularity among Americans who actually took up arms against the British army. In 1775, after New England militiamen had routed the redcoats at Concord, American soldiers established defensive positions outside Boston. George Washington had not yet arrived in Massachusetts to assume command of the Continental forces. General Israel Putnam was in charge. During the lull in fighting, his troops decided that they needed a proper battle flag. The creation of an official standard represented an important development in American resistance, for before this time, the militiamen had primarily identified with small communities—with Acton or Lexington, for example. Only slowly did they come to appreciate the need for a symbolic expression of national unity.

Several accounts of the unfurling of the flag survive. The ceremony occurred at dawn. According to one witness, the American soldiers assembled "on Prospect-Hill, when the Declaration of the Continental Congress [calling on Americans to take up arms] was read; after which an animated and pathetic [expressing tenderness] Address to the Army was made by the Rev. Mr. Leonard, Chaplain to General Putnam's Regiment, and succeeded by a pertinent Prayer." Leonard begged the Lord to preserve the "people of this land ... [who] have been reduced to the dreadful alternative of submitting to arbitrary laws and despotic government; or taking up arms in defense of those rights and privileges, which thou, in thy goodness, hast conferred upon them as men and as Christians."[14]

As soon as Leonard finished, Putnam gave a prearranged signal to raise the flag. "The whole Army shouted their loud Amen by three Cheers, immediately upon which a Cannon was fired from the Fort, and the Standard lately sent to General Putnam was exhibited[,] flourishing in the Air, bearing . . . this Motto, 'AN APPEAL TO HEAVEN.'"[15] A loyalist spy confirmed the news. He reported to the British general Thomas Gage in Boston that "our people [have] got a famous New large Standard," and when it was first exhibited, "all of us huzzahed at once, then the Indeans [sic] gave the war hoop and to conclude, of[f] went [the] Cannon." It was indeed an impressive ceremony "that was worth you seeing."[16]

One doubts that missing the event seriously disappointed Gage. He had other pressing issues on his mind. But if he had visited the American camp, he would have seen a flag emblazoned with a single pine tree against a white background. Underneath the evergreen ran the words AN APPEAL TO HEAVEN. The inclusion of the tree in the design of the flag poses no interpretive mystery. It had a long, iconic history in Massachusetts. As a symbol of the colony, the tree made its first appearance on coins minted in the mid-seventeenth century.

The meaning of "an appeal to heaven," however, is less straightforward. Although the militiamen surely hoped that God would favor their cause in the controversy with Great Britain, the words represented more than an expression of hope. Indeed, the phrase is a reference to an incident from the Old Testament, one that grounded John Locke's arguments in the *Second Treatise,* and perhaps quite independently of Locke, one that provided American ministers during the Revolution with a compelling scriptural basis for explaining how political resistance to oppressive rulers might receive the Lord's blessing.[17]

Locke's use of these words is instructive, since like the ministers who tried to make sense of the American Revolution, he confronted a despotic English ruler. The phrase "Appeal to Heaven" appeared many times in Locke's text. He linked the phrase with the biblical account of Jephtha in the eleventh chapter of Judges. When the Israelites pleaded with Jephtha, "a mighty warrior," to support them against the Ammonites, he in turn asked God to decide the controversy. In other words, Jephtha made an appeal to heaven. "Let the LORD, who is judge, decide today for the Israelites or for the Ammonites."

References to Old Testament events provided Locke with much-needed political cover, since on the eve of the Glorious Revolution he was in fact trying to justify the removal of James II from office. Such ideas were as subversive in 1688 as they would be in 1776. Like many contemporaries, Locke believed that the Stuart monarch had abandoned the rule of law. Directly addressing a growing threat of tyranny, he drafted the *Second Treatise*, one of the more radical defenses of revolution to appear before the nineteenth century. Locke counseled those grown weary of James II that in extreme cases, the people had a right to take their political grievance to the Lord. Such cases included a king who had forfeited the trust of the people and judges who had compromised their integrity by siding with the despised monarch. Like Jephtha, Englishmen could make an appeal to heaven.

As Locke interpreted the biblical story, the people had absolutely no assurance that God would in fact support their cause. Resistance to established civil authority was always a gamble. God might even declare an aggrieved people to be rebels, in law mere criminals. In the penultimate paragraph of the final chapter of the *Second Treatise*, entitled "Dissolution of Government," Locke describes the dilemma facing all revolutionaries:

> If a Controversie arise betwixt a Prince and some of the People, in a matter where the Law is silent, or doubtful, and the thing be of great Consequence, I should think the proper *Umpire*, in such a Case, should be the Body of the People. For in Cases where the Prince hath a Trust reposed in him, and is dispensed from the common ordinary Rules of the Law; there, if any Men find themselves aggrieved, and Think the Prince acts contrary to, or beyond that Trust, who so proper to *Judge* as the Body of the *People* . . . how far they meant it should extend? But if the Prince, or whoever they be in the Administration, decline that way of Determination, The Appeal then lies no where but to Heaven.[18]

For Locke, the Glorious Revolution of 1688 ended well. James II abandoned the Crown, fled to France, and with the blessing of Parliament William and Mary became rulers of a nation determined to restore the rule of law. They agreed to abide by the English constitution. Although it would have been a stretch to depict the members of Parliament as the true representatives of the people—they were after all the wealthiest land-holders in England—they in fact claimed that mantle, and after public order had been restored, they proclaimed the doctrine of parliamentary sovereignty. The transformation of political culture gave the people assur-ance that they no longer had to fear despotic monarchs. British subjects throughout the world applauded these political developments, often citing them as evidence of enlightened progress. Colonial Americans joined the chorus, singing the praises of a constitution that seemed to protect per-sonal liberty. During the first half of the eighteenth century only a few critics in England pointed out that Parliament itself might succumb to forms of corruption that could compromise freedom. No one paid much attention to these marginal voices. And however central Locke's ideas about popular resistance may have been in 1688, they were soon shunted aside in a complacent political environment in which a landed aristocracy controlled the levers of power.[19]

All that changed on the eve of the Revolution—at least, it did for the Americans. Locke's work experienced a sudden new burst of popularity. A Boston publisher judged that a restive colonial marketplace would be re-ceptive to the *Second Treatise*, an analysis of popular resistance to tyranny, even though the work had been ignored for almost a century. George III was no James II, but his refusal to treat Americans as the equals of Englishmen within the empire indicated that a Jephtha moment might be at hand. As a Boston newspaper advertisement for the *Second Treatise* announced: "Per-haps there never was a Time since the Discovery of this new World, when the People of all Ranks every where show'd so eager a Spirit of Inquiry into the Nature of their Rights and Privileges, as at this Day." The printer believed that in these troubled times "it has therefore been judged very seasonable and proper to put it in the Power of every free Man on this Continent to furnish himself at so easy a Rate with the noble Essay just now re-published."[20] It is significant that enslaved African Americans also appreciated the dominant political language. When a black man living in Essex County, north of Boston, drew up a petition for the freedom of slaves in August 1774, he began quite appropriately with an argument about rights. "This is a time of great anxiety and distress among you [colo-nial rulers], on account of the infringement, not only of your Charter rights, but of the natural rights and privileges of freeborn men." Why, the slave asked, "will you not pity and relieve the poor distressed, enslaved Africans?—Who, though they are entitled to the same natural rights of mankind, that you are, are nevertheless groaning in bondage."[21]

It is doubtful that the ministers in small congregations throughout the colonies rushed to purchase Locke's treatise. Like him, when confronted with an unprecedented political crisis so huge that it raised the possibility of armed resistance to a king, they turned to the Old Testament. They spoke a language that ordinary Americans understood. They felt a responsibility to speak out, whatever the reception might be. The Reverend Andrew Lee admitted that there were people who thought that ministers should stay out of politics. Like so many privileged people throughout history who have preferred not to have their sources of privilege questioned, Lee's critics claimed that if ministers "treat in public upon any thing of civil nature, 'that they are meddling with what does not concern them: that their business is to preach the gospel, and not politics.'" To which Lee responded, nonsense. Politics is the concern of God. And in his sermon he pledged to use "plainness" so that the supporters of American liberty would understand his arguments.[22] The Reverend Samuel Baldwin adopted a less adversarial tone but agreed with Lee. Baldwin thought that ministers should discuss politics with their congregations. He appealed to heaven in the hope "it might have some Tendency to keep up the Spirits of the People in the important and dangerous Struggle in which we are now engaged . . . [especially since] the present is doubtless the most calamitous Day the British Colonies ever beheld."[23]

Some ministers took the concept of the appeal much farther than had Locke. For them, it was more than an expression of hope that God would give their request a hearing. They wanted to justify the actual use of arms. One can understand their anxiety at this moment. On June 2, 1775, for example, Nathan Perkins, pastor of the Fourth Church at Hartford, Connecticut, delivered a powerful sermon to a company of soldiers "Being the Day before they marched from this Place." According to the title page, Perkins's work was published "at the Desire of the Hearers." He informed the volunteers who would soon face combat "Never, never did so dark, so gloomy, so alarming, so terrible calamities hang over America as at present." People had assumed that the assault on their rights would be resolved without violence. But that had not occurred. "When therefore our money is demanded of us," Perkins explained, "by the gentle arguments of fleets and armies, or with the bayonet at our breasts, we are warranted by all the laws human and divine, to defend ourselves . . . & appeal to heaven for the justice of our cause." Of course, Perkins was calling for more than a review of the sources of discontent. He appealed to arms, to the sword, trusting that a merciful God would not fault Connecticut's soldiers at the moment of battle.[24]

The Reverend Jonas Clark added anger to his appeal to heaven. One can appreciate his fiery rhetoric. He delivered a sermon entitled *The Fate of Blood-Thirsty Oppressors* a few months after he had witnessed British troops shoot down members of his Lexington congregation. He was not willing to forgive the atrocity. Drawing on passages from the Book of Joel, one of the more obscure sections of the Old Testament, Clark announced that "The sword is an appeal to heaven,—when, therefore, the arms of a people are eventually successful, or by the immediate interposition of providence, their enemies and oppressors are subdued or destroyed— When a people are reinstated in peace, upon equitable terms, and established in their just rights and liberties, both civil and sacred: then may it be said, that the Lord hath cleansed their innocent blood." However uncharitable it may have sounded, Clark wanted revenge. Taking up arms—using them—was the substance of the appeal. As he told his grieving parishioners, "Blood is said to be cleansed, or avenged, when justice hath taken place, and the murderer is punished."[25]

The logic of an appeal to heaven resonated widely among Americans on the eve of independence. Indeed, this single phrase repeated over and over in sermons—often those delivered before soldiers—became a kind of shorthand cry for resistance to Great Britain.[26] Unlike the formal revolutionary pamphlets that have received so much scholarly attention, the scripturally based claims addressed directly three central issues that troubled both ministers and their parishioners.

First, as we shall discover, the argument placed the main burden of political judgment on the people: Were Americans justified in resisting their rulers? They were solely responsible for deciding whether the accumulating grievances were so serious, so unlikely ever to be redressed, that they had no other choice but to employ violence against the offending authority. This widespread perspective on popular resistance reinforced fundamental assumptions about republican government, since as the minsters insisted, by judging the competence of their rulers, the people affirmed that they were the source of all political power.

Second, because many Americans—not just their pastors—feared that rebellion could promote lawlessness, even anarchy, the ministers framed their appeals to heaven in terms of a process. One could not legitimately run off half-cocked simply because one objected to this or that statute. The idea of an appeal to heaven gave the people pause, forcing them to justify their actions. In a curious way, godly resistance preserved civil order by slowing the people down. Resistance had to be reasonable rather than impulsive.

And finally, the plea to heaven offered a means to achieve a sense of assurance, confidence at a time of peril, for if the people in fact judged the situation rightly and if they took their time in doing so, they could go forward knowing that they might secure the Lord's support.

IV

When called upon to explain the breakdown of imperial authority, Protestant ministers relied almost exclusively on the Old Testament. A host of biblical figures appeared in their texts. According to the Reverend Ezra Sampson in a sermon he preached before Colonel Cotton's regiment at the Roxbury Camp, "A variety of beautiful examples as well as admirable rules for the regulation of our conduct in life . . . are scattered in the divine oracles."[27] Sampson praised the wisdom of Moses, Joshua, and David. Other ministers spoke of Nehemiah and Mordecai as well as many ancient rulers who had oppressed the Jews.

The ministers treated stories from the Old Testament as directly and immediately applicable to the American crisis. Scriptural history was real history, not a collection of mythic tales. It had as much relevance to current events as did recent English history. When Jonas Clark told his Lexington congregation about how the "*children of Israel*" had persuaded themselves to leave the "gardens of *Egypt* or the fertile lands of *Goshen* only after their burdens had been increased to an unreasonable degree, by the violence and cruelty of those that oppressed them," everyone in his church knew that they too were being forced to leave Goshen. The battles of Lexington and Concord served as evidence that they were sharing the travails of the followers of Moses.[28]

Unlike the authors of formal revolutionary pamphlets, the ministers saw no reason to turn to secular political theory to justify resistance to Great Britain. Scripture provided all the evidence they needed. The Reverend Samuel Cooke, for example, was only stating the obvious when he insisted that the Old Testament remains "a light to our feet and a lamp to our path."[29] One studied the story of Nehemiah rebuilding Jerusalem not for inspiration, but to understand better how George III had hatched a design "to enslave and oppress us."[30] For David Jones, a minister in Pennsylvania, the whole point of drawing attention to Nehemiah was to demonstrate that "in some cases, when a people are oppressed, insulted and abused, and can have no other redress, it then becomes our duty as men, with our eyes to GOD, to fight for our liberties and properties."[31] Joseph Montgomery agreed. In a sermon delivered in 1775 at Christiana Bridge, Delaware, he observed, "There is not a period of the Jewish history but what informs us either how we ought to behave ourselves in prosperity, or what we ought to do in order to avert impending Judgments, or what conduct becomes us if we would desire to have heavy and distressing afflictions removed from us."[32]

It was entirely predictable that many ministers would take the next logical step in the analysis. The Americans were in a real sense modern Jews, a chosen people with special responsibilities to the Lord. In *Rabshaken's Proposals Considered*, delivered before "the officers of the companies of Minutemen" in Groton, Massachusetts, Samuel Webster recounted, "The Jews submitted not—and, how in his own time and way, the Lord delivered them." The lesson was clear. The Jews had "trusted in God; and so may we,—opposing the power of God to Britain's force."[33] After all, another clergyman insisted, like the Jews "the people of America [are] . . . a covenanted people."[34]

However favorably God may have viewed the unhappy colonists, he did not demand that they resist tyranny. That decision was entirely their own. It was a burden that they accepted as part of the human condition. Only they could judge whether a ruler had deprived them of their rights or engaged in an intolerable level of corruption. In a sermon delivered in Philadelphia David Jones insisted that "the people must be the judges whether the laws are good or not."[35] The idea that the people were the true source of power had a long history, but in 1775 abstract theory about the popular foundation of government suddenly acquired practical and dangerous application. Americans were not only called upon to appraise the actions of king and Parliament, but also urged to prepare for war. According to the ministers, because God distanced himself from everyday political affairs, it was the obligation of the people to attend to secondary causes, acquiring weapons and drilling soldiers, for example. Zabdiel Adams reminded a Lunenburg, Massachusetts, congregation that God "expects that we use all lawful methods in our own power for our security and defense; after which we may leave our righteous cause with heaven, in humble hope that he will uphold and protect it."[36]

The problem, of course, was that the ministers never clearly defined the precise tipping point, the exact instant when the denial of rights or the passage of a new tax warranted an armed response. Different judges could reach different conclusions about such matters. Still, the insistence that ordinary people were responsible for the preservation of their God-given rights fostered a rough sense of equality. John Allen, a Baptist minister, boldly addressed this point in the dedication to a sermon delivered in Boston. He informed the Earl of Dartmouth, then secretary of state for the Colonies:

> As a fly, or a worm, by the law of nature, has a great right to Liberty, and Freedom, (according to their little sphere in life) as the most potent monarch upon the earth: And as there can be no other difference between your Lordship, and myself, but what is political, I therefore, without any further apology, take leave to ask your Lordship, whether any one that fears GOD, loves his neighbor as himself, (which is the true Scripture mark of a Christian) will *oppress* his fellow-creatures?[37]

The revolutionary pamphlets that have shaped our understanding of basic principles that encouraged Americans to fight for independence fail to show how abstract theories about constitutional law and republican virtue played out in communities where people faced the unwelcome prospect of suddenly treating old friends as dreaded enemies. It was this tension, this profound reluctance to break with tradition and experience, that caused so many people to call the fight with the Mother Country an "unnatural war."[38] Even faced with a violation of fundamental rights and the arrival of a large British army, supporters of revolution felt the tug of memory, of former loyalties, and although some accounts of the run-up to the Revolution depict the patriots as almost instinctively taking up arms against king and Parliament, the mental strain of resistance was in fact very real. As David Jones in Philadelphia forcefully reminded his congregation, we are now "called to take the bloody weapon of death in hand."[39]

The ministers did not evade this profoundly human problem. They knew that the emotional elements that reinforced allegiance and identity could not be taken for granted. Lingering doubts about using the sword in a political cause could potentially undermine revolutionary mobilization, for if one was unable to imagine former friends as enemies, as targets of lethal violence, then resistance was compromised before it got off the ground. Joseph Montgomery, in a sermon delivered to a newly formed military unit, openly addressed the issue. "Our enemies are our fellow-subjects, our brethren, and our kinsmen," he observed, "and whilst the laws of nature, and the voice of God, conspire to excite us to assert our rights and privileges at the risk of our lives and fortunes; yet it is with the greatest reluctance, that we have drawn the sword." The whole conflict seemed so strange, so unnecessary, since "there never was a people more strongly attached to the King than the Americans were to the illustrious house of Hanover." Indeed, as the fresh recruits well remembered, "We boasted in the name of English-man." Whether Montgomery's resolution of the problem was entirely satisfactory is unclear. He urged the American troops going to war against "our fellow subjects" to turn to the Old Testament to discover how best to resolve the challenge of shifting allegiance.[40]

Other ministers insisted that England had changed. The country and culture that the Americans had loved for so long had shifted in ways that compromised traditional emotional ties. As Zabdiel Adams explained in a sermon entitled *The Grounds of Confidence and Success in War*, Great Britain "who was the nurse in our infancy, the guardian of our youth, and the boast of our riper years, has now become the invader of our liberties." Adams confessed that the colonists could have agreed to become the slaves of a distant mother country and be done with it. But they rightly rejected that course. "Though we all profess allegiance to Britain's King, and have ever discovered ourselves as loyal subjects as any in his dominions, yet so just an idea have we of the importance of our rights, that we seem resolved to defend them at the risque of everything dear."[41]

Jacob Duche assured a company of American soldiers—the "*First Battalion*" of Philadelphia—of "the righteousness of the cause," but he admitted to the men facing battle that their appeal to heaven carried a heavy emotional burden. After all, they would soon face "the hard necessity of standing upon our defense against our brethren, children of the same family, educated in the same manners, the same religion with ourselves, bound together by a long participation of common blessings, and of common dangers and distresses, mutually protecting and protected by each other."[42] During a sermon before "the officers of the companies of minute men" in New Hampshire, Samuel Webster offered a more earthy argument for breaking away from England. British rulers claimed that the mother country had defended the Americans during the Seven Years' War and therefore had earned loyalty. Webster responded, rubbish. This was no time for second thoughts. The English treated the colonists "as a flock of sheep to wolves, that have secured them by their howlings, tho without design, from foxes and small dogs, and then devour them for their pay."[43]

Perhaps because so many Americans—not just those of loyalist persuasion—still felt the attraction of former allegiance, the ministers worked hard to persuade the people that they were engaged in a truly just war. When the colonists made their appeal to heaven, they knew that God might or might not support their cause. It was a gamble. But surely, if they launched a preemptive strike against their opponents, if they took up the sword in a self-serving attempt to obtain more land or resources, if they were not confident in the righteousness of their own cause, then God would most likely not take their side. The ministers repeatedly claimed that the colonists had not wanted war. An aggressive parliament had forced their hand. During the protests before declaring independence, they had tried to reason with England's rulers by formally petitioning king and Parliament. Only after all these actions had failed to yield relief had they armed themselves in self-defense. Elisha Fish assured the members of committees of safety for Worcester, Massachusetts, "Having first endeavored by all moderate, peaceable, and rational methods to secure their rights, and finding no redress, in a day of oppression ... they can, and often have, appealed to God in the way of self-defense."[44]

No doubt, the men who served in Lord North's cabinet found these justifications for rebellion hard to accept. Not surprisingly, the American clergy advanced a different interpretation. They may have sensed that it is almost always easier to mobilize a people in a defensive cause than in an offensive one. Soldiers fight with more conviction when they believe that they have been wronged and now must preserve families and farms. One essay addressed to the people in 1775 stated the point from the colonists' perspective. "For my own part," the writer observed, "I think there is very great reason to doubt, but that seven thousand, even of the best troops, are able to conquer [defeat] two hundred thousand of the most disorderly peasantry upon the earth, if they are animated in defense of every thing they hold most dear and sacred."[45] A month after the Battle of Lexington, a Connecticut author published *The American Crisis*. He insisted that the Americans had obeyed every legal act of Parliament. But there was a limit to patience. They rejected the "late cruel Edicts, to strip us of all our Liberty, and all our Property." Americans were the victims. "Having tried all other Means in vain," wrote this anonymous author, "and compelled, at last having no Alternative but Death, or abject Slavery, with deep Considerations we make the last grand Appeal to Heaven, and the impartial World."[46]

By going through all the steps of negotiation from formal petitions to gathering arms, the people could be confident that at the very least God would give their cause a sympathetic hearing. As one minister explained, "a defensive war is sinless before GOD."[47] Nathan Perkins developed the point as fully as did any other minister. Addressing "the soldiers who went from West Hartford [Connecticut], in Defense of their Country," Perkins admitted, "We are reduced to the sad, deprecated necessity of defending our rights at the point of the sword." Although the prospects were terrifying, Americans could find solace in the knowledge that "As ours is then a defensive, it must be a righteous war. Should a ruffian meet me on the road, demand my purse with a dagger at my throat, or a pistol at my breast, if by any means I could strike him dead, I should think myself warranted to do it, by the laws of God and man."[48] Since many of the soldiers in the congregation did in fact view British troops as ruffians, they did not have to worry that God would condemn them for shooting one. In an early use of the word "revolutionary," Joseph Montgomery informed American militiamen in July 1775 not only that "defensive war is lawful," but also that "revolutionary principles justify resistance against unlawful power."[49]

A radical streak ran through the sermonic literature. Some ministers openly attacked the whole concept of monarchy. It is impossible to gauge how many Americans subscribed to antimonarchical views before Thomas Paine published *Common Sense* in January 1776. The mere fact that some clergymen openly expressed opinions that would have brought them to the attention of authorities if they had been living in England, however, suggests that subversive ideas were circulating among ordinary people, at least among those of New England.[50] We have already seen how Dan Foster praised the execution of Charles I and the republican rule of Oliver Cromwell. He was not alone. John Allen insisted that when kings failed to advance the common good, they had to be removed from office. Charles I had abandoned the people, and he came to an entirely justified bad end. "He fell into the hands of wicked men," Allen noted, "and they [the people] cut off his head for it."[51]

For those intent on making an appeal to heaven, English history demonstrated that kings could not be trusted. Although many Americans in 1775 still stoutly maintained allegiance to the Crown—it was Parliament that had betrayed them—some ministers entertained views strikingly subversive in character. Such open criticism of kingship represented a major break with the colonists' long political experience. One writer supported the point with a statistical argument, as if he had really polled the American people. "I believe," he stated, "there are at least ninety-nine Americans in an hundred, who think Charles the First was an execrable tyrant, that he met with no harder fate than he deserved, and that his two Sons [Charles II and James II] ought in justice to have made the same exit."[52] Jonas Clark reminded his parishioners in Lexington that the "Freemen, Christians and a free *People*" of England had judged the policies of Charles I and found him wanting. "*Charles* would not have lost his kingdom, and finally his life upon the Scaffold, by the hand of the executioner," Clark declared, "nor *James* been obliged, in disgrace, to quit his throne and abdicated the government of the kingdom, had it not been for their own violent counsels and measures, to oppress and enslave the people, whom they were called to govern and protect."[53]

The problem was not simply a history in which some kings were bad kings. Monarchy itself was the issue. As Andrew Lee explained to a congregation in Norwich, Connecticut, "Man was not made for absolute power or monarchy." Lee listed Tiberius, Caligula, and Nero as examples of tyrants who had used their power for evil, not exactly a group with whom George III would have eagerly identified. Some Americans, however, found the parallels convincing. Kings became autocrats; they could not help themselves. After all, according to Lee, "it is very dangerous to a person that is exalted, to be set above control; elevated to that degree, that there is none on earth who can call him to an account."[54]

Although the ultimate success of an appeal depended entirely on God, American clergymen urged their parishioners to avoid behavior that might needlessly provoke the Lord. That they called for a general moral reformation comes as no surprise. Religious leaders had been doing that for centuries. The situation in 1775 and 1776 generated greater intensity. It demanded more than routine contrition. The ministers warned that however worthy the fight against Great Britain might be, God sometimes punished people for "disobedience, ingratitude, and unfruitfulness."[55] Shared rituals of repentance buttressed community solidarity. In a revolutionary environment, public recognition of sin, of a failure to fulfill Scripture, became a political act. Americans who defended their rights had to ask themselves whether their declarations of self-righteousness in the fight against Great Britain were just a shameless rhetorical strategy masking selfish goals. "An empty profession of religion and liberty" only compromised the political cause, "for such a profession, may be yet joined with the most odious slavery to the corrupt lusts of the heart."[56] Proof of an authentic willingness to reform involved acts such as a boycott of luxury goods, most of which had been imported from England. People who sacrificed material pleasures for political ends understood that "patriotism without piety is mere grimace; and that zeal for the rights of mankind, unless joined with the love of order and the laws of God, will degenerate into the turbulence of faction."[57]

According to the ministers, moral patriotism required unity. Perhaps even more than America's political leaders, clergymen admonished ordinary men and women that public dissent would destroy whatever chance they had to escape tyranny. Division was a sign of weakness. "Seditious discourse" compromised effective mobilization at the community level. History proved the point. Expressions of doubt—even complaint about the demands of war—had almost always "been the ruin of the most free states that ever lost their liberty."[58] The Jews of ancient Israel had learned that lesson. In a sermon aptly entitled *The Happy Effects of Union*, Enoch Huntington reminded his congregation that "the final overthrow of the *Jewish* nation, the desolation of their capital city, their temple and their country, was chiefly brought on by their divisions and factions; and they did ten times more to their undoing than all their foreign enemies and invaders."[59] Disagreement over small issues had the potential to get out of hand, kindling a "civil war among ourselves, which would be more dreadful than with Great Britain." In fact, dissent could return the American people to a horrible state of nature in which "the inhabitants, would have the opportunity, every man to kill his neighbors, and turn the country into a field of blood and desolation."[60] George Washington and many political leaders also called for unity, since it seemed unlikely that unless the thirteen colonies stood together they could defeat the British. But the ministers' appeal was different in character. It was focused on friends and neighbors actually making hard decisions in common.

Two additional aspects of American society seemed to undermine the people's appeal to heaven. Although criticism of slavery was not widespread, a few ministers—mostly in New England and the Middle States—argued that the brutal treatment of African Americans not only made a mockery of popular protests against British oppression, but also insulted God. At issue here is not a claim that the country was seriously contemplating freeing the slaves. It was not. But some historians have insisted that we should not blame the founding generation for its failure to end human bondage. The argument seems to be that times have changed and that forms of exploitation we find morally reprehensible today were not pressing issues for the people who mounted a revolution. Whatever the merits of this view, it is significant that some ministers publicly linked slavery and the slave trade to the demand for liberation from imperial oppression, insisting that cries for political freedom for white people without acknowledging the suffering of black people amounted to hypocrisy.[61]

Several published sermons made precisely that point. *A Discourse on the Times*, published in 1776 in Norwich, Connecticut, observed that resistance to Great Britain was meaningless if God found the Americans morally deficient. To avoid that judgment, the author declared, we must "set at liberty those vast numbers of *Africans*, which have so long time been enslaved by us, who have as good right to liberty as we have—We must no longer exercise that cruelty and barbarity toward them, as we have heretofore done."[62] Levi Hart, a clergyman in Preston, Connecticut, launched an even more impassioned critique of slavery. In 1774 he asked "the gentlemen of the law"—in other words, the colony's political leaders—"whether the admission of slavery in a government so democratical as that of the colony of Connecticut, doth not tend to the subversion of its happy constitution."

He pointed out that "the African slave-trade [was] a flagrant violation of the laws of nature, of the natural rights of mankind." And so, as ordinary New Englanders prepared for war, Hart reminded them "with what a very ill grace can we plead for slavery when we are the tyrants, when we are engaged in one united struggle for the enjoyment of liberty; what inconsistence and self-contradiction is this! Who can count us the true friends of liberty as long as we deal in, or publicly connive at slavery?"[63] Like so many social wrongs that persist despite broad awareness of their existence, slavery endured, divorced for most Americans from their justification for making an appeal to heaven for their own rights.

Eliphalet Wright, an obscure and outspoken clergyman from Killingly, Connecticut, boldly asserted in *A People Ripe for an Harvest* that another issue besides slavery was seriously eroding revolutionary unity. He raised the problem of economic class, a sensitive topic that the authors of revolutionary pamphlets seldom touched. Wright took up the cause of the ordinary American soldier who risked his life in battle and yet did not receive adequate financial support for his troubles. Why, he wondered, were these men required to shoulder heavier burdens than were the wealthier individuals in the community? He did not identify the "great men" who refused to sacrifice for the common good, but whoever they were, they were in Wright's estimation hypocrites. Everywhere one encountered "our great men crying out, that our liberties are all at stake, and yet they will not turn out to fight for the defense of our liberties without vast wages." From this perspective the appeal to heaven was a sham. "As affairs are now going on, the common soldiers have nothing to expect, but that if America maintain her independency, they must become slaves to the rich. It seems as if our rich men, like so many hard millstones, had agreed to grind them to death."[64] To be sure, Wright's was a lonely voice. That his sermon ever reached print is something of a surprise, and the one surviving copy is missing key pages. Perhaps assumptions by the rich to special privilege, like the visible continuation of slavery, encountered public indifference. There is no way to tell. But whatever the case, Wright—much like Dan Foster—viewed abstract political principles through a lens of everyday social experience.

On the community level America's ministers provided the people with assurance. They insisted that ordinary men and women had a right to judge the performance of their rulers, and if these leaders were found wanting, the people could make an appeal to heaven, a decision that meant that they would determine their own political futures. The sermons demanded action, reform, and commitment. And yet, however enthusiastically the clergy justified resistance to tyranny, they seemed uneasy that they might be riding a tiger, one that might carry them to chaos and anarchy. How far, they wondered, could one encourage the people to take charge of their political lives without risking the destruction of the bonds that sustained civil society?

No one knew the answer. Joseph Perry weighed the alternatives facing revolutionaries. On the one hand, there was liberation and freedom, on the other, disorder and lawlessness. Perry wanted to steer a middle course. "I am far from supposing insurrections never do any good," he wrote in May 1775, "or that they are not sometimes even necessary." He was certainly unprepared to condemn popular resistance to political authority. What he had witnessed "manifested a truly patriotic spirit." But still an element of doubt persisted. After all, "matters may have been carried too far."[65] A minister in Lancaster, Pennsylvania echoed these concerns. We must maintain social order, John Carmichael advised, "for it is certain that nothing next to *slavery* is more dreaded, than the anarchy and confusion that will ensue, if proper regard is not paid to the good and wholesome laws of government."[66]

As we shall discover in later chapters, the tension between order and disorder, between radical reform and social anarchy, permeated American political thought. The question of how much to trust the people to make the right choices—to give stability to the people's government—was present from the beginning of the Revolution. The issues have not changed greatly over the years. We still praise the power of the people while fearing that somehow we might return to the state of nature.

V

On the eve of independence America's ministers served as gatekeepers linking a threatening external political world to the daily life of small communities. They provided their neighbors with a coherent, persuasive explanation of the crisis that had engulfed them all. Some modern Americans may prefer an explanation of revolutionary mobilization based primarily on formal political theory and legal reasoning. This traditional intellectual focus requires revision. The aim in restoring the ministers to a central place in the revolutionary story has not been to argue that theology provided the sole key to understanding the rise of popular resistance to Great Britain. Rather, the goal has been to locate our understanding of the Revolution in the communities—the true sites of resistance—and to show how respected clergymen in sermon after sermon, week after week, addressed the people's doubts, giving them assurance in the righteousness of their cause and encouraging them to sacrifice for the common good. The writings of the Founders, however inspiring they may be today, do not adequately depict the emotional struggle or personal turmoil that ordinary soldiers experienced as they faced a daunting military challenge. The ministers did that, defining the burden of political allegiance within a perilous environment.

The ministers spoke to ordinary Americans in a language that they readily understood. In the sermons we encounter the triggering element that turned an often inchoate sense of wrong into an obligation to make hard political decisions about resistance. It was one thing to praise abstract principles—to celebrate rights and freedom—and quite another to transform those words into action. The ministers sensed the need to move beyond rhetoric. They achieved this end by equating political passivity with sin.

Few Americans at the time could ignore the ministers' logic. Depicting political allegiance as a choice between obedience to God and sin forced ordinary people to come forward, to make a decision about resistance. When sin was involved there could be no middle ground. As Enoch Huntington explained, Providence called upon ordinary men and women "to shew and convince the world, that tamely to submit to the arbitrary, lawless, oppressive claims, of kings and courts, when the rights, welfare and happiness of the people are at stake, is so far from being a duty, that it is *sin* . . . every one is called upon to make a resolute, virtuous resistance."[67] The argument defied rebuttal. Nathan Perkins instructed a group of soldiers going to war that "tamely and unresistingly to give up the liberties, with which God and nature have blessed us, and which we hold dear as men, and sacred as Christians, must be a crime in us."[68] The militiamen had no choice. Their souls were at risk in a political controversy. It was in this spirit that another minister informed a unit of New Hampshire Minutemen, "My friends, though I am not able to assure you of all the events of our present controversy—yet sure I am that you are called, in common with the rest of the world, to a contest in which you must conquer or die eternally."[69]

About the experience of war, the ministers were surprisingly candid. Combat was dangerous; many men listening to the sermons would die. Nathan Perkins told the soldiers in his congregation: "The most of you are strangers to the dreadful horror of battle. An army drawn up in battle array, the roaring of cannon, the smoke and confusion, the cries of the wounded, groans of the dying, and all the dreadful horrors of battle are things to which you have not been accustomed." Even faced with death the American troops should remember that they were fighting for "your native land, your dearest friends, your just rights, all you hold dear." As Perkins stated, "If these motives do not fire your souls in your country's cause, what can!"[70]

The ministers offered something more. They imagined a people who had won a long and difficult war. They had achieved freedom. They controlled their own government. In a sermon delivered in December 1774, William Gordon described a future that warranted sacrifice. The United States would recover prosperity, he believed, and soon "become far more glorious, wealthy and populous than ever, through the thousands and tens of thousands that will flock to it, with riches, art, and science acquired by them in foreign countries. And, how will the surviving inhabitants and their posterity together with refugees, who have fled from oppression and hardships, whether civil, or sacred, to our American sanctuary, daily give thanks to the Sovereign of the universe, that *this general asylum* was not consumed."[71] Gordon described a tolerant, diverse, free society worth fighting for. It certainly justified the risk of making an appeal to heaven.

CHAPTER THREE

FEAR

In the narratives of revolution it is striking to discover how quickly the hope for liberation has given way to fear. The emotional shift is not surprising. Nor is it necessarily an indication that the people have lost faith in the principles that initially sparked resistance. After all, a palpable sense of insecurity puts ordinary men and women on guard against an array of the physical dangers suddenly unleashed by political unrest.

It is also the case, however, that fear itself can become a problem. It has the capacity to erode the bonds of mutual trust, generate lethal rumors, and turn the defense of noble ideals into hate. The negative potential of revolutions is well documented. In small communities often separated by great distances from a nation's capital—be that Moscow or Paris—a feeling of dread has almost always accompanied the overthrow of discredited regimes, and in the absence of accurate information about unfolding events fear has triggered spasms of violence that later generations find embarrassing or inexplicable. Americans came close to following this destructive path. And yet, with a few notable exceptions, they refused to allow hate to define their revolution. Their commitment to a rudimentary rule of law during a time of partisan hostility deserves—now more than ever—a place in the history of our political origins.

A comparative perspective helps us to achieve this goal. We know that in unstable environments suspicion puts trust at risk. Neighbors who have lived peacefully for years in the same village allow real or imagined threats to their safety to justify lashing out at others. They persuade themselves that villagers or just passing strangers might in fact be secret agents intent not only on harming them, but also on betraying the entire revolution. In France and Russia—two well-studied examples—peasants welcomed the prospect of radical reform, but within a very short time, social and political resistance on the local level acquired an ugly character.[1] Doubt and anger fueled denunciations, which in turn made reports of insidious conspiracies more credible.

Whenever fear has infected beleaguered communities, otherwise rational and fair-minded people have sought to identify the human sources of disappointment and suffering. They demand names. Who is threatening us? And then, proclaiming their own self-righteousness or ideological purity, they have persecuted witches, priests, Jews, Japanese, aristocrats, or African Americans—an evolving list of targets that over time and in different cultures has included almost every group that could plausibly have been responsible for a state of affairs that no one at the time fully understood.

In comparison with other major revolutions, the American experience may seem a tame affair—that is, it does so if we focus attention on the white majority. For this group, nothing remotely similar to France's Great Fear or Terror occurred. Even in the South, where at the end of the war people murdered neighbors with frightening abandon, nothing happened that can be plausibly likened to the horrific purges that occurred during the Russian Revolution. Such comparisons must, of course, be qualified. White revolutionaries visited terrible violence far more frequently on African Americans and Native Americans than on loyalists, with whom they often shared a common cultural and ethnic heritage. This was predictable.[2] Racial tensions were fundamental to the American story, and they were at the core of extremely repugnant episodes involving the slaughter of Native American villages—western New York witnessing particularly heinous atrocities. The contrast with the settled areas of the country could not have been greater. In places where the British and American armies battled, where Tories and revolutionaries clashed, where slaves were tightly controlled and the Indians a distant threat, mass murders like those we associate with other revolutions did not occur.

This anomaly is harder to interpret than it might at first appear. There is certainly no reason to assume that the apparent absence of large-scale atrocities provides evidence that Americans had no taste for violence.[3] Arguments of this sort only serve to deflect attention away from the fact that most Americans between 1775 and 1777 lived in a constant state of apprehension. Violence or the threat of violence was just as much a part of their revolutionary experience as it was in other countries that experienced bloody excesses.

Accounts of the American Revolution that concentrate on the work of the members of the Continental Congress or the strategies of military leaders fail to capture how this chronic sense of personal insecurity came to characterize daily life from New Hampshire to Georgia. For the ordinary people of all races the war introduced frightening vulnerability. It generated mistrust and doubt. Even in communities located far from major battles, men and women worried about partisans who might at any moment burn their barns, kill their cattle, or assault friends who openly supported the Revolution. The dangers were real, especially in places such as Delaware, New Jersey, and Long Island, where the Tories—Americans who proclaimed allegiance to king and Parliament—organized guerrilla operations that put the revolutionaries' lives and property at risk.

Restoring fear to our revolutionary story is crucial in developing a more accurate understanding of how Americans gave meaning to their own participation in the war. Although one could cite many reasons why they managed to defeat the British in the end, the explanation most easily overlooked is how successfully their communities dealt with large numbers of internal enemies, people described at the time as persons "notoriously disaffected" to the American cause.[4] By treating fear as a fundamental aspect of political upheaval, we gain clearer insight into how the Revolution actually worked on the ground. It was in small communities where those Americans who supported independence were forced to decide who were friends, who enemies, and how to define allegiance in a politically uncertain environment. As we shall discover, fear justified what may now strike us as unfortunate episodes that involved the banishment of people without the benefit of due process. And in one case, fear was responsible for the creation of an internment camp whose very existence has been erased from our shared memory of revolution.

Severe political crisis forced revolutionaries to confront the prospect of employing violence against other Americans identified as domestic enemies. Even during times of grave danger this was not a welcome prospect. To participate in combat against soldiers of an opposing army is one thing; it is quite a different physical task to discipline fellow townsmen for what might be called ideological crimes. If gangs of Tories were operating in the area, revolutionaries often had no other choice. Partisans were roughed up, others occasionally murdered. In these situations it was psychologically essential to demonize adversaries, to deny their shared humanity, to label them in derogatory ways, and to accuse them of engaging in atrocities so brutal, so savage, so beyond the range of civilized interaction that they deserved whatever punishment they received.

The dangers were not imaginary. Tories did in fact carry out raids in which innocent people were killed. But the rhetoric of resistance did more than just report what had occurred in this or that attack. It exaggerated what had actually happened. Inflated tales about women raped or babies brutally killed circulated as truth in this environment, transforming neighbors who merely disagreed about political loyalties into objects of fear. They had to be watched. They could never be trusted. More than any other activity, participation in the Revolution required constant vigilance. As one Maryland writer who signed a newspaper essay "Rationallis" confessed, "My soul glows with the warmest resentment against our wicked, perfidious, and cruel open foes, but in a much greater degree accumulates my detestation and abhorrence of our *secret* enemies. . . . A native traitor is a villain of the blackest hue."[5] Hatred was not in itself capable of sustaining revolution, but it helped.

Reflections on the rhetoric and reality of revolutionary enforcement raise provocative questions about the formation of political identity.[6] There is no doubt that Americans felt a sense of pride at the end of the war. Against all odds they had created a new republic. However much they disagreed on specific government programs, they shared a spirit of nationalism, at once powerful and positive. But political identity has a negative side, an intense, often quite repellant awareness of who were and who were not citizens. African Americans were excluded from civil society. So were Native Americans.[7]

What we might consider is how Americans worked out their own political identities during the war within a poisonous environment of doubt and suspicion. It was in this context that they developed a powerful new sense of nationalism. The experience of insecurity—the fear that secret enemies might strike at any moment—not only encouraged revolutionaries to define political allegiance in terms of them and us, but also helped those who still harbored lingering affection for Great Britain to sever the last emotional ties to the mother country.[8] As a newspaper published in Fishkill, New York, during the war insisted, reports of terror and violence served a beneficial purpose: "By weaning us from those attachments which many of us still had, to a people from whom we originally sprang."[9]

I

Of the revolutionary accounts of ordinary people that have survived, few rival the painful intensity of the Reverend Nicholas or Nils Collin's *Journal*. Although he wanted no part of revolution, he discovered—as did so many other Americans—that he could not escape the miasmic fear that permeated his small New Jersey community. Others, no doubt, witnessed the kinds of terrifying events that Collin recorded. What made him unusual was the fact that he kept detailed notes chronicling violence and denunciations, betrayals and revenge.

Collin journeyed from Stockholm to Philadelphia in 1770, a young, well-educated man destined to become a pastor of a Swedish church in America. He viewed his move to the New World as an adventure. His enthusiasm for the enterprise remained high even after he reached his final destination, a small community in New Jersey then known as Raccoon but now as Swedesboro. As the pastor of the local church he faced a depressing challenge. Although some members of his congregation spoke Swedish, many no longer maintained meaningful ties with their country of origin. Collin, of course, spoke excellent Swedish, and, fortunately for him, he also was fluent in English and German. To make the situation in Raccoon even less inviting, many residents seem to have drifted away from formal religion altogether, and Collin had to spend time reviving the basic tenets of Christian faith. Still, he did not complain. Only a year after accepting his new post, Collin gave the Raccoon settlement a backhanded compliment: "America is quite pleasant and not as terrible, as many in Sweden believe. By the help of God, I shall not regret that journey. Swedish pleasantries and splendid enjoyments cannot be had [here], but we cannot expect all good things at once."[10] Late in 1773 Collin was promoted to rector of the local church, and even though he missed the cosmopolitan world that he had left behind, he remained optimistic about his future.

Collin's situation took an unpleasant turn in 1776. Although he stoutly maintained that he owed political allegiance only to the king of Sweden and that he had no interest in local political affairs, he could not ignore the growing partisan conflict that suddenly engulfed rural New Jersey. After the British army had overrun New York City in August 1776, it seemed only a matter of time before the people of Raccoon would be drawn into the violence of war. Collin's parishioners took sides, and as formal government authority broke down, extralegal groups sprang up demanding support from frightened residents. No one knew whom to trust. Panic was in the air. This was no time for learned debates about constitutional law or abstract political theory. Life or death decisions had to be made about negotiating the demands of revolution. "Formerly, nearly all had been eager [to take part resisting Great Britain], but now as the fire came closer, many drew away, and there was much dissension among the people. Many concealed themselves in the woods, or within their houses, other people were forced to carry arms, others offered opposition and refused to go. The people were afraid to visit the church, because the authorities took the opportunity to get both horses and men." Collin begged those supporting the American cause to show restraint by curtailing "the mad, un-Christian behavior."[11]

Collin's appeal for reason had no discernable affect on the people of Raccoon. All he could do was try to stay out of harm's way, and although he received death threats, he carried on with extraordinary personal courage and confided in his journal the steady disintegration of civil society. The most depressing period occurred in 1778, soon after the British army abandoned Philadelphia. The events that had preceded General Howe's occupation of that city had created huge uncertainty among Collin's parishioners. No one dared predict the war's outcome, and in this unstable environment, people hedged their political bets, changing sides as the military situation unfolded.

Ordinary people were armed and frightened. As Collin reported, "Everywhere distrust, fear, hatred and abominable selfishness were met with. Parents and children, brothers and sisters, wife and husband, were enemies to one another." It was hard to distinguish revolutionaries from loyalists, since both groups plundered, vandalized, and seized their neighbors' property. Nothing was safe. The roving bands destroyed "everything in a barbarous manner, cattle, furniture, clothing and food; they smashed mirrors, tables and china, etc., and plundered women and children of their most necessary clothing, cut up bolsters and scattered the feathers to the winds, burned houses, whipped and imprisoned each other." To Collin's dismay the heartless culprits even had the audacity to surprise "people when they were deep asleep."[12]

At one point Collin concluded that a rogue militia company led by "a man of a rather bad character" intended to assassinate him. A group of revolutionaries took him prisoner on a cold February morning and allowed him "only 15 minutes" to prepare for a difficult trip of almost one hundred miles. The officer in charge ordered Collin to walk the entire distance, but he stoutly refused to do so. Secured on a horse, the pastor "followed them under close guard by a strong escort with loaded guns and fixed bayonets." He anticipated death at any minute, "especially as many were drunk and fired several salvos for their own amusement." In any case, as Collin was keenly aware, "the approaching darkness would easily have hidden the true murderer."

Collin later learned that the plan was to goad him to attempt an escape, and then, as he made his break for freedom, his captors would shoot him down. As luck would have it, just when it appeared that Collin had no chance, Doctor Otto arrived on the scene. About him we know very little. According to Collin, Otto not only served as a local magistrate, but also was "a kindhearted man belonging to the German Lutherans." The doctor secured bail, and after the militia officers forced Collin to swear allegiance "to the new government," he returned home angry at what he interpreted as a violation of his self-proclaimed political neutrality. "Among a more civilized and generous people," Collin insisted, "this adventure could never have happened to me. . . . [After all] I took no part in their factions, but to chastise their godless persons and to prevent arson and theft is the duty of a true servant of the Lord, even if it costs [him] his life."[13]

The king's supporters behaved no better than did the revolutionaries. When the English briefly occupied Raccoon, Collin made the mistake of assuming that he was no longer in personal danger. When he left his house one day on an errand, a guard ordered him to halt, but "because of the noise and confusion," Collin did not hear the command. The soldier "was on the point of shooting me." Once again, the pastor avoided disaster, but his neighbors were less fortunate. "Many people here were plundered on this occasion," Collin noted in his journal. He recognized that such treatment of civilians was politically counterproductive. Indeed, excessive brutality was "one of the main reasons for their [the British forces] slight success, because often both friend and foe were robbed in the most despicable manner."[14]

A particularly gruesome event heightened fear in Collin's community. A few Americans in the area who were desperately short of money entered into a clandestine trade with the British. Revolutionary authorities had no patience with commercial exchanges that supplied the enemy with food. However, dire warnings against the practice failed to discourage the people from trying "to obtain specie coin, as well as sugar, tea, syrup and strong liquors." In mid-March 1778 the predictable crackdown occurred. The revolutionary militia arrested fifteen suspected traders and held them "in the schoolhouse at the Raccoon Church."

A few weeks later, the military situation suddenly shifted. "At daybreak on April 4, [1778] 300 refugees [Americans fighting for the British] and English troops arrived in three divisions to surround the militia, which escaped with great difficulty," reported Collin. The British troops and loyalists "burnt down the schoolhouse for the simple reason that their friends had been kept prisoner there." Soon, thereafter, the violence became lethal. Collin rushed out of his house when "a terrific cry was heard near the church." He immediately encountered "a terrible sight." The terse journal entry reminds us what happens when fear stokes anger. "A man, married to a woman of Swedish parents and in a way belonging to the congregation," Collin discovered, "was tied to a pine tree and was being whipped. He fainted at times, but when he recovered, the flogging continued both on [his] sides and back, so that the flesh was said to have been entirely crushed [and cut up]. Some days later he died. His crime was that he had profited by the forbidden trade."[15]

Collin survived the war and lived for almost fifty more years. He became a respected religious and intellectual figure in Philadelphia. But it is hard to imagine that he ever successfully erased from his memory the events that he had witnessed in Raccoon. Violence leaves scars. He summarized what he had endured in his journal. "From all this, it is apparent how terrible this Civil war raged," Collin observed late in 1778. "Both parties fought not like real men with sword and gun, but like robbers and incendiaries." Perhaps if regular troops had been assigned to keep order in the area, the fear that accompanied prolonged insecurity might have been addressed. But that had not happened. Near-anarchy "contributed greatly toward such barbaric license, as the province was too wild and of less importance, so that straggling parties under lesser and poor officers were allowed to proceed according to pleasure."[16]

We have no way of knowing how many other Americans experienced the Revolution in these traumatic ways. No doubt, people living near active war zones had more reason to fear personal harm than did other revolutionaries.

But it was always a matter of degree. Fear was pervasive. A minister who traveled through Westchester County, New York, during the autumn of 1777 encountered ordinary men and women who had been deeply and adversely affected by chronic violence. What he reported would probably not strike anyone who has looked at—either in newspapers or on television—the faces of the survivors of modern revolutionary terror as particularly unusual. But we do not generally associate such disturbing images with the American Revolution.

Like Raccoon, Westchester endured constant partisan activities. The inhabitants "often were actually plundered, and always liable to calamity. They feared every body they saw, and loved nobody." They had become paranoid. "To every question," the minister asked, "they gave such an answer as would please the inquirer.... Fear was, apparently the only passion by which they were animated. The power of volition seemed to have deserted them. They were not civil, but obsequious; not obliging, but subservient." Expressing sympathy for their condition did little good. "If you treated them kindly," the traveler discovered, "they received it coldly; not as kindness, but as a compensation for injuries done them by others."[17] This was a revolutionary society perpetually on guard, suspicious of strangers, always alert to hints of danger.

II

To calculate with certainty the number of Americans who opposed independence would be impossible. The figure seems to have been large, as much as 20 percent of the population. But this is guesswork. With the outcome of the war in doubt, people of loyalist sympathies were wise to hide their political allegiance. Moreover, what we know about the Tories defies meaningful generalization. They came from all social classes; they resided in all the states. They lived in small country towns; they were wealthy urban merchants. To be sure, some religious bodies had a greater proportion of loyalists than did other Protestant sects. Many Scots who had recently immigrated to North Carolina supported the king. But within every group, one encounters exceptions.[18]

We shall probably never establish with confidence why ordinary Americans chose one side or the other. What makes the challenge of establishing political identity even more difficult is that not all Tories expressed discontent in the same way. Some of them fought for the British. They committed what we would now label war crimes. Others were just trying to survive the conflict as best they could, often backing whichever group seemed at any given moment the most dangerous or the most likely to succeed. Of course, many loyalists gave voice to genuine ideological commitment. Some prominent Americans fled to London and spent the war trying to persuade the British government to maintain the fight.

Far more people simply kept their heads down, trimmers calculating as best they could which way the political winds were blowing. On one day a person could perhaps give aid and comfort to a Tory on the run, and then, at some later time, swear allegiance to revolutionary authorities. Politics on the ground were fluid and pragmatic.[19] It is not surprising, therefore, that many Americans wanted against all odds to remain neutral. One can understand their desire just to make it through their days without inviting trouble. The revolutionaries, however, hated the neutrals as much as they hated the Tories. They seemed like free riders trying to take advantage of the wartime sacrifices of other Americans. In 1777 a writer who styled himself "An American" informed newspaper readers: "A *doubtful* character is a despicable one, and therefore every man who does not in such a day, as the present, distinguish himself as a firm friend to his country, ought to be considered as an *enemy*, and recorded as such. We know there is no medium between freedom and tyranny."[20] Another piece appearing in the *Maryland Journal* condemned neutrals or moderates. "The man who by his neutrality deserts the cause, is a traitor to his country. I consider every man an enemy to the state who will not give his assistance to maintain the *new* government."[21]

In more recent times the Tories have enjoyed more sympathetic treatment. Histories of the Revolution often depict them as somewhat tragic figures, principled individuals who courageously defended the king even though that decision inevitably involved great personal suffering. Openly expressing loyalty to Great Britain invited banishment and loss of real estate. But however much we might empathize with persecuted supporters of the Crown, we should recognize that ordinary revolutionaries would have had little patience with such positive appraisals. During the early years of the war, they classified the Tories as dangerous enemies. They saw nothing admirable in their behavior. In an essay addressed "To the People of Maryland" in 1777, a writer asserted, "It is an uncontroversial fact, that each county [in Maryland] produces some persons disaffected to the independency of this state, and its present government; it is also a truth, that a few are to be found not only inimical of its government, but whose residence among us is dangerous to the state." The threat to the security of the public was real. "To our internal foes we are indebted, in a great measure, for the present war, the immense expense incurred, and the devastation, ravage and ruin suffered by us in consequence of it."[22]

As we have learned, Nicholas Collin chronicled ongoing partisan violence in one small community. There was nothing unique about his experience. Tories brought a reign of terror to New Jersey, Delaware, the Connecticut shoreline, and the Hudson Valley; in the South political differences sparked cycles of bloody revenge.[23] Assessing the peril in 1776, a writer in the *Boston Gazette* announced, "The state of our Government I think is alarming. I do not mean from our enemies in Britain, I am less afraid of them, than of our enemies among ourselves—They are the most dangerous—The Tories are the persons I most dread."[24]

He had a point. Throughout the country the fight for independence had set off civil war. In 1776 a committee of safety in Baltimore sounded the alarm. "We are sorry to inform you [the state council of safety] that the spirit of violence and opposition to the measures which have been adopted for our common safety, grows extremely daring and outrageous in this county, so that the officers appointed to carry into execution the Resolves of the [state] convention dare not proceed without further assistance." Something had to be done "to destroy the rising hopes of internal enemies."[25] In Albany the people were overcome by fear. The local committee of safety informed the Provincial Congress of New York that Albany County "is crowded with disaffected persons; the woods are full of them, and not withstanding every effort that has been made by our militia, and the rangers, to apprehend them, they still have eluded our search." Civil society seemed to be breaking down. "The disaffected persons in the county have proceeded to open acts of violence; they have plundered some of our soldiers of their arms in the road in open day, broken into houses of the inhabitants in the night time, and robbed them of their arms, ammunition and blankets, and even rescued our prisoners from the hands of those who were guarding them."[26]

Accounts of this character did little to calm widespread fears that the enemies of revolution were on the rise. The accuracy of the reports is not our immediate concern. No doubt, violent events had occurred. But in the telling the details were enhanced. People were encouraged to imagine the Tories as far more dangerous than they probably were in fact. The reason for exaggeration is clear. In a revolutionary situation in which it was vital to maintain commitment to a common cause, there was a psychological need to demonize the opposition, to describe the loyalists as not fully human and certainly as capable of acts against innocent revolutionaries that no truly civilized person would condone. There was nothing unusual about the vilification of foes. After all, in almost every war our country has fought over the last two centuries, Americans have demeaned their opponents, giving them derogatory names and associating them with evil.

The Revolution was no exception. The loyalists were not simply neighbors who had adopted objectionable political principles. They were worse. Contemporary documents portrayed the Tories as "a set of avaricious miscreants," "a banditti of hungry traitors," "internal enemies," "professed detestables," "wicked, perfidious, and cruel open foes," "villainous parricides," "apostate citizens," "murderers, traitors, spies and thieves," "sons of tyranny and despotism," "execrable miscreants," "dangerous, perfidious, and serpentine domestic enemies," "Pests to Society," and "bosom vipers."[27] In 1776 one author who blamed the Tories for "blood-thirsty designs" urged "all Americans who love Liberty, and hold their Country dear" to beware of the "infernal monster" determined to undermine independence. "Let me tell you," he insisted, "words do not convert lions into lambs, serpents into doves, nor Tories into Sons of Liberty; Remember, as our Savior was betrayed by one of his disciples, so in our country by her pretended friends."[28]

Another story originating in Kingston, New York, during the war explained that eight Tories accused of "putting families in fear" had been arrested. What, the newspaper asked, could Americans living in other communities learn from this incident? "Thus does the infernal designs and proceedings of the court of Great Britain assimilate to their own character all those who espouse their cause, not only seducing them to become base treacherous thieves, robbers, murderers, &c. but divesting them of humanity, and converting them into Savages and perfect Devils in human shape."[29] Hyperbolic rhetoric of this sort did not necessarily propel the Revolution forward, but it made it a lot easier for people to turn fear into hate and to entertain ways to control political enemies that they would normally have rejected out of hand.

Revolutionaries had ready explanations for why other Americans would turn against them. Political opposition revealed their inherently flawed character. In this political narrative the Tories could not help themselves. They were evil people utterly incapable of supporting a good cause. Boston's *Independent Chronicle*, for example, claimed, "The first and prevailing species of the herd of beings, called Tories, is actuated entirely by selfish, ambitious views, and therefore [they] will sacrifice everything social and sacred to their mean *selves*."[30]

A second, less cynical theory depicted internal enemies as simply ignorant. Somehow they had not fully understood how Great Britain had become a source of oppression. It is a curious phenomenon that attacks on the Tories' alleged failure to comprehend current events provides one of the better insights into what the revolutionaries themselves actually believed, since they accused the loyalists of discounting the very principles that the patriots allegedly held most dear. In September 1776 a Maryland paper ran a piece that had originally appeared in the *Connecticut Gazette*, arguing among other points, "Most of the TORIES, as far as I learn, are criminally and grossly ignorant, yea, enveloped in midnight Darkness." The author listed the Tories' key ideological errors. They did not, for example, "respect the natural and unalienable Rights of Mankind," comprehend "The Corruption and Wickedness of the British Parliament, and the Electors of Britain," acknowledge "The blood thirsty and vindictive Spirit of the Tyrant of Britain," or accept "The Benefit accruing to both Countries from the Independence of America." One could not expect better of the Tories, since "Their obstinacy chains them down in Egyptian Darkness,—a darkness that may be felt, and deeply lodges them in the strong holds of ignorance, where nothing salutary and enlightening can come nigh to them." The writer who ironically styled himself "Lenity" concluded, "Show me a Tory, and I will show you a Traitor, one who daily commits High Treason against his country, and [we must ask] is such a one fit to live? No, it is a Joke on the welfare of the country to suppose it."[31]

Passionate revolutionaries knew exactly how to deal with the country's domestic enemies. Get rid of them, they insisted. No one advocated killing the Tories, just that they should be banished, and swiftly. Some enthusiastic commentators sounded like vigilantes, suggesting that ordinary people might be forced to take the initiative in protecting their communities.[32] The public danger justified employing extreme measures. It is hard to verify some of the actions reported in the newspapers. One Boston journal claimed that a group of local men "appeared early in the morning, masked and armed, cap-a-pee [covered from head to foot], and paraded the streets . . . dragged six Tories out of their beds, placed them in a cart, and drove them out of town." Apparently, no one died in this incident, but the revolutionaries warned if any of the Tories dared return they "would put every one of them to death."[33] In 1778 a writer in the *Connecticut Journal* ominously reminded readers how God had responded to a group of rebellious angels who once threatened the peace of heaven. "Notwithstanding the infinite mercy of God," the author explained, "we know he banished forever those rebel angels, who dared to take up arms against heaven, *their native country.*"

Could revolutionaries facing a similar situation show greater leniency than had the Lord? Appeals for mercy made no sense in such situations. After all, the Tories were "the betrayers and murderers of thousands." They deserved "to be banished forever from the land, which they have so plainly forfeited, endeavored to enslave, and have actually stained with the blood of their murdered brethren."[34] An incendiary Boston radical who adopted the pen name "Joyce, Junior" warned that the time had come for "some Well-wisher to his Country" to cleanse the city of revolutionary betrayers. All that was needed was a "spirited Asserter of the American Cause" who would encourage like-minded citizens "to clear this Town of all noted and suspicious Persons, who are so injurious to this State in particular, and the United States in general."[35]

In this threatening political climate it is perhaps not surprising that some fearful Americans contemplated even harsher forms of treatment for "our most dangerous, perfidious and serpentine domestic enemies." "An Enemy to Tories" suggested in a New Hampshire paper that the community build a large ship, and "after putting on board some Provisions—Set them [the local Tories] adrift, & make it Death for any of them to ever land on any Part of the American Shore that is inhabited by FREEMEN."[36] Someone who addressed the people over the pen name "Public Compassion"—with no apparent sense of irony—urged fellow revolutionaries to sell the Tories into slavery. Experience taught that "gentle measures" did not work, and even though selling Tory neighbors into bondage might seem a step too far, Compassion insisted that they deserved to be "transported to some place that tolerates slavery," which of course at the time included all thirteen states.[37]

The ships carrying "detestables" never set sail. Nor were white Tories sold into slavery. However much ordinary Americans hated the country's domestic enemies and gave credence to inflated reports of atrocities, they showed little enthusiasm—except perhaps in the South at the end of the war—for personal revenge. They expected officially sanctioned bodies—be they committees of safety or local governing units—to enforce the Revolution. As we shall discover in Chapter 4, the desire to work within a framework of community authority acted as a constraint on anger generated by fear. Ordinary people generally cooperated with the revolutionary communities, watching for suspicious characters, denouncing neighbors for disloyalty, but they had no taste for actions that threatened to unleash anarchy. Even a firebrand such as Joyce, Junior confessed that however tempting it was to administer a kind of rough street justice, "the Method of extirpating Tories, would come better from Government."[38]

Popular excesses seemed as unattractive as did acceptance of British rule. In a widely circulated article appearing originally in the *Pennsylvania Packet* in 1777, a writer claimed that he could distinguish five separate political groups in the United States. Predictably, the most offensive were the "rank Tories" who called for unconditional submission to Great Britain. Next came the "moderate men," who "think freedom too dear when purchased with the temporary loss of tea, coffee, sugar, wine and rum." The "timid Whigs" supported the Revolution only so long as the Americans were clearly winning. The next category comes as a surprise. The author had no use for "furious Whigs" who "think the common forms of justice should be suspended towards a Tory criminal, and that a man who only *speaks* against our common defense, should be tomahawked, scalped, and roasted alive." Those who best understood the true spirit of revolution were the "staunch Whigs" since "they are friends of order and good government and are just and merciful in the exercise of power."[39]

In communities overcome by fear, however, restraint was never easy. It serves no useful purpose for us to hazard a guess as to whether the revolutionaries' distrust of the Tories was justified, or in specific circumstances even accurate. People accommodated as best they could to insecurity, real and imagined. Confronted by a surge of violence, some residents of

Amenia Precinct, New York, for example, wondered whether the staunch Whigs really understood the revolutionary challenge. They informed the provisional state government that they had identified "a number of people" who were clearly "enemies and traitors to the United States of America." Something had to be done, and that, very quickly. "The people here in general are so exasperated against them [the Tories] for fear of being murdered, burnt or destroyed in the night, that they seem determined to rise in a body, and kill all the Tories they can find in the county, unless some effectual measures are very soon taken with them."[40] The residents of Amenia were barely hanging on, and in their desperate appeal for help, they remind us of what it was like to live through a revolution.

III

Although various committees and courts eventually took on the responsibility for meting out punishment for alleged crimes against the Revolution, the burden of identifying domestic enemies fell mainly to Americans who brought suspicious characters to the attention of authorities. This is an extremely important point for understanding how people who were not directly threatened by pitched battles experienced the war. They became observers, slightly nervous and constantly alert to unguarded words or actions that might reveal a person's true political allegiance. The pressure to maintain surveillance transformed traditional community life. Local gatherings that had time out of mind encouraged candid, even inebriated conversation suddenly involved a high level of personal vigilance. Evenings at a tavern, relaxed talk after militia training, or visits to neighboring families, for example, became revolutionary sites that could spark doubts about the loyalty of individuals who had previously seemed trustworthy.

Such exchanges between friends and associates often provided justification for public denunciations, since in an environment marked by fear, revolutionaries felt compelled to come forward with reports of politically questionable behavior. Vigilance was a duty. Within American communities it served as a measure of genuine patriotism. As "A FREE AMERICAN" announced in the Independent Chronicle, "In the present critical situation of public affairs, it becomes the duty of every individual to contribute his best endeavors toward the public welfare of the community, of which he is a member."[41] Another writer who addressed the people as COMMON

SENSE—not Thomas Paine—drew attention to "the necessity of always fitting out internal police to the circumstances of the times we live in." What that task meant in practice in Philadelphia was careful monitoring of "a strange variety of men and characters." He advised readers "in the present crisis, we ought to know square by square, and house by house, who are in real allegiance with the United Independence States, and who are not."[42] In Norwich, Connecticut, fear of "internal enemies" promoted a call for a special night watch "for the happy purpose of frustrating the secret machinations that may be formed by those villains [the Tories] to subvert the wise plans laid and laying for the good of these American States."[43]

It was all well and good, of course, to encourage public vigilance. In practical terms, however, it proved very difficult to identify actual internal enemies. After all, they looked like other Americans, and if they went about their business without raising suspicion, they could easily mask their allegiance. In that way they were perceived as being like the witches who once plagued Salem, Massachusetts. People convinced themselves that Tories were present in their communities. But they operated in secret, invisible to the public eye, and were all the more dangerous because of their ability to hide in plain sight. Samuel Adams, who was then serving in the Continental Congress, found the problem of exposing real Tories extremely frustrating. "They are the most virulent, & I am of Opinion, the most dangerous Enemies of America," Adams informed a correspondent. "They do not indeed openly appear in Arms, but they do more Mischief secretly."[44]

Adams was not alone in warning against "internal *secret* enemies."[45] In the absence of reliable information about what the Tories were up to, revolutionaries occasionally allowed imagination to substitute for proper intelligence. In September 1776 the *New-Hampshire Gazette* assured readers that Tories were hatching conspiracies in their midst. He reported that these dangerous characters "had particular toasts" and "significant nods and smiles" that they used in public to communicate with fellow travelers. There was even more worrisome news. The Tories "keep up a secret correspondence thro' the colonies in order to comfort one another, to keep up their sinking spirits, and to propagate falsehoods."[46]

Most disconcerting for the people who supported independence was the certainty that the Tories held clandestine meetings in which they plotted to undermine the Revolution. The evidence for such gatherings was admittedly thin, but lack of solid information did little to dispel the conviction that conspiracies were afoot. And there was no question of what went on at these political covens. The Tories met to plan violence against their neighbors. A 1776 assembly of representatives from thirty-two towns in Middlesex County, New Hampshire, warned "confederacies are judged to be formed or forming in many parts of the county, and may be strengthened, and many other great inconveniencies ensue from such persons who are inimical to the cause of American Liberty." The unsubstantiated source of this disturbing information apparently did not reduce its impact. The group pledged to "use our best endeavors to prevent such persons assembling together."[47]

From Boston came a report—again, lacking firm evidence—that an anonymous person had "certain Information of a Gang of Tories, who have Weekly Meetings at particular Houses in this Town under the cover of Night, and there consulting and wickedly contriving to ruin, if possible this once happy Land."[48] Another appeal from Boston called upon all persons "who are friends to their country" to support efforts to expose the "many private meetings" the Tories organized "with others in other Towns (with the ill design as we have too much reason to think)."[49] Revolutionaries in Norwalk, Connecticut, begged the state government to help them deal with local Tories who were "plotting and planning, in a secret manner."[50] From Albany came news that "our suspected enemies in this city are continually drawing off in a secret manner into the country, perhaps collecting together and awaiting the departure of our friends to fall upon the remainder of us."[51] Fear legitimated these stories. A conspiratorial mentality took root and, as we shall discover, gave license to remedies that ran counter to the rule of law.

Considering that the Tories operated in secret, the revolutionaries had to devise ways to identify real domestic enemies. As with the infamous witch trials, the challenge was detecting external behavior that revealed an evil political character. One hint that a person might be a Tory sympathizer was that he or she simply looked like a Tory. This curious logic was certainly at work in the state of New York, where local authorities arrested strangers on the grounds that they appeared "to be of suspicious Character" or might be conceived "from their appearance and Conversation to be suspicious Characters."[52]

More reliable indicators of political affiliation were actions—witnessed by ordinary citizens—that threatened the American cause. The easiest to document were cases in which an individual left a community and volunteered to fight for the British. Empty houses or uncultivated fields provided visible signs of desertion. An example from Massachusetts reveals how people in one small town identified a former neighbor, now a Tory. They observed that Charles Callahan "has absented himself for more than three Months from his habitation & has left [an] Estate Real & personal to the value of more than Twenty pounds within said Town [Pownalborough] and from the best Intelligence we can obtain, we verily believe the said Charles Callaghan [sic] went voluntarily to our Enemies and is still absent."[53] Thousands of other Americans made the same decision. They fled to areas controlled by the British army, or less frequently, travelled to England.

Failure to appear for militia practice was sure to arouse suspicion. Since many of the young men called to serve in the local forces made a living as farmers, they often decided that harvesting a crop or putting out seed justified skipping these drills. In other words, absence did not indicate for certain that a person sympathized with the British. But whatever the reasons for staying away, it caught the attention of neighbors who turned up for the exercises and suggested to them that truancy was an expression of political dissent. After all, service was not a choice; it was a duty. When the British army mounted an attack on New York City late in 1776, the Philadelphia Council of Safety announced "No excuse ought to be admitted or deemed sufficient against marching with the Militia at this time, except Sickness, Infirmity of Body, Age, religious Scruples, or an absolute Order from the Authority of this State." The Council added a poignant political observation: "It is the opinion of this Board, that every Person who is so void of Honor, Virtue, and Love of his Country, as to refuse his Assistance at this Time of imminent Danger, may justly be suspected of Designs inimical to the Freedom of America."[54] Still, as the records of many localities show, Americans frequently found reasons why they need not show up for militia practice, and their behavior was denounced by those who did.[55]

Fortunately for those who worried about what the Tories were doing in secret, the conspirators occasionally revealed themselves in public. These dramatic moments often occurred during everyday community gatherings such as militia practice or drinking at a local tavern. Ill-considered words— perhaps uttered in anger or frustration—were sufficient to demonstrate that a neighbor might in fact be an ideological enemy. For people who were already feeling insecure and prone to believe reports of secret Tory plots, these events served to strengthen the support of ordinary people for the American cause. It was in these situations that they discovered that whatever they believed they did not agree with the Tories. Or that it was too dangerous to do so. Political loyalties were defined against visible opponents who, like confessing witches, unexpectedly voiced their offensive ideas in public. Dramatic exchanges of this kind were in fact profoundly shaping events in many communities. It is in the voices of obscure people that we gain a fuller understanding of how abstract notions about revolutionary resistance were tested and confirmed against outspoken dissenters.

There was no problem identifying Robert Gassaway as a person of interest. He lost self-control during a militia exercise on February 1, 1776. A resident of the Middle District of Frederick County, Maryland, he surprised other soldiers when he "publicly and loudly declared before . . . two Companies, and in the Presence of several other Spectators, that it was better for the Poor People to lay down their Arms, and pay the Duties and Taxes laid upon them by the King and Parliament, than to be brought into Slavery and to be commanded and ordered about as they were." People asked Gassaway what he meant by slavery if it was not Great Britain. To that question, he responded "a Parcel of great men." He described an extraordinary conspiracy of so-called patriots, proving that the same accusations ran in both directions. For Gassaway, it was the leaders of the Revolution who were plotting secretly against the common good. According to him, these great men had destroyed the tea in Boston and, fully aware that they "had done wrong," had then "ordered all America to be brought under Arms, and say now my brave Boys fight away." Witnesses urged Gassaway to calm down. They reminded him "that this was only his own Opinion and that he had better keep it to himself."

Gassaway initially refused to walk back his charges, defiantly proclaiming that he was right. He then urged the Maryland militiamen "to lay down their Arms, and petition the Congress to petition the King and Parliament" for reconciliation. He added "he wished the Eyes of the Multitude were opened." No one seems to have found Gassaway's performance persuasive. He was fined for "an Offense that might have been of dangerous consequence." By this time Gassaway had reconsidered. He saw that the other soldiers and spectators had no intention of paying taxes levied by Parliament. And so, before the community, he admitted voicing serious political errors. "I confess," he declared, "that I am sory to think that I should have said enni thing that should have given enny purson reson to think that it was my deiser to disunite the peopel and, And acknowledge my error in so doing, and do promis for tim to cum to behave myself carfully" [sic].[56] Gassaway need not have worried too much. His intemperance had forced others to reflect on what independence from Great Britain meant to them.

Another man from Baltimore County claimed to have knowledge about widespread secret opposition to the Revolution. Like Gassaway, Alexander Magee ran his mouth in public, voicing "dangerous and inimical" political opinions, which were of particular concern since "he appears to have some influence among the Common people." What he announced—and this was two months before the Declaration of Independence—was that armed resistance to king and Parliament had no justification. In fact, he informed his neighbors, "it was owing to the Lenity & forbearance of Great Britain why she had not convinced us of our Error ere now." A day of reckoning would soon come. Of that he was sure. Magee claimed to know that many people who pretended to support the Revolution were actually disguising their true allegiance. In any case, he had no intention of assisting the American cause, and more, if local authorities tried to levy a fine on him for his actions, Magee "would shoot any person who should attempt to execute his effects for the purpose."[57] He did not in fact shoot any members of the Baltimore committee, but the possibility that an individual of such violent temperament might sway the loyalty of common people added to the sense that larger numbers of invisible enemies were waiting to strike.

About the same time a similar event occurred in a small Connecticut town. Andrew Patchin, who lived in Brookhaven, was returning to his home after a routine militia exercise. The experience of drilling seems to have exhausted Patchin's patience, for it soon became known in the community that he not only vilified local military officers—men selected by soldiers—but also questioned whether the Continental Congress knew what it was doing. As in other examples of this sort, Patchin's behavior on a day in May reminds us how ordinary Americans were drawn into revolutionary politics. His impulsive words turned other militiamen into witnesses. During an investigation, Daniel Nash swore "he heard Andrew

Patchin say (as he was going home from General Training) the Congress goes on as they ought not to Do." Nash remembered that Patchin also "damn'd the Congress in all their unlawful proceedings & used much more unfriendly discourse." Another witness confirmed this account. He reported that Patchin "particularly Dam'd Col. William Floyd, saying he came from the Congress on purpose to make Disturbance and the Devil would have him, for he would go to hell for what he had done, & so would Captain Nathan Rose & Lieutenant William Baker; and persuaded all present to agree to go to no more trainings, saying that neither he, or any of his should; and said all those who would not so agree was worse than Infidels."[58] What happened to Patchin is not known. He may have been expressing only temporary irritation at being forced away from preparing his fields in the spring. But one never could tell for certain whether he was merely having a bad day or had revealed a parcel of domestic enemies determined not to fight for their country.

Whether alcohol removed normal inhibitions and encouraged men such as Gassaway or Patchin to speak their minds in public is not known. There is no doubt, however, that drink certainly helped beleaguered communities identify possible secret opponents who kept their political opinions to themselves when sober. Excessive drinking was not the problem. Inebriation could be forgiven. It was what tipsy neighbors said under the influence of alcohol that added to the climate of fear. Their indiscretions suggested that members of a fifth column might be operating in one's immediate neighborhood. Thomas Carman certainly seemed suspicious. He came to the attention of New York State authorities when people observed him declaring undying loyalty to the king. According to one witness, Carman "exclaimed against the Cause of America and damned the Congresses and Committees and drank a Health to King George and he would stand by him and fight for him." Moreover, Carman was fond of repeating to whomever would listen a short doggerel: "They seek'd for my Life and plundered my Estate, But I am for his Loyalty King George the Great." One has the sense that locals did not consider Carman to be a serious political danger. After all, as another witness explained, when he sang praises to the king, Carman had been "intoxicated with Liquor."[59] But there was always lingering doubt.

In New York Samuel Witten made injudicious comments while under the influence of liquor. After sobering up, however, he had second thoughts, insisting "the Americans are right in their resistance by arms & that he is willing to take up arms & defend the Country."[60] Samuel Townsend of Kingston, New York, tried to pass off his inimical political views as a joke. He told investigators that he "some few Days ago went from home upon some Business & happened to Gett a Little Intoxicated in Liquor." Riding along a road, Townsend fell into company with a congenial stranger. That person began boasting of recent Tory successes. Townsend should have shut up, but "being merry and in Liquor, Wantonly and in a Bantering manner told him that in the Lane through which they was then Riding five & twenty Whigs would not Beat five & twenty Tories." With this "joke" the two went their separate ways. When his words came to the attention of others, he insisted the whole incident had only been a humorous attempt to keep up the conversation and not the act of a conspirator. From a local jail he begged "his Intoxication & Looseness of his Tongue will Be forgiven . . . as it would not have been expressed by him in his sober Hours."[61]

There were other ways that ordinary revolutionaries could expose enemies in their midst. If they caught a neighbor spreading false news about the progress of the war, they felt entirely justified in labeling the person a threat to the community. After all, deceitful stories could undermine American resistance. Most people accused of dispersing deceptive reports were in all likelihood not British agents charged with putting forth propaganda.[62] They seem to have been individuals who unwisely repeated gossip in public and thereby contributed to a chronic sense of insecurity. Several people in Rockingham, Virginia, revealed their true Tory sympathies by "speaking disrespectful and disgraceful words of the Congress" and "propagating some News tending to raise Tumult and Sedition in the state." Thomas Vance of Rockingham, Virginia, came before local authorities for "Declaring himself a Tory, publishing false news and speaking words to terrify the people."[63]

Albany faced the same problem. Abraham Wendell of that city confessed to "having industriously propagated Intelligence respecting the Enemy which tho' false may nevertheless tend to dishearten weak and ignorant Persons." After local authorities confronted Wendell, he promised on oath "not to spread any such Reports in future."[64] On another occasion an Albany committee observed the Tories played on the fears of ordinary people. They advanced "artful arguments" that had "great effect on weak minds." One false story certainly undermined resistance in Ecopus, New

York. Tories encouraged frightened people to take refuge in New York City, "assuring them, that when they had shewn themselves there, they would be suffered to return immediately to their farms; that in a fortnight Gen. Howe and army would penetrate Ulster County, and reward their loyalty by giving them possession of their Whig-neighbors' farms."[65] How many people actually believed such tales is impossible to know for certain. More to the point, they had to be wary of false news, judge the source, listen carefully, and remain alert to the possibility that stories circulating in taverns and on the street might have been planted to deceive gullible revolutionaries.

Anxieties about ascertaining reliable intelligence about the war came to a head in Stoughton, a small community south of Boston in eastern Massachusetts. The problem surfaced initially in early December 1776. Local officials felt obliged to investigate, "A Report having been spread among the Good People of Stoughton." A terrifying story circulated through the town that "the Congress were Surrounded by the Enemy, that nine of the Southern Governments had revolted, that Connecticut was on the Point of doing so, that General Washington had turned Devil, and the General [Charles] Lee had wrote the above Intelligence to the General Court of this State." If any of this was true, then the fight for independence was over before it got off the ground.

To make matters worse, the residents of Stoughton accepted the report largely because a respected member of the community and a member of the Massachusetts Assembly, Henry Stone, certified it was all true. When a committee interrogated Stone, a successful blacksmith, he maintained that he had not intended to mislead his neighbors. The evidence, however, was somewhat dodgy. Stone claimed to have heard from another man who possessed a letter allegedly written by General Lee. That correspondence related how "the ministerial Army were march'd for Philadelphia to the Congress, and that He [the person who received the letter] did not doubt but that the Congress was by that very Minuit surrounded if not taken." And, the letter added that "the Southern Governments had left us," and "Connecticut would give up too." Washington had apparently deserted the cause. Stone compounded an unfortunate situation by repeating the news to anyone he encountered. In the end he managed to escape punishment by placing the blame for the false news elsewhere. Stone was merely an ir-responsible gossip.[66] The episode touched the entire community. Stone was the focus of the affair, but a considerable number of villagers came forward to give evidence about who had said what to whom. The ordeal at Stoughton serves as a reminder of how ordinary people experienced the Revolution on the local level, a world of rumor and suspicion, mistrust and insecurity.

During the war ordinary Americans were well advised to be extremely wary of travelers. Strangers had a long history of generating suspicion in small communities. In an environment in which people had grown cautious of domestic enemies, these fears were amplified. The person one encountered on the road might be engaged on legitimate business, but by the same token, he (travelers were seldom women) might be on his way to join British forces or gathering intelligence for military preparation. Perhaps because Connecticut was so exposed to British attacks from New York City and Long Island, its governor and state committee of safety decided in 1776 to halt the free movement of potentially dangerous travelers. Authorities there warned that "many persons inimical to the United States of America, do wander from place to place, with intent to spy out [upon] the state of the colonies, whereby confederacies may be formed and strengthened." No one could claim exemption. Revolutionaries had a responsibility to challenge all persons "unknown or suspected, whether they appear in the character of gentlemen, expresses, travelers, or common beggars." When questioned, the suspect had to produce "a certificate from some congress, committee of safety or inspection, some magistrate, justice of the peace, or General, or Field Officer in the Army, therein mentioning the same is traveling, and that he is friendly to the liberties of American States." If a citizen encountered someone without a proper pass, he was instructed to "carry [him] to the nearest civil authority" immediately. And for good measure, the ordinance requested Connecticut towns to post special night watches to intercept dangerous travelers who hoped to avoid exposure.[67] New Hampshire passed a similar law compelling "all persons traveling" to have passes "denoting their friendliness to the American States." Communities were responsible for drawing up provisions "for taking up and examining all suspected persons."[68]

How many revolutionaries actually confronted strangers on the road is not known. Records about such matters are scattered and incomplete. Great Barrington, Massachusetts, seems to have been especially vigilant about confronting travelers. A town meeting decreed that no transient persons should be permitted to remain in town, or to traffic or trade, for more than ten days without the consent of a local committee. To make sure that the order was enforced, it appointed a special committee "for the purpose of inspecting into the political character of such persons."[69] And in Albany a revolutionary body announced that it had empowered Major Henry Van Veghten "to stop every Person whom he may find traveling through this City and whom he may conceive from their appearance and Conversation to be of suspicious Character."[70]

These various regulations and responsibilities—all intended to overcome chronic personal insecurity—encourage us to entertain a powerfully new sense of how revolution affected the lives of ordinary Americans. They did not spend their days following the activities of the Continental Congress or even the reports from distant battlefields. To be sure, those subjects mattered. But most of the time participation in the Revolution was a profoundly local concern. On this level, as Nicholas Collin and others have reminded us, just making it through one's day involved unprecedented tensions. For them, it was an anxious, uncertain moment. Everyday interactions—sharing a drink after militia exercises, conversing with neighbors in a local tavern, or encountering strangers on the road—were fraught with danger. A comment made in anger or a joke about the state of political affairs could raise suspicions. Invisible enemies had to be identified, and failure to find any did not mean that Tories were not in fact lurking in the woods or holding secret meetings. It was this tormenting sense of doubt about political allegiance that defined the revolutionary experience. And it was in this strained atmosphere that some Americans made decisions about secret enemies that they may have later come to regret.

IV

However justified they may seem at the time of their construction, internment camps strike most Americans as an embarrassing aberration in our nation's history. They remind us of moments when fear—most often associated with anxiety about possible military attack—has persuaded the government to suspend normal legal procedure and incarcerate people whom they judge to be threats to public security. The experience of Japanese

Americans during World War II provides a notorious example. Other, more recent cases quickly come to mind. Apologies after the fact never quite excuse what has happened.

We do not usually associate the American Revolution with such events. That is surely a lapse of memory. At the very moment that the country declared independence, people deemed suspicious were arrested, and without proper trial—even without the benefit of full investigation—relocated to internment camps where they could be closely watched and presumably rendered incapable of giving aid and comfort to enemy agents. These were not military prisons. Captured British soldiers received quite different treatment. The camps housed American citizens.

A particularly disturbing case occurred in Pennsylvania. In 1777 the British general William Howe decided to seize Philadelphia, then the city where the Continental Congress met. The entire expedition turned out to be a colossal mistake. Howe's superiors in London expected him to join General John Burgoyne's large force then moving down toward Albany from Canada. If the two armies had in fact secured the Hudson Valley, they would have cut off New England from the other American states and probably brought the war to a close. For reasons that remain unclear, that did not happen. Howe transported an army from New York City to the northern Chesapeake area, where he began a slow march on Philadelphia.[71]

News of the growing military threat caused panic throughout the city. Revolutionaries lashed out at readily available scapegoats, imaginary enemy agents who seemed to be supporting the British advance. Local authorities immediately targeted members of leading Quaker families. Their religious scruples, long a source of annoyance among supporters of independence, served as an excuse for public vilification. The Friends were pacifists. More galling, even as the British were just then approaching the city, Quakers refused on religious grounds to take oaths of allegiance to the new nation.

Relying initially on an incriminating document that turned out to be a forgery, frightened people in Philadelphia concluded that secret conspiracies were afoot. A general in the Continental Army announced on the basis of the false evidence that "Quakers at their Meetings Collected Intelligence & forwarded [it] to the Enemy." Like other revolutionaries, he concluded the Quakers were "the most Dangerous Enemies America knows & Such as have it their power to Distress the Country more than all the Collected Force in Britain."[72] The reaction was perhaps predictable. James Allen, who kept a diary during this period, recorded a contagion of fear. "When General Howe was expected to Philadelphia," he wrote, "a persecution of Tories . . . began; houses were broken open, people imprisoned without the color of authority by private persons, & as, was said a list of 200 disaffected persons made out, who were to be seized, imprisoned, & sent off to North Carolina."[73]

Many suspects were indeed dispatched to North Carolina.[74] But the greatest danger seemed to come from a small group of Quakers. Local officials concluded that the city would not be secure unless the Quaker men were carted off to Staunton, Virginia, a distance of over three hundred miles. We know a lot about the accused because they aggressively rehearsed their ordeal before the public. These were well-educated men who knew the law. They petitioned city officials; they published detailed denials of treason in the local newspapers. In one powerfully worded statement entitled *An Address to the Inhabitants of Pennsylvania* (1777), the twenty-some prisoners questioned whether their persecution resulted from "intemperate zeal and personal animosities." They had not been allowed habeas corpus. There was no "General Warrant, specifying no matter of offense against us, appointing no authority to hear and judge whether we were guilty or innocent, nor limiting a duration to our confinement." No wonder that the Quakers complained that they were the victims of "modern despotism."[75]

These appeals made little impression on their accusers. Escorted by armed guard the Quakers were carted off to an internment camp in Winchester—not Staunton as it turned out—and for many months they endured hardship. They complained bitterly about separation from their families. Throughout their exile they showed remarkable courage. They certainly refused to compromise religious principles. An offer of freedom for anyone who would swear an oath to the state had no takers. After Howe departed Philadelphia and the city's inhabitants no longer gave into fear, the suspects were summarily released. No one apologized for what had occurred. There were no monetary settlements, not even for the funds the Quakers had spent for food and lodging in Virginia.[76] For their tormentors the entire episode was soon forgotten; for the Quakers who worried that a sudden military reverse might again enflame fear, the scars of internment remained.

Fear led to the creation of a much larger domestic prison in Exeter, New Hampshire. Although this camp held many more men than did the one in Winchester, almost nothing is known about its brief history. The reason for its obscurity is clear enough. Those housed here were ordinary farmers who lacked the education or resources required to sustain an effective public defense. Their names appear on long lists. About their lives before or after incarceration we know almost nothing. But however obscure they may have been, their experience should be restored to the story we tell ourselves about the Revolution.

As was the case in Philadelphia, events in Exeter were the product of military desperation. During the fall of 1777 the British opened two separate fronts in New York State. Their army easily conquered New York City, and from this strongly fortified position, the British threatened communities located in the lower Hudson River Valley. Especially vulnerable were villages in Dutchess and Westchester Counties. Tory bands operating with the support of British Regulars terrorized the entire region. The loyalists, of course, had a different perspective. They believed that local revolutionary militias were entirely responsible for the region's insecurity. As the people who lived there went about their business, it probably did not greatly matter who was to blame. Violence stalked every farmstead. Death and destruction of property were common. In the area north and west of Albany the military situation was even more ominous. British supporters, allied with well-armed bodies of Native Americans, frequently raided frontier settlements.[77]

Faced with the frightening prospect that the British and their allies could soon overwhelm the ill-prepared revolutionary forces, the state's provisional government established an emergency committee charged with identifying and punishing domestic enemies. The body possessed extraordinary powers. On September 19 the New York assembly—itself acting without a constitutional mandate—explained that "the great laws of self-preservation" justified awarding almost unlimited authority to the new committee. The group's appointed members included John Jay, who later figured centrally in President George Washington's cabinet. The expectation was that the committee would do whatever was necessary "to defeat

the barbarous machinations of their domestic, as well as external enemies."
That responsibility allowed it "to send for persons and papers; to call out
such detachments of the militia or troops in the different counties as they
may, from time to time, deem necessary for suppressing insurrections; to
apprehend, secure or remove such persons whom they shall judge dangerous to the safety of the State."[78]

Jay and his colleagues threw themselves into the task. According to
committee minutes, in less than a month after its creation the committee
warned New Yorkers to be alert for "notoriously disaffected persons."
These people, it advised, "should be immediately removed . . . to one of the
neighboring States, till such times as proper courts shall be instituted in
this State for the due trial and punishment of such treasonable practices."
One can admire the committee's confidence in better days to come, but
with the British scoring so many victories, the establishment of proper
courts of law must not have seemed imminent.

The appeal to identify domestic enemies encouraged terrified revolutionaries to come forward. They named suspects. In fact, exposing neighbors who supported the British became a measure of patriotism. Ordinary
farmers from Dutchess to Albany Counties shared the committee's view
that "it is the duty of every virtuous citizen when a mortal blow is aimed at
the liberties of his country to stand forth in an open & spirited manner &
to assist by his example, his council, or by his arms in vindicating and defending her cause."[79] Denunciations entailed personal risk. The committee
addressed the problem, insisting that it would keep the identities of informers secret so that they would not suffer the "malice and resentment" of
those whom they had exposed.[80]

Local groups arrested scores of people. How many of these individuals
had actually supported the British can never be ascertained. Some of them
may have engaged in serious violence against outspoken revolutionaries.
Others may have simply expressed doubt about the course of the war or
questioned the wisdom of declaring national independence. In any event,
the jails filled rapidly. These were generally small structures, cold and
unsanitary. Even in the best of times incarceration took a toll on the prisoner's health. But this was wartime. Buildings that served as jails were
overcrowded and insecure. A few accused Tories were dispatched to
Pennsylvania, Connecticut, and Massachusetts, but those states could not
accept large numbers. As the arrests continued, people suggested other,

even bizarre ways to solve the problem. An Albany committee noted that it had just learned "a number of French armed vessels are arrived at some of our ports." They presented a splendid opportunity. "If our Tory neighbors were exchanged for as many of their sailors," the committee believed, "a number of useful men might be engaged for our ships, and our internal enemies removed." It seemed an especially good plan, since "the punishment would strike terror in others."[81] Not surprisingly, nothing came of this proposal.

As the prisoner crisis grew more pressing, New York authorities hit upon an idea that appeared to solve the problem. Large numbers of suspects could be shipped off to New Hampshire, where they would no longer pose a serious threat to public security. The emergency committee then meeting in Fishkill, New York, interviewed Colonel Joseph Welch, who happened to be in the area with a contingent of New Hampshire troops. In a letter dated October 31, 1776, Welch explained the logic of the situation. His comments deserve to be quoted in full. "Numbers of disaffected persons have been taken up and sent to the States of Pennsylvania, Connecticut, and Massachusetts-Bay, but their numbers are still great, and the committee, at a loss where to send them to prevent their mischievous designs from hurting the common cause, applied to me to know whether I thought they might venture to send any to the State of New-Hampshire." To which, Welch responded, "I informed them that our State was well disposed to the cause of America, and it was my opinion would readily give their assistance to this affair."[82]

No sooner had Welch spoken—indeed, on the very same day—the committee transmitted a message to the General Court of New Hampshire. The members begged the recipients to understand the extraordinary challenge facing New York. "The Committee appointed by the Convention [Provisional Government] of this State for the purpose of inquiring into, detecting, and defeating all conspiracies which may be formed therein against the liberties of America, find it indispensably necessary to remove a number of dangerous and disaffected persons, some of whom have been taken in arms against America, to one of the neighboring States." Welch confirmed New Hampshire's willingness to provide assistance. In fact, he "was of opinion that the zeal which your honorable body have uniformly manifested for the American cause, would induce you cheerfully to receive and dispose of them, in such a manner as to prevent the further execution of their wicked and malicious designs." Such fulsome praise combined with a promise of a 200 dollar payment to cover the costs of housing the prisoners no doubt helped make the New Hampshire group even more cheerful.[83]

One New Yorker viewed the move as a kind of ideological therapy. Transferring those people accused of political crimes to a new location would redeem them from their former opinions. In December William Duer, a prominent member of the New York committee, apologized to the members of the New Hampshire General Court for dumping so many prisoners on the other state. "It was with great reluctance," he insisted, "that this Committee found themselves necessitated to trouble you with men whose principles are so dangerous to the liberties of mankind." But extreme measures could produce beneficial results. Forced exile might "wean them from those poisonous tenets which have been instilled into many of them, by associating with crafty and designing abettors of the wicked usurpations of the British King and Parliament."[84] Of course, there was another, quite different possibility, as later generations have learned from bitter experience. Banishment often serves only to reaffirm one's original convictions.

Exeter is located about 250 miles from Fishkill and only a little closer to Albany, two places from which the New York prisoners departed. It is hard to establish with confidence the exact number of people involved. A good estimate would be a few more than two hundred. Since the total population of Exeter at this time was about 1,750, the influx of exiles from New York must have had a major impact on flow of daily life in the New Hampshire town.[85] The prisoners walked from the southern Hudson Valley to New Hampshire, a difficult journey in the best of times but much more challenging in the late autumn. One man who left an account of the trip anticipated a violent reception in Exeter. "On our march through Conn[ecticut]," wrote Joshua Gidney, "we were told that the people of Exeter would deal with us according to our deserts, by close confinement, if not by hanging, as every Tory deserved." That did not happen. To Gidney's surprise, the locals treated the arrivals "with civility, and by some with Respect."[86] He was fully justified in expecting hostility. As the prisoners were arriving, a leading political figure in New Hampshire wrote to his friend, Josiah Bartlett, then serving as a state representative in the Continental Congress, that he hoped the newcomers would be treated well. His heart was not in the pleasantry, however. He really wanted to get rid of the entire group. Scotland would do if only they could be compelled to stay there. What then would he recommend? "I can think of but two ways of effecting this," he informed Bartlett, "that is death or transportation, & Humanity inclines me to the latter. Indeed, we had better send them to the Enemy's army than to let them continue among us."[87]

Continue they did. Although the New York committee had no control over the prisoners once they had reached New Hampshire, it advised authorities in Exeter to divide the entire group into two separate classes. On the lists of suspects banished from New York, a clerk placed an asterisk next to the names of those people designated as particularly dangerous. What exactly they had done to merit this mark of distinction is not known, but perhaps because the committee possessed information now lost, it recommended that these men should be confined in jail. Other names appeared on the lists with no additional comment.

Once they had reached Exeter, however, New Hampshire officials devised a different plan. They organized the prisoners into three bodies. A small number of prisoners were in fact consigned to the Exeter jail, where they spent the winter under close guard. A much larger group was allowed to rent rooms "within six miles of the State House in the Town of Exeter." They quickly found lodging in villages near Exeter. In Kensington twenty prisoners resided in six homes. Gidney was among these people. He was pleasantly surprised to discover that the New Hampshire committee "gave the major part of our number, of whom I am one, Liberty of seeking lodging within six miles of the state house, a Liberty we did not expect."[88] And the third class consisted of Quakers, people swept up during the wave of arrests in New York and probably guilty of nothing more serious than pacifism. They were allowed to live anywhere they pleased in New Hampshire so long as it was "with the People of that Society."[89]

New Hampshire officials drew up strict rules of conduct for the prisoners. They had to pay for their own food and housing. They were advised to "support themselves by labor," which meant in practice that they probably found temporary work on local farms. During the period of incarceration, they were not allowed to correspond with anyone, including members of their families. The local committee resolved that "none of the Prisoners sent into this State from the State of New York have leave to write or send Letters to any person or persons whatever or wherever with the same being inspected." And most significant, considering what happened later, the men scattered in villages around Exeter were prohibited from having political conversations with the local residents. They were enjoined from using "words or arguments to people they may converse with tending to hurt the Interest of the States of America, or in opposition to the present contest with Great Britain."[90]

The irony of the situation was that authorities in Exeter had no clearer idea why these men had been exiled from New York than did the prisoners. The New Hampshire committee begged for more information. Surely, they explained, there must be some proper legal documentation about the crimes that the men on the list had allegedly committed. The New Yorkers dragged their feet. Although the silence annoyed people in New Hampshire, they showed remarkable patience. They simply accepted that Jay and his colleagues were acting in good faith. To be sure, they received no hard evidence, but they noted that an agent sent from New York to negotiate payment for the prisoners' support "appeared [to be a] Gentleman & generous, disinterested supporter of American Liberty."[91]

Although most prisoners followed the rules of conduct, they did in fact raise hard issues with their new neighbors. They did not defend king and Parliament. Nor did they make any attempt to convert local revolutionaries. Rather, in conversations in kitchens and on village streets, they complained that they had been denied basic legal rights that every American took for granted. They had not received due process; no one in New York had bothered with habeas corpus. And people in New Hampshire listened to these complaints. All of this ran counter to what organizers had envisioned for the internment camp.

The New Hampshire committee first raised the alarm on December 27, 1776. In a letter to William Duer, it reported "Great uneasiness prevails among them [the prisoners] & their clamors of being sent here without an examination at home, and consciousness of their innocence which they assert, has had considerable influence among the People in these parts in their behalf." The suspects maintained in public that they had done absolutely nothing that would make "any person to Suppose them unfriendly to the American cause." Growing increasingly anxious about snakes in the garden, the New Hampshire committee demanded help. "We wish an Impartial Enquiry might be made into their characters, and if any appear innocent who was taken up and sent from their homes in the Confusion and unavoidable hurry that you was involved in at that time, that an order may be sent for their discharge."[92]

Sensing that they had found a sympathetic audience, the prisoners did what so many others have done in their situation. They started to submit petitions for release to the New Hampshire legislature. Soon a few documents became a flood. So many petitions for liberty reached the representatives that they could not conduct normal business. The New Hampshire committee informed New York: "Perhaps not less than Quires [papers folded to form eight leaves] of these Petitions are on file here." New York's response to fear had suddenly become New Hampshire's problem. "We earnestly desire some further direction relative to them," the Exeter officials wrote, "and if you think fit for them to be longer detained that you would send some particular charge of their crimes." Such a move might at least quiet prisoners demanding their legal rights. Indeed, if New York would only document the specific crimes allegedly committed by each person, the local committee could *poke the same down their Throats, to stop their petitioning, as they all plead not guilty.*"[93]

The internment camp had collapsed by March 1777. At that time New York officials ordered the return of all prisoners. By the end of the year all of them had left Exeter. Many had already escaped. New York belatedly settled its accounts with New Hampshire. Most suspects went home. A few men accused of violent crimes against the Revolution were placed in New York jails. The conflict with Great Britain continued for several more years, and domestic enemies remained a problem along the Hudson River. The great fear that had disrupted the lives of hundreds of people became no more than a minor footnote in the history of the American Revolution.

V

During the early years of the war, Americans experienced revolution through the lens of fear in their own communities. Sometimes it touched their lives in the form of sporadic violence, neighbors terrorizing other neighbors as in Raccoon. On other occasions, it persuaded local authorities that they needed to suspend normal legal safeguards in the name of security. The prospect of being overrun by British forces certainly heightened fears, but the sense of personal danger was well rooted in this society before the appearance of an invading force. Ordinary people knew—or thought they knew—of atrocities committed by domestic enemies. The threats to their personal safety were both real and imagined. And, of course, one did not have to be sent to Winchester or Exeter to suffer the sensation of dread, the anxiety that someone who wants to do harm is hiding in the woods or organizing a gang determined to steal livestock or burn a barn. Just making it through the day involved fear.

The story of how Americans handled that fear helps explain why during moments of extreme tension revolutionaries did not allow the threat to personal security to excuse massive retaliation against alleged political enemies. That they hated Tories is not in question. But time after time and in different regions of the country, Americans stopped short of instituting a reign of domestic terror of the sort that we associate with other revolutions. The temptation to lash out was ever present. Instead, they practiced restraint. When confronted with the likes of Robert Gassaway or Andrew Patchin—men who in front of soldiers openly challenged allegiance to the new country—revolutionaries called for testimony, accepted apologies, and moved on without further inflaming divisions within their communities. Of course, the establishment of internment camps in New Hampshire and Virginia ignored the fundamental elements of a rule of law. Perhaps more important in understanding the creation of a new political culture were the ordinary farmers of Exeter. These citizens listened sympathetically to the political prisoners from New York who appealed for justice when the success of revolution hung in the balance.

CHAPTER FOUR

JUSTICE

How Americans sustained justice during the Revolution inspires a kind of Alice-in-Wonderland proposition. Indeed, it invites us to imagine a history that never occurred. The curious exercise has a point. Counterfactual narratives yield unexpected insights. They bring into sharper focus questions about the past that we should perhaps have been asking all along but did not do so because traditional accounts seemed to suffice.

The American Revolution prompts just such a reassessment. For a very long time no one has seen much reason to challenge a familiar history that seems to flow effortlessly from the fight at Lexington to the signing of a peace treaty in 1783. It is an account of courageous and enlightened leaders supported by patriotic people willing to sacrifice personal comfort in the name of liberty.

But what, Alice might ask, would have happened had Americans grown so tired of war that they decided to compromise with Great Britain? What if many, even most, just gave up? In this fanciful history some elements would follow the traditional script. For example, Continental Congress would still seem fumbling and incompetent and George Washington slow to knock out enemy forces. These elements would turn widespread impatience with the course of the conflict into a demand to restore an earlier, allegedly happier time when tensions over imperial taxes and trade could be negotiated without violence. Moreover, even in this counterfactual telling, we would want to note how the colonists were initially eager to support the American cause. The prospect of easy victories after Bunker Hill brought out large numbers of young men who Thomas Paine would later ridicule as "summer soldiers and sunshine patriots." But over time, even zealous revolutionaries discovered that popular commitment to independence could not be sustained. Appeals to sacrifice the pleasures of everyday life fell on increasingly deaf ears. And after a year or two, possibly by 1778, the people concluded that George III and the Parliament were not as objectionable as they had appeared during the first rush of revolutionary enthusiasm.

Explaining why the American Revolution did not follow this imagined script is more challenging than it might appear. There are, of course, entirely plausible reasons for why the rebellion did in fact succeed. One could argue, for example, that revolutionaries persevered because of their deep commitment to a bundle of fundamental ideas about constitutional rights and personal freedom. Or, one could draw attention to the ability of charismatic leaders such as George Washington to keep an army in the field. But whatever the merits of these explanations, they fail adequately to address what needs to be explained—why did Americans not call it quits? After all, the war lasted eight years, and after the excitement of actually declaring independence had cooled and reports from the battlefield suggested that the British might win, many men and women expressed serious doubts about the wisdom of continued resistance. Neither a small group of celebrated leaders nor a devotion to a bundle of abstract political principles was sufficient to sustain effective mobilization over such a long period. Something more was required to keep the Revolution moving forward, especially when the prospects for victory seemed so bleak.[1]

The missing piece in the puzzle was local enforcement. This is not a word that one normally encounters in histories of the American Revolution. The term somehow seems alien to our values. It suggests that victory over Great Britain depended in no small way on the ability of revolutionary authorities to police political dissent. But in a history of real events that was exactly what happened. With the courts largely closed, various committees sustained revolutionary commitment long after Congress had declared independence. Curiously, these extralegal groups—especially the committees of safety and observation—have received very little attention in the histories of the Revolution.

This is unfortunate. After all, the committee system provides the key to explaining the success of the Revolution. It most certainly did not disappear after the fighting began. Committees continued to recruit soldiers and collect weapons. More important for our purposes, they functioned throughout the war as an effective ideological police force, as basic units in a larger revolutionary infrastructure, and even when major battles occurred in distant places, local committees continued to interrogate and punish suspects identified as domestic enemies. From a comparative perspective—thinking about other revolutions that have transformed the world over the last two centuries—these groups carried out what we might identify as revolutionary justice. By monitoring their neighbors' support for the new regime, they did more than merely police internal dissent. Even when the war was going badly and people grew weary of sacrificing the comforts of daily life, the committees reaffirmed in small communities a commitment to revolution.

Modern Americans may understandably feel somewhat ambivalent about the critical role that the committees played in achieving independence. They would be fully justified in associating such forms of community enforcement with vigilantes or kangaroo courts, extralegal bodies that claim to administer justice but systematically ignore the rule of law. It is certainly true that revolutionary committees in America operating under difficult wartime conditions sometimes neglected basic procedural safeguards we now take for granted. Frequently absent from their deliberations was a concern for habeas corpus, legal counsel during hearings, thorough collection of evidence, cross-examination of witnesses, or protection for the accused from self-incrimination. Individuals suspected of *inimical* behavior—the most common charge—had to demonstrate before committee members why they were innocent, not the other way around. One might conclude from this record that the pressures of revolution seriously eroded the conventions of normal civil society. In the context of the American Revolution, this is an uncomfortable finding to be sure, but precisely the sort of thing that one encounters in the history of other revolutions.

There is another, less alarming side to the story of the committees—at least, in revolutionary America. We might observe that the alternative to the committees was not access to normal courts. In most states they were closed during the early years of revolution. Rather, we should acknowledge that if the committees had not filled the vacuum, had they not addressed political crimes in a time of war, it was possible that personal vendettas and cycles of revenge could have sparked chronic instability on the ground, even anarchy. This was not a fanciful claim. As we discovered in the previous chapter, the contagion of fear that swept through the country during the early years of war could have created a Hobbesian world in which "the condition of man is a condition of war of everyone against everyone." We should take the threat of disorder seriously. The collapse of imperial institutions could have resulted in breakdown of civil society. The suggestion may seem extreme, but we should remember that contemporaries saw the balance between order and disorder in precisely these terms. If ordinary people had taken the law into their own hands, they could have destroyed a shared national sense of purpose and thereby jeopardized the entire revolution.

Even more noteworthy, the committees did not in fact operate like the kangaroo courts so often encountered in despotic regimes. As much as local wartime conditions allowed they tried to avoid the appearance of abandoning a rule of law. There were some lapses, to be sure, but the committees were sensitive to complaint. They seldom sanctioned gratuitous physical punishment, much less torture. Whenever possible these local bodies exercised remarkable constraint, for example, by accepting pledges of future good behavior from accused persons, administering oaths rather than demanding incarceration, allowing people who confessed to political crimes to be paroled in their own communities, and accepting extenuating personal matters as a justification for leniency. Committee members recognized that when the war was over, they would have to live with neighbors who had made wrong political decisions. Some alleged enemies of revolution were, of course, more dangerous than others. They murdered neighbors or destroyed property. But not all offenses were equivalent. After all, it was one thing to join the British army, quite another to voice unpatriotic opinions at a friend's house or in a tavern. Within a revolutionary context requiring restraint, the committees not only kept the Revolution going, but also kept it from spinning out of control.

The story of revolutionary committees involves both continuity and change. As we have seen in an earlier chapter on *rejection*, hundreds of local committees sprang up during the period before the Declaration of Independence. They were the products of a huge spontaneous popular response to imperial policies perceived as oppressive. Various groups—often called committees of safety and observation—recruited Americans into a totally new political forum. The people who came forward had seldom held office before the imperial crisis. Under extraordinarily trying circumstances, they managed to organize effective boycotts of imported British goods, locate guns and powder, and communicate a powerful sense of purpose to other committees. Confrontation with king and Parliament generated unprecedented levels of participation in political affairs.

These trends continued after the fighting began. Committee members without much practical knowledge about managing political affairs wrestled with very difficult challenges. One of these was dealing with domestic enemies. These activities alert us to another point that must be emphasized. An impressively large number of people who served on revolutionary committees not only acquired a greater sense of self-confidence in their ability to govern, but also learned what it meant to exercise authority in a new system in which no one could claim privilege because of noble birth or royal patronage. For a revolutionary generation, the transition from a monarchical system to one based solely on the will of the people was a fundamental aspect of the wartime experience. Again, we encounter on the local level ordinary Americans defining revolution on their own terms. By so doing, they contributed as much as did the Founders to the creation of a new political culture.

I

A disquieting incident that occurred late in the war brings into dramatic relief how the demand for justice—a process highlighting the tensions between passion and constraint—played out during the Revolution. It involved a trial in Frederick County, Maryland, where the ongoing conflict with Great Britain had strained local resources and created an atmosphere of anger and fear. Frederick was the site of a large prisoner-of-war camp that housed many Hessians. Sometime in August 1781 reports reached Judge Alexander Hanson that a group of Tories in the area had recruited a sizable force of armed men prepared to fight for Britain. Descriptions of the plot were vague, but one witness bragged that as many as six thousand loyalists would come forward when they received the proper signal. Intelligence sources provided the names of seven key conspirators. They had done something a lot more serious than speaking loose words at a tavern or failing to show up for militia drill. Recruiting men in the service of the enemy was treason, a capital offense. With so many prisoners of war residing in the community, the danger from Tory insurgency was especially threatening.

Born in 1749, Hanson came from a distinguished Maryland family. He had received an excellent legal education in Philadelphia, and as a young man with a promising future he gave his enthusiastic support for national independence. People elected him to serve on a committee of observation for Frederick County, an indication of high standing in revolutionary circles. Several years later, he was appointed a member of the state's General Court. Although few records of Hanson's decisions have survived, nothing suggests that he was exceptionally zealous in carrying out his duties. One would probably describe him best as a very talented lawyer with a bookish interest in codification and jurisprudence. But whatever his professional history, the alleged Tory plot against the American Revolution elicited a surprisingly strong emotional response from Hanson. Maryland, he insisted, could not tolerate so many "disaffected and Dangerous Persons going at Large."[2] Even before the trial, Hanson concluded that the leading conspirators deserved harsh punishment. All that was needed was a jury willing to convict the suspects of treason.

That turned out to be a formidable challenge. About the seriousness of the offense or the weight of the evidence the jurors had little doubt. The seven men were clearly guilty of betraying their country. The problem was the judge's insistence on obtaining conviction for treason, a crime that under Maryland law mandated capital punishment. The jurors hesitated, uneasy about condemning the conspirators to death. Hanson had no patience with such scruples. Did the jurors not understand the law? Had they failed to comprehend fully what it took to enforce the Revolution? From the bench, the judge lectured the jury. "You are convened," he observed, "to execute a trust of the last importance to your country. It is a trust which no good citizen would wish to decline, when he reflects, that, upon the faithful administration of just laws, the safety of individuals, the preservation of government, and the being of society ultimately depends." The jury carried a heavy burden. After all, "A considerable number of persons, charged with an unnatural conspiracy, to assist our enemies in subverting the liberties of America, are confined in the goals [gaols]." Their crimes, he reminded the jurors, were covered by a 1777 Maryland act "to punish certain crimes and misdemeanors, and prevent the growth of Toryism."

Hanson's advice apparently had little impact. He found the jurors' sullen reluctance to accept his arguments extremely annoying. What could explain such hesitation? Was there a chance that some of the jurors knew the suspects or were related to them through an extended family? Perhaps flattery would do the trick. Hanson continued, "I cannot suspect that you, gentlemen, who have been selected for your spirit, intelligence and patriotism will, by an unpardonable neglect of duty, or an ill-judged tenderness to the lives of traitors, encourage the perpetration of the most atrocious crimes. Those strong and decisive feelings, which actuate the bosoms of honest Whigs, will promote you to a jealous discharge of your duty."

Another potentially embarrassing problem soon arose. Hanson may have sensed that some jurors knew more about the law—or more precisely, about the law pertaining to treason—than he had anticipated. In exchanges between judge and jury, Hanson drew attention to some irregularities in the gathering of evidence. There was, in fact, a law on the books that seemed strikingly relevant to the case. That statute declared that "no person shall be convicted by a petit jury, unless by the oath of two lawful witnesses, to prove each separate and distinct fact, charged in the indictment, as treason . . . except the prisoner, willingly and without force or violence, confess the same in open court." These provisions were not observed during this trial. The prisoners maintained their innocence. Two witnesses to each and every alleged crime had not come forward. Hanson dismissed such concerns. Like other judges—then and now—who refuse to allow procedural niceties to stand in their way, Hanson strongly admonished the jurors against allowing "a rule of evidence . . . [to] afford impunity to wretches, of whose guilt a candid mind could not entertain the smallest doubt." And just in case anyone in the courtroom questioned Hanson's behavior, he protested that he was free from "any unreasonable prejudices."[3]

The jurors eventually succumbed to Hanson's bullying. A guilty verdict should have marked the end of the affair. But, as soon became clear, Hanson was not finished with the traitors. Giving vent to his own passion, he decided to make them examples of revolutionary justice. What triggered the outburst was Hanson's belief that the prisoners were mocking the whole proceeding. Moreover, there was a rumor circulating in the community—Hanson called it "a delusion"—that the men would eventually receive light sentences. Even though "an impartial jury" had rendered a proper judgment, the accused Tories "have adopted a vain idea propagated by the enemies of this country, that she dare not punish her unnatural subjects for engaging in the service of Great Britain." Hanson would have none of it. Mercy had no justification during a time of war. "I think it is my duty," he continued, "to explain to you your real situation. The crime you have been convicted of, upon the fullest and clearest testimony, is of such a nature that you cannot, ought not to look for pardon. . . . the ends of public justice, the dictates of policy, and the feelings of humanity, all require that you should exhibit an awful example to your fellow subjects, and the dignity of the State with everything that can interest the heart of man, call aloud for your punishment." The only hope for such a despicable group was a "pardon from the Almighty Being, who is to sit in judgment upon you, upon me and all mankind."[4]

Whether anyone in the courtroom foresaw Hanson's next move is doubtful. He decided that none of the convicted men deserved a hanging, then considered a simple, humane execution. He demanded a level of savagery associated only with the most despotic Old World regimes.[5] Looking directly at the prisoners, Hanson announced the sentence: "You shall be carried to the goal [gaol] of Frederick County and thence be drawn to the gallows of Frederick-town and hanged thereof—You shall be cut down to the earth alive and your bowels shall be taken out and burnt, while you are yet alive, your heads shall be cut off, your bodies shall be divided into four parts, and your heads and quarters shall be placed where his excellency the governor shall appoint."[6]

Soon thereafter something happened that Hanson had insisted could not occur. The governor of Maryland, Thomas Sim Lee, did not show interest in distributing the body parts of the condemned men throughout the community. Instead, he pardoned four of them. Three others were executed behind the courthouse, but the sheriff who administered the sentence apparently had no stomach for disemboweling the prisoners. They died by hanging.[7] The entire episode exposed the conflicts among those who administered revolutionary justice. Even after hearing the evidence, the jurors had qualms about executing the suspects. The governor may have been aware of political pressures that Hanson ignored. For him the situation required balance, between passion and constraint, between the requirements of the law and the sensitivities of ordinary people who had their own notions about revolutionary justice. Even the local sheriff had his own ideas on the subject.

II

After 1775 an elaborate court system that had evolved over the long colonial period collapsed.[8] Writs issued in the king's name suddenly made no sense in a country rapidly moving toward independence. While most revolutionaries wanted to continue a system of justice based on common law, they had other, much more pressing concerns to deal with. Some states such as Massachusetts re-established courts able to treat civil and criminal litigation more quickly than did others. It was not until 1777, for example, that local and county courts in Pennsylvania reopened.[9] In this unstable political environment, provisional state governments—state constitutions would come later—focused on the immediate demands of war, allowing committees of safety to address cases involving domestic security. Some frightened Americans urged the army to interrogate and punish civilians who had aided the British or expressed opinions thought to be inimical to the success of a new republic. Military and political leaders, however, discouraged appeals to extend martial law to the general public.[10]

The organization of the committee system that developed after fighting began defies easy generalization. Each state responded to the challenge in ways that reflected its own history and geography. South Carolina created a powerful state committee of safety. In Maryland a state committee oversaw decisions taken by separate county committees. New York developed an even more complex structure in which small precincts reported decisions they had made to county committees. In turn, the county bodies communicated with a central state committee. In Massachusetts scores of committees that had sprung up as early as 1774 continued to police ideological dissent. Within a short time after independence state-sanctioned courts began to supplement the work of local committees, and although a state committee tried to bring order and consistency to this network of local committees, one has a sense that local bodies exercised a considerable discretion in dealing with people deemed "unfriendly" to the Revolution.[11]

In theory at least, authority in matters of domestic security in the United States flowed down from the Continental Congress. Of course, that body did not have the resources needed to monitor what was happening in local communities throughout the country. Several months before declaring independence, it did, however, recommend that the American people establish procedures for controlling opponents who were attempting to undermine the war effort. In a resolution dated January 26, 1776, Congress initially counseled patience. It urged local bodies to treat individuals who openly supported Great Britain with understanding. Perhaps opponents did not understand the true political issues driving resistance? Re-education seemed a generous response to ignorance. In that spirit, Congress resolved the following: "it be recommended to the several Committees, and other friends of American liberty in the said colonies, to treat all such persons with kindness and attention, to consider them as the inhabitants of a country determined to be free, and to view their errors as proceeding rather from want of information, than want of virtue or public spirit." Congress concluded that open and candid discussions about "the origins, nature and extent of the present controversy" would be sufficient to convert naïve and ignorant countrymen to the American cause.

But tellingly, in the very same resolution, Congress admitted that education alone might not do the trick. Military clashes had encouraged some Americans who remained loyal to the king to give aid and comfort to the enemy. Moreover, Tory sympathizers were busy spreading lies about the true origins of discontent. To counteract such dangerous conduct Congress called upon "the different Assemblies, Conventions, and Committees or Councils of Safety . . . by the most speedy and effectual measures to frustrate the mischievous machinations, and restrain the wicked practices of these men." Local revolutionary bodies were instructed to disarm and imprison the most dangerous suspects. However, even as it appealed for strict vigilance, Congress worried that organized efforts to promote domestic security might invite ordinary people to take the law into their own hands. Vigilantes who lashed out against ideological enemies under the cover of patriotism were still vigilantes. Cries for personal revenge only served to stir up needless local violence, a development that would inevitably compromise the unity and cooperation on which the Revolution depended. Be assured, Congress insisted, "that whenever retaliation may be necessary . . . this Congress, will undertake the disagreeable task."[12]

Congress could not possibly make good on such an assurance, neither in 1775 nor at any moment during the rest of the war. It published resolutions about domestic security, but it did not and could not know what groups would actually take responsibility for enforcing revolution. The curiously imprecise list in this document—"different Assemblies, Conventions, and Committees or Councils of Safety"—revealed the difficulty of identifying exactly who would address "wicked practices." And so, although authority to police political dissent seemed to flow from Congress, each community more or less was left to establish its own procedures. The decentralization of political power that was the hallmark of an emerging federal system placed the committees in an awkward situation. In part they owed their existence to the Continental Congress, but at the same time they claimed a measure of legitimacy as the representatives of the people.

Although these claims were not mutually exclusive, committee members who had been elected rather than appointed to office began to think of themselves as the agents of the people.[13] In this sense, the committees were genuinely revolutionary bodies. Election gave them legitimacy. They brought new people into the political process. One person who served on a committee in Harford County, Maryland, understood this logic. He warned his colleagues that they would violate popular expectations if they did not immediately call for a new election. It did not matter that the Maryland Convention (a transitional legislative assembly) urged the sitting committee to stay in place. The people, he declared, looked upon the legislature's request for the members of the committee to continue their work "beyond the time for which they were elected by the people to be unconstitutional and laying a foundation and precedent for one of the most alarming stretches of power."[14]

Other Americans shared these sentiments. The committees were expressions of a new political culture. In 1777 a writer in the *Maryland Journal* identified only as a "Friend to Liberty and Common Sense" argued not only that ordinary people knew as much about the workings of politics as did their social superiors, but also that committees afforded them a chance to voice their sentiments in public. Only tyrants would attempt to silence the members of a rising political class. After all, despots "have made it their great business to persuade the mass of the people into a mean opinion of their own understandings, while they have used every art they could devise to inspire them with the most exalted sentiments of the understandings of their rulers, very well knowing that if they could induce the people to think themselves fools, and that their rulers were the only wise ones on earth, they would readily submit themselves to their arbitrary domination." Ridiculing the abilities of the people was Tory propaganda. "Hence it is," the Friend asserted, "that collections of the people in Town-Meetings, Associations, Conventions, &c. have been so exceedingly offensive to the tyrant of Britain, and his minions." Progress was slow. Even as ordinary Americans assumed responsibilities on the committees, some gentlemen in Maryland clung to the old authoritarian ways. These enemies of revolution were none other than "the remaining tools of that tyrant

[who] make use of every insidious art to exclude the middle class of people from public offices in these States."[15]

Another person, writing in the *Pennsylvania Packet*, put forward a much more radical argument linking the committee system directly to the will of the people. Although the "Pennsylvanian," as the anonymous writer wished to be known, may have taken an extreme position, the persuasiveness of his appeal owed much to popular beliefs about natural rights. He recognized that some readers might be skeptical. "We have seen Committees and Constitutional Bodies of men appointed by the people," he observed, "who have suspended the prevailing laws of the land." In fact, the committees "have exercised the most sovereign authority." In ordinary times such developments would have been a matter of great concern. But these were not ordinary times. The war raised unprecedented challenges to normal civil society, and formal institutions of government had demonstrated that they were ill prepared to protect the people's rights.

In this situation ordinary Americans—or the committees that owed their existence to them—had to define the meaning of real justice. This task required understanding that *"political and legal* rules are very different, and perhaps never can be reconciled." The committees enforced the political rules, in full recognition "that there are crimes at this time actually existing, which are not declared so by any other laws than those of Heaven, necessity and justice. [These were] laws which are antecedent to all social laws, eternal and immutable in themselves, and of course superior to all others in their moral obligation. Amid the exigencies of national war many unexpected things happen in which our receding from the ordinary course of law may in the whole of its consequences be an act of duty, and a mercy done to helpless thousands." The writer claimed that however the committees went about enforcing natural law, the people had nothing to fear. After all, these groups encouraged industry, patriotism, and—most of all—popular justice. "In short," he concluded, "if real disinterested public virtue is to be met with in any civil institutions it must be in these. 'Tis true their power is great, but as they draw it immediately from the people, it cannot fail of proper respect."[16] The Pennsylvanian was pushing the boundaries of popular participation. The celebration of extralegal authority most assuredly would have disturbed more moderate persons worried that revolutionary justice was in fact just an invitation for anarchy.

Whatever threat to a normal rule of law the committees may have represented, the various states showed no reluctance in awarding them almost unlimited power to deal with domestic enemies. In a preamble to a resolution creating an enforcement committee, for example, the New York government demanded rigorous vigilance, since the state was menaced by "certain inhabitants and subjects of this State, [who had been] either seduced by the arts or corrupted by the bribes of the enemy, or influenced by unmanly fear, [and] profess allegiance to the King of Great Britain." Political neutrality was no defense. People who took neither side in the conflict were just as bad as violent Tories. Their ambivalence justified a rigorous response, for as the New Yorkers insisted, it is "consonant to the usage of all civilized states, to withdraw their protection from, and punish such of their subjects as refuse to do their duty in supporting the liberties and constitutional authority of the state of which they are members." Therefore, the new committee would have "full power and authority to disfranchise and punish all such unworthy subjects."[17] At the time, no one felt a need to spell out methods for discovering suspects or protocols governing interrogation and punishment.

The New Hampshire assembly also concluded that the danger to public safety demanded swift action. "Whereas at a time when the public Enemy have actually invaded some of the United States of America, and threatened an invasion of this State," exclaimed the New Hampshire representatives, "the safety of the Commonwealth requires that a power be somewhere lodged to imprison or otherwise restrain any persons whose enlargement [freedom] is dangerous to the Community." Without providing procedural detail, the New Hampshire Assembly gave the Committee of Safety authority to arrest possible enemies, search their property, and keep them in prison for as long as seemed necessary.[18]

The acts and resolves pertaining to the creation of committees in other states were remarkably similar in character. Local authorities—especially during the first two or three years of war—possessed largely unencumbered discretion to handle political opponents as they saw fit. Even before the Declaration of Independence, Virginia established tough regulations. Local authorities had tried to reason with people labeled moderate Tories, but that strategy had not worked. Therefore, the Virginia legislature concluded, "it is become necessary to declare what are and shall be considered as offenses, to the end a regular mode of punishment may be established, and equal right and justice administered to all persons within this colony." It immediately became clear that race figured into the calculus of allegiance. According to the ordinance, "if any white person, or persons, shall hereafter aid or assist the enemy, by enlisting soldiers, giving intelligence, or furnishing them with arms, provision, or naval stores, or shall bear arms against this colony; all and every such person, or persons, so having borne arms, or hereafter offending in manner aforesaid, shall, upon being convicted . . . be liable to be imprisoned, or otherwise confined in such manner as the Committee of Safety may direct."[19]

Officials who drew up the various state guidelines seem to have assumed that those who came to a committee's attention were probably guilty. A Connecticut Assembly act of 1776, for example, provided directions "for apprehending and securing such inimical Persons as shall be deemed and judged dangerous to the State." According to the legislation, the "Civil Authority, Select-Men, and Committees of Inspection, within the several Towns in this State, shall have Power to confine within certain Limits, or remove all such Persons within their respective Towns as they shall, upon due Enquiry and Examination, judge to be inimical and dangerous to the United States."[20]

A few Americans wondered whether the committees should restrict their inquiries to people accused of giving aid and comfort to the British. Perhaps there were other kinds of domestic enemies. What of officials who took bribes? Why should such persons be allowed to hold power during a revolution that encouraged ordinary people to speak out about political matters? In 1777, a writer with the pen name of "Meanwell" grew frustrated with this kind of radical populism, and in a bitterly sarcastic newspaper essay he railed against a regime of democratic despotism. How many Americans shared the perspective that Meanwell attacked is impossible to judge, but his argument suggests that some of them viewed the experience of serving on committees through a broadly inclusive lens. It was in these groups that one encountered the voice of the people. Writing in the *Maryland Journal*, Meanwell insisted that "Every Township, or at least every County, should always have under what *rational* Title pleases them best, an INDEPENDENT *Committee of Safety*, for keeping a watchful Eye over the Officers of Government, within their own their Own Districts, as well as over the Officers, whose functions extend throughout the State at large." No one was exempt from suspicion. The members of these political cells "should carefully observe the Motions of any Persons connected with those Officers, by Kindred, Friendship, or Interest."

Through constant and zealous vigilance, Meanwell imagined nothing less than a guarantee that the people would control their own government. "They should examine," Meanwell advised with tongue in cheek, "whether the Legislature do not, even in the most indirect Manner, usurp the Rights of the People." If there was any evidence that state or local rulers had acted in bad faith, the committees had a responsibility "not only to warn the People to make suitable Representations, but, whenever it may become necessary, to *invite* all the Committees instituted on the same Principle, within the same State, to join in their Remonstrances." Nothing escaped their notice. Under this surveillance system—one is reminded here of the radical committee structures that developed in revolutionary France and Soviet Russia—"Oppressors of every Rank, and Species" would be subject to investigation. "It is by such Acts of real Usefulness, that Independent Committees can make themselves respectable."[21]

That the committees in any state aspired to such vast inquisitorial powers over everyday political affairs is highly doubtful. With the possible exception of a period late in the war when some committees claimed that state officials treated people identified as Tory sympathizers with too much leniency, the committees avoided conflict with local government authorities—indeed, generally cooperated with them—and devoted their attention to military issues and alleged crimes against the Revolution. Meanwell's fear that the committees might become authoritarian agents for enforcing public virtue only indicates how much the Revolution depended on an expansive network of local bodies that recruited soldiers and collected military supplies as well as policed domestic enemies.

III

The Revolution had its greatest impact on Americans in the communities where they lived. This claim may come as a surprise. We often frame the revolutionary experience in terms of military service, and while it is certainly true that thousands of men either joined local militia units or, less frequently, signed up for tours of duty in the Continental Army, far more people witnessed the transformation of American political culture much closer to home, be it in large cities such as Philadelphia and Boston or in scattered townships or county seats. The records of these committees—as one might expect, few complete sets survive—read like modern police files that have been written in haste: choppy, abbreviated, and thin on detail.

Records of this sort do not lend themselves to concise generalization. Examining them is like flipping through a collection of random photographs. There seems to be no connection between entries, no obvious narrative. Names appear once, sometimes twice, and then they are gone, presenting a series of separate moments when obscure Americans were forced to explain why someone else found their behavior suspicious. In addition to the actual members of the committee, these sessions included persons who had brought a complaint, occasionally witnesses to an alleged crime, and spectators from the community who watched the drama play out and silently calculated whether the new revolutionary regime could provide the security they so desperately desired. In that sense the actions taken by these committees served as a general test for the legitimacy of the new political order. It would be impossible to establish the total number of people who experienced revolution in this context. But it was surely large. A powerful state committee in New York, for example, adjudicated over a thousand cases, and that figure does not include many county and precinct sessions held throughout the state for which documentation is incomplete.[22]

Estimates of the number of Americans participating in revolutionary enforcement expand quite significantly when local militiamen are included. As a fighting force the militia repeatedly proved unreliable. Ill-trained and inexperienced men seldom perform well on the battlefield. They went home when the spirit moved them; they did not always carry out orders from officers. It is not surprising that George Washington quickly decided that he could not depend on soldiers of this character to defeat the British Regulars.[23] However justified these aspersions may have been, they should not be allowed to detract attention from the militia's major success. In most places, most of the time, they functioned as revolutionary police, arresting individuals deemed dangerous—or just suspicious—by a local committee.[24]

They performed in this capacity in Connecticut and New York. In New Jersey they provided security for committee men holding sessions in areas where Tory insurgents were active.[25] The presence of an armed militia made enforcement of committee decisions a lot easier. It did something more, however. The militia discouraged Americans who had expressed only lukewarm support for national independence from joining the Tories when the prospects for American military victory seemed remote. This is a key point in understanding how the Revolution worked in small communities. Just by being a highly visible agent in political affairs, the militia helped the committees sustain popular support for independence. Or, to put the point another way, it made it very hard for domestic enemies to organize an effective counterrevolution.

Early in the war almost every state—some of them still calling themselves colonies—ordered Americans to record a formal pledge of allegiance.[26] Local or county officials usually oversaw the process, which provided a reasonably accurate indication of revolutionary support, even if some lied. The number of people who masked their true political sentiments was probably not large, however, since in this religious society swearing an oath of allegiance, often on a Bible, was not a matter one took lightly. The collection of the names of possible enemies of the regime— even if such people only had moral or religious scruples about swearing oaths—greatly assisted the work of the committees. Those men who refused to pledge allegiance, of course, immediately became suspects. The Maryland legislature explained why it was necessary for all men living in the state to make a public declaration of their political sentiments. According to "An Act for the Better Security of the Government" (1777), it could be assumed that "in every free state, allegiance and protection are reciprocal, and no man is entitled to have the benefit of the one, who refuses to yield to the other." From this claim it followed that every white male "should give testimony of his attachment and fidelity to this state." The exercise also served to reveal the names of individuals who had recently left the community. Local authorities believed that absence marked them as deserters, most likely as committed Tories who were living in areas controlled by British forces.[27]

The procedures for recording oaths of allegiance varied from state to state. Massachusetts distributed printed forms to town clerks who gave ordinary people an opportunity to sign the document. The subscribers had to "profess, testify and declare before God and the world, that we verily believe that the war, resistance and opposition in which the United American Colonies are now engaged against the fleets and armies of Great-Britain, is on the part of the said colonies, just and necessary." The lists were kept in the clerk's office so that interested parties could ascertain who was or was not to be trusted.[28] Several states such as Pennsylvania ordered male citizens to join an Association formed to advance the revolutionary cause and discourage opposition to independence. Maryland expected "every free male person" above the age of eighteen to take an "oath of fidelity and support the state." Country clerks had to maintain detailed records of oath takers and the date that they took the oath. There is no question that revolutionaries in Maryland paid attention to whose names appeared on these lists. One person complained, for example, that "the trustees and visitors of King William School" had met without taking the required oath of fidelity. "Some of them," he observed, "have ever been looked on as Tories, and others of them bear a very suspicious political character. If the Tories can infringe our laws with impunity, our government is not only weak, but ridiculous." Something had to be done immediately. After all, "can Whig parents permit a Tory schoolmaster to educate their children?"[29]

New Hampshire launched an even more ambitious program for identifying popular revolutionary support. In March 1776 the state required male residents to "engage and promise that we will do the utmost of our power, at the Risque of our Lives and Fortunes, with Arms oppose the Hostile Proceedings of the British Fleets and Armies, against the United American Colonies." Thousands of people signed the New Hampshire lists. It is significant that citizens who refused had to explain their actions before local authorities. One man, identified as a Scotchman, "Declines obliging himself to take up Arms against his Native Country, but declares he will neaver [sic] take up Arms against America, & is willing to bear his Proportion of the publick taxes with his Townsmen." Another person, Moses Welch, "refused to take up arms & pleads Conscience for an excuse." Twelve individuals in another community "Appear to be fearful that the Signing of this Declaration in some measure to be an infringement on their Just Rights & Libertys [sic] but they Appear to be Friendly to their Country & Several of them have ventured their lives in the American Cause." Indeed, three of those who did not sign had just volunteered for the Continental Army.[30]

And so it went, town after town, person after person; New Hampshire's male population had to justify personal political beliefs. Although the exercise helped discourage counterrevolutionary activities, the state's communities could never afford to be complacent. A petition to the legislature from a group in Portsmouth dated almost a year later called for every person "without distinction to swear allegiance to the State, as it is the only Touch-stone we know, who are supporting the Independency of America, and who are not." In fact, Portsmouth revolutionaries thought that oaths "would be of Infinite service at this crisis, as every honest, upright man would with cheerfulness take the oath, & those that would not, its high time, in our humble opinion, should be secured as Prisoners of War."[31]

The state of Connecticut devised a devilishly complex plan that employed local lists of suspected Tory sympathizers as a means to reimburse revolutionaries who had suffered loss of property as a result of repeated loyalist attacks from the water. It was a longstanding problem. Throughout the war enemies in search of livestock and other farm produce, which was used to provision British troops stationed in New York, plundered Connecticut towns located on the Long Island Sound. Often these raiders landed in an exposed community, seized animals or grain, and departed in small boats before the local militia could organize a response. These episodes happened so often that people began to ask whether some locals hoping to make a quick profit were assisting this illegal commerce. In desperation, the state legislature ordered the selectmen of those towns "who may think themselves in Danger of being robbed or plundered by any Attempts of such open or secret Enemies, to make out a List of Names of such Person or Persons within their respective Towns, who in their Opinion are commonly supposed to encourage, countenance, or carry on any contraband Trade or illicit Communication with the Enemies." All the selectmen needed to add a name to the list was their belief—really no more than hearsay—that a certain person "be generally reputed to be dangerous or inimical." The record was then housed in the town clerk's office, and when the raiders next appeared, anyone who claimed to have suffered a loss could demand an appraisal "by three judicious and disinterested Freeholders." The estimated amount of damages was then charged to the people on the enemy list. The Connecticut act served not only to compensate local revolutionaries, but also to identify publicly neighbors who had somehow managed to raise political suspicion.[32]

In political environments torn by fear and suspicion, committees tried to avoid making arbitrary decisions. It is true that in the pressure of the moment, they ignored basic protections that the courts had observed during the colonial period. People accused of crimes against the revolutionary states did not receive legal counsel. Nor could they demand to confront or cross-examine their accusers. Appeals from local committees to higher state committees occurred, but such actions were rare. There were, however, some controls. Whenever possible the committees interviewed witnesses—often persons who had brought a problem to the attention of authorities—and these gave testimony after swearing on a Bible to tell the truth. Despite its intimidating name, the New York Committee for Detecting and Defeating Conspiracies, often chaired by John Jay, a trained lawyer, did a reasonably good job of distinguishing between private feuds and genuine threats to public security.[33] The New Jersey Council of Safety also insisted on interrogating witnesses.[34] A New Hampshire act (18 June 1777) "for taking up, imprisoning or otherwise restraining persons dangerous to this State" ordered that no arrests could be made without an official warrant delivered to a sheriff from the Committee of Safety. Before that could happen, the committee alone had the power to identify persons who "the safety of the Commonwealth requires should be restrained of his personal liberty, or whose enlargement [freedom of movement] within this State is dangerous." The law authorized committee members to question prisoners, "and if any or all the persons so committed shall appear innocent of the crimes alleged against them, then [the committee was permitted] to give order for their enlargement or otherwise to continue them under imprisonment at their discretion."[35]

How well the committees managed in practice to protect people accused of political crimes is hard to estimate. Surviving records suggest that suspects were generally assumed to be guilty. The task for committee members was determining the seriousness of the alleged offense and the danger that a particular person posed to the safety of the community. The burden of proof was on the accused; they had to persuade the committees that they in fact had done nothing wrong. It was a difficult challenge. A fragmentary document from Cheshire County, New Hampshire, reveals how a committee conducted business. During one session a number of suspects appeared; each one took an oath and pleaded not guilty. Four witnesses gave testimony against Elijah King. According to Seth Walker, King "said he Look'd upon the Country in a wrong cause: said if he must take up arms, he should do [it] on the other side." Lieutenant Johnson reported that King "Said he did not like Independence." The other witnesses confirmed that King was inimical to the American cause. Then, Captain Smith insisted that he was not guilty of any crime. Six witnesses told a different story. One claimed that he had heard Smith "declare, That he was on the King's side, and when any News in our favour, he would say, 'Twas a Damn'd Lye: he said he never had nor would take up arms. Diverse times heard him utter word Discouraging; have heard him protest against the common cause." John Butrick was surprised when Smith praised George III. "I said to him," Butrick remembered, "if you Cannot think like other people do, you had better not speak." But Smith failed to get the message. "He then Damn'd the Blue Skins (meaning the Liberty People) said Hell was gaping for them now." The only evidence against Josiah Butler was that "His general character is a Tory." Abner Sanger did himself no good when he resisted arrest. William Barran "Says, That when the Committee order'd him [Barran] and some others of the Militia to bring Sanger in order to examine, that he swung his Axe at them and told them to disperse you Damn'd Rebels; and when they had taken him, that on the way he drank a toast to the King and success to his Majesty's Arms and confusion to Americans." Sanger added that in his opinion "the Congress were a Disgrace to a Gibbet [the gallows];—and said we were all fools." The Cheshire committee decided to send some of these people to the county jail. Others were fined.[36]

Although, as we shall discover, the committees often demonstrated remarkable restraint and occasionally compassion, they were under pressure to take a hard line against suspected domestic enemies. The author of a piece published in the *Connecticut Journal* asked why Americans should "show mercy to our enemies." To do so represented an abuse to justice. In normal times "we see the murderer, the traitor, and ravisher executed at the cry of justice, and in mercy to the community." Why not treat political criminals in the same way? "On what imaginable pretense then can the betrayers and murderers of thousands, of their country, who have taken up arms against their brethren, their parents, and assisted a cruel enemy in sheading the blood of our dearest relations, how can such criminals expect a milder fate, than to be banished forever from the land, which they have so plainly forfeited, endeavored to enslave, and have actually stained with the blood of their murdered brethren [who] cry from the ground for vengeance against them."[37] However justified such angry rhetoric may have been, it is interesting to note that the writer who called for the execution of murderers and rapists urged only banishment for Tories.

Newspaper writers in other states expressed similar contempt for leniency. A piece published in a Baltimore journal insisted that people "who oppose, or seek to betray it [independence], must expect the more rigid fate of the jail and the gibbet." And why should they not? "A lax manner of administering justice, falsely termed moderation, has a tendency both to dispirit public virtue, and promote the growth of public evils."[38] Readers of the *Constitutional Gazette* (New York) learned from the article "To all Americans who love Liberty, and hold their Country dear" that suffering "those who contradict the true interest of their country, at this important struggle, to go unconfirmed, or to enjoy their former property upon a slight confession, or promise of reformation, is to give them the advantage to sport with our liberties, as well as to appear ridiculously stupid ourselves."[39] A person airing his opinions in a Rhode Island paper agreed. People "charged with being a Tory, or unfriendly to the cause of American liberty" deserved no mercy. If authorities dared to treat domestic enemies lightly, "the public may expect that they are abused, cheated, and betrayed; resent it, and determine that they will have justice done them, though they take the execution in it into their own hands." The writer warned local officials responsible for revolutionary justice that if they wanted to "prevent confusion and disorder," they would then "do your duty."[40]

Tough rhetoric came from frightened citizens. And however much local justices and members of committees may have shared such sentiments, they knew that they could not dispense justice simply on the basis of raw emotion. For one thing, they did not have authority to mete out harsh physical punishment. No one advocated the use of torture, even though at an earlier moment in English and American history criminals had endured branding, nose slitting, and ear cropping. Throughout the war, military panels carried out executions, but only in exceptional cases involving treason did states sanction capital punishment. Moreover, while many people convicted of political crimes were in fact sent to jail, incarceration offered only a very limited and temporary way to control domestic enemies.[41] For one thing, prisons were small and poorly maintained. They were inadequately heated and unsanitary. Confining a person to jail often amounted to a death sentence, and, unsurprisingly, prisoners regularly escaped. To provide round-the-clock guards or to build more substantial prisons would have cost local authorities more money than they were willing to spend.

IV

Within a precarious wartime environment the committees—in some areas, local justices—struggled to maintain the rudiments of a rule of law while at the same time resisting the powerful temptation to seek revenge. These two elements characterized the entire revolution on the community level. Sustaining resistance over eight years required a balance between passion—emotions generated by anger and fear—and constraint. However serious the provocation, the committees tried as much as the situation allowed to negotiate with domestic enemies, favoring remedies that seemed to hold out a possibility for reconciliation rather than those that created permanent marginalization. Whenever they could do so, committees selected a lesser punishment over a harsh one. In some cases, of course, leniency was out of the question. But in most states—for reasons we will explore—the committees hoped, at least at first, that reason and understanding would persuade the king's friends and those who just wanted to remain neutral to support the American cause. It was only when such people remained recalcitrant or lied to authorities that more stringent measures came into play.

Committees occasionally attempted to reason with suspects. If only they could be made to see their political errors, they might still be allowed to interact in normal ways with neighbors. One of the more celebrated examples of a committee's efforts to effect a change of mind occurred in New York State. Late in 1776 Peter Van Schaack, a wealthy and well-educated gentleman, made it clear that he could not in good conscience take an oath of allegiance to the new regime. He did not come out in open support of Great Britain. Rather, Van Schaack insisted that he be allowed to remain neutral. The Committee for Detecting and Defeating Conspiracies found Van Schaack's plea indefensible. It summoned him and others of similar convictions for an official hearing. The committee resolved to ask these people "whether they respectively consider themselves as subjects of the State of New York, or of the King of Great Britain; if they answer that they consider themselves as subjects of the State of New York, then to tender to them the oath of allegiance, and, on their taking and subscribing the same, to discharge them." Van Schaack refused the offer. The committee did not back down. Persuaded that it had given him ample opportunity to make his peace with the state's provisional government, it banished Van Schaack to Massachusetts, where he remained throughout the war.

Van Schaack deeply resented a punishment that separated him from home and family. Even in exile, he protested the committee's actions. No doubt, as a person trained in the law, he scored some points. He asked how the committee could ask him to swear an oath to what at the time was only a provisional government. Was this a legitimate institution? On what grounds could a temporary revolutionary legislature demand obedience? Van Schaack also called into question the procedures of an extralegal body. "If I was to be condemned on suspicion," he wrote in 1777, "I expected at least that my informers and judges should have been under oath; and if a test was necessary, I expected it would be in consequence of some general law, putting all men who are in the same class in the same situation, and not that it should be left at the discretion of particular men to tender it to such individuals as malevolence, or party, family, or personal resentment should point out."

Van Schaack's petitions had no effect on the verdict. The committee thought it had treated him generously. It had explained the issues involved. All he had to do was take an oath. After all, he was not a Quaker or member of another religious group that had scruples about swearing oaths before civil authorities. None of this made the slightest difference to Van Schaack. Even after Great Britain signed a peace treaty, he still complained about the committee's conduct. Gouverneur Morris, then a leading figure in New York politics and friend of members of the committee, showed some sympathy, admitting that mistakes could have been made during the war, but considering that an enemy threatened to overrun the state in 1776, he concluded that Van Schaack should perhaps have had a better understanding of the situation. Morris explained how he viewed revolutionary allegiance. "While the appeal lay to reason, I reasoned," he recounted; "when it was made to the sword, I thought it my duty to join in the great issue. When the breach was so widened that no hope remained of cure, I solemnly pledged my faith to support the independence of my country, which had then become essential to her liberties." Van Schaack could have supported the cause. But he had not done so, and now, the only consolation was "it is your misfortune to be one out of the many who have suffered."

John Jay had been more directly involved in the Van Schaack interrogation. After the war, the two men tried to re-establish a friendship. While it was clear that Jay looked forward to a cordial future, he reminded Van Schaack how revolutionary justice had worked. The committee had been under extreme pressure to identify domestic enemies. Decisions had to be made quickly. "Your judgment," Jay observed, "and consequently your conscience, differed from mine on a very important question." What Jay remembered from his work on the committee was that "no man can serve two masters: either Britain was right and America was wrong; or America was right and Britain wrong. They who thought Britain right were bound to support her; and America had a just claim to the services of those who approved her cause. Hence it became our duty to take one side or the other." Van Schaack's motives for refusing to take an oath may have reflected honest, even admirable beliefs, but during wartime it had been almost impossible for the committee to separate Van Schaack from others who "left and took arms against us, not from any such principles, but from the most dishonorable of human motives.... Against these men, every American must set his face and steel his heart."[42]

Confession of a crime before a committee accompanied by a promise to behave in the future often were sufficient to permit a suspect—even one who had attacked the honesty of committee members—to return to the community, usually with no more than a warning. Such was the case of Thomas Wigdon, who appeared before the Northampton, Pennsylvania, Committee of Observation and Inspection in July 1776. Two people serving on the committee had ordered Wigdon locked in the local jail for speaking "disrespectfully of this Committee and the Chairman." When the full committee met some days later, it heard the complete charges against Wigdon. He had openly called the honesty and patriotism of the chairman, Lewis Gordon, into question. The evidence left little doubt that Wigdon "had uttered false & opprobrious words against this Committee in general as being Tories and disaffected to the Common Cause of American Liberty." To make matters worse, during the interrogation Wigdon "not only justified the said indecent Language but openly and publickly called the Chairman a Scotch Bugger."[43] But at the last moment Wigdon apparently had second thoughts. He begged a pardon, which he received along with forgiveness for fees he had incurred while in jail. Perhaps the committee concluded that Wigdon had had too much to drink. Therefore, however he slandered the chairman, he represented no serious threat to the security of the community.

Even more striking was how leniently the Northampton Committee dealt with a group of men whose vocal support of Great Britain could not be blamed on imbibing too much beer. The incident began one evening in December 1776. A member of the committee and a friend were traveling home from Easton, Pennsylvania, when they overtook "a party of men" who "behaved in a very rude and indiscreet manner." According to witnesses, three persons stood out from the others "by damning the Congress, Convention & Committee—saying that they were a parcel of Damned Rascals & were Selling the people's Liberties or words to that affect." When the full committee learned about the exchange, it ordered a militia officer to arrest the culprits. After a full examination, several suspects were sent to jail. Later, another individual who had insulted the committee appeared, but "he not seeming to give any sufficient satisfaction for the same is Ordered to Gaol." A few nights in the local jail seems to have encouraged a remarkable change of mind, for three of the accused "Petitioned this Committee Setting forth that they were heartily sorry for their past Conduct and praying to be released, &c." The show of remorse resulted in freedom. The only conditions placed on them were to provide security for an entire year and publicly acknowledge their fault and to promise "to behave better in the future."[44]

That was all. Insulting the men who dispensed revolutionary justice received only minimal punishment. This occurred at a moment when the British army was driving George Washington's forces from New York City, and American prospects looked very bad. The committee in this case—and in many others of similar description—seems to have used discretion to soften the letter of the law, giving possible domestic enemies a second chance rather than driving them into implacable opposition. The New York Committee of Safety appears to have adopted that approach. In March 1777 it interrogated Colonel Van Allen, who by his recent actions "had been such as to give just grounds to suspect that his sentiments were not altogether friendly to the liberties of America." A conversation that had taken place at the home of one of Van Allen's neighbors triggered suspicion. Someone observed that a person they all knew had just gone over to the British. To which Van Allen exclaimed, "I don't give a donder or hagel [thunder and hail] about it, if we could but have peace; otherwise it would yet perhaps cost the lives of thousands." The local committee decided to send the case up to a state committee, and after closely questioning Van Allen, it concluded that since Van Allen "has heretofore borne a good character as a true friend to his country, and being willing to take the oath of allegiance to this State," the state committee allowed him to return to his community a free man. His only punishment for wanting peace was giving up his commission as lieutenant colonel in the militia.[45]

People in other states who demonstrated genuine contrition before a committee usually fared as well as Van Allen. In January 1776, for example, a Delaware committee demanded that Joseph Cord explain why he had "used certain expressions deemed inimical to the welfare and true interests of America." Evidence that came before the committee revealed that Cord had in fact announced in public that he did not know whether British troops planned to invade the region, but if they did, "he would spend the last drop of blood with them, and after that was gone, and as for the Committees and Congresses, damn them, he valued them not." Considering the seriousness of the offense, it was not surprising that the Sussex County Committee censured Cord "for his unfriendly speeches." That action, coupled with seeing his name published in a local newspaper as an enemy, seems to have cured Cord's disloyalty. In an apology before the committee, Cord admitted that the language he had used "is the language of the worst enemies to America." He promised to behave better in the future, and that was the end of the matter.[46] A group of suspected Tories appeared before authorities in Pittsfield, Massachusetts, and after they were questioned, they made a confession of political errors, took an oath of allegiance to the United States, and "were received as the friends of these states."[47]

Confessions sometimes involved a large number of people. Size presented no problems for the committees, which ruled that the suspects could return to a community if they candidly retracted mistaken political ideas. Twenty-five lukewarm patriots confessed to such dangerous thinking before a New Milford (Connecticut) Committee of Inspection. They "expressed their regret at the unhappy divisions in this country; acknowledged they had said and done many things to strengthen the division on the part of those who opposed the liberties and rights of a free people." The apology included a pledge to obey the laws of the nation and the state of Connecticut and, in addition, a declaration that "their bosoms [were now] warm with friendly sentiments to the rights and privileges of the

Americans." The committee found the performance convincing and "restored the twenty-five persons to the usual favors of their fellow men."[48]

The Baltimore Committee confronted an even more difficult situation. In November 1776 it warned Maryland authorities that it could no longer maintain order. Tories in the area had organized a dangerous counterrevolutionary force. In desperation, the Baltimore Committee begged for armed support from the state. "We are sorry to inform you," it wrote, "that the spirit of violence and opposition to the measures which have been adopted for our common safety, grows extremely daring and outrageous in this county, so that the officers appointed to carry into execution the Resolves of [the state] convention dare not proceed without further assistance." Only swift action, the committee reported, could "destroy the rising hopes of internal enemies." It was in this highly unstable political environment that James Bosley, a militia captain, served as an agent for revolutionary justice in Baltimore County. He faced an almost impossible challenge. Bosley had to collect a fine from Vincent Trapnell—spelled several different ways in the records—for not signing the Maryland Association.

In a deposition taken later Bosley recounted what happened. "As soon as I came within a small distance of him [Trapnell], as he was at work looking at me, he swore he would blow my brains out and quickly stept [sic] to his door, when he was hindered by his wife urging and begging him not to get his gun." Trapnell gave up on the gun, but still in a violent passion, he "picked up a large stick swearing and cursing and with both hands struck my head." Bosley defended himself as best he could with "a small cane I rode with, otherwise the consequence might have been worse." Trapnell continued to throw stones at the committee's representative, "swearing he would kill" Bosley. After barely escaping from Trapnell's farm without further injury, Bosley turned back, telling his adversary "I would acquaint the committee of his acting today; he answer'd the committee and I might kiss his arse and be damned, pulling his coat apart behind, for a parcel of roguish damn'd sons of bitches, and if they came here he would use them in the same manner as I have done you &c. &c. &c."

When the committee heard the news, it ordered depositions from a surprisingly large number of people who had witnessed the attack on Bosley. They confirmed the obvious. Trapnell had lost all self-control, "cursing and swearing like a mad man." There was more unsettling information to come. If he had only had a tantrum, Trapnell might have expected a warning about behaving better in the future. But he had taken a step too far. The committee learned that while "Jumping up and knocking his heels together," Trapnell had bragged before friends "he could raise 500 men by night and 1500 men by Saturday night. It was also proposed by some of the Company then assembled to pull down Capt. Bosley's house and destroy his Living, which proposition Trapnell acquiesced in." Trapnell went to jail, where he mounted a spirited defense. From prison he insisted that the entire incident turned on a personal controversy with Bosley and not a lack of true patriotism. In a petition asking for release, he explained, "what I did was only in resentment to the person and no ways designing any ill against the State of affair of the American cause. I have, Gentlemen, associated and likewise given to the relief of the distressed of Boston. I bear, Gentlemen, no allegiance to the King of England, nor have any connection with those that embrace his maxims and am ready and willing to pay all due allegiance to this State." Later, he observed in a mild expression of contrition that "passion overcame me."[49] Trapnell received surprisingly light punishment, considering that he had threatened to raise a small army of loyalists. He returned to the community and, years later, argued again in court with Bosley, this time over a failed commercial deal.

Lying to a committee was never a good idea. Cornelius Newkerk and William McDarmoth, two extraordinarily clumsy schemers, thought they could manipulate the Committee of Safety and Observation for Kingston, New York. Their timing was poor. In April 1777 the entire Hudson Valley was under siege, and local committees throughout the region were on full alert for enemies who might be providing military intelligence for the British. The two men may have believed the Kingston committee would show leniency no matter how serious the charges brought against them. Their names had originally come to the attention of the committee while it was investigating a group of Tories who had established a chain of safe houses where they hid people trying to join British forces in occupied New York City. During one examination, the committee learned not only that Newkerk was associated with this group, but also that he had proclaimed, "he was a man for the King and his boys had got guns and every thing ready." Acting on the suspicion that Newkerk and his friends were conspiring against the American cause, the committee interrogated Newkerk and McDarmoth, both of whom protested their innocence. Their testimony must have been persuasive, since the committee decided that they could be released as soon as they took an oath of allegiance to the state of New York. The wording of the oath left no doubt about the expectations of the new revolutionary regime. Each man did "most solemnly swear that I renounce all allegiance to the King of Great Britain, that I will be a good and true Subject to the State of New York, that I will Discover all Plots & Conspiracies against it which may come to my knowledge and Pray God Almighty so to keep me as I do faithfully and sincerely keep this Oath and Declaration." As soon as they had fulfilled their part of the bargain, they hurriedly departed, happy to be free.

Perhaps as a result of arrogance or naïveté, Newkerk and McDarmoth failed to leave well enough alone. In the gathering dusk, they rode away from Kingston. Coming to a creek that they did not think safe to ford in darkness, they elected to stay at the home of Joseph Ousterhoudt. They were in luck. They went to their room completely unaware that they were sharing it with another traveler, Elizabeth Yeomans. When they entered, she "Drew the Curtains of the bed Close Together so that she could not be seen by Newkerk & McDarmoth." What followed seemed like a scene taken from a Renaissance farce. According to testimony recorded later, the two men "Laid Down supposing themselves alone in the room [and] began to talk about the Transaction of the Day before the Committee."

Yeomans did not miss a word. Newkerk, who appears to have been the most forward of the pair, bragged that he had fooled the Kingston committee into thinking he was a good Whig, in other words, a friend of revolution. McDarmoth claimed he too had passed himself off as a genuine patriot. But he was still uneasy. The business about the oath was not something to be taken lightly. To this, Newkerk explained that he had no reservations, since before the clerk for the committee read the oath Newkerk stuffed his ears with wool. He apparently thought that if one could not hear the words, one was not bound by the pledge. McDarmoth expressed amazement, not about Newkerk's audacity, but rather, about the source of the wool. Where, he asked, did Newkerk find it? Newkerk answered that whenever he anticipated having to swear an oath, he carried a few bits of wool to plug his ears. McDarmoth admitted that he was not so clever. Still, he thought the oath presented no moral problem, since the committee had asked him "to be True to the Country." His conscience was clear. "I could do that and free my Conscience," he explained, "for it is our Country where we were born [and] the King is the Ruler of the Country."

When they turned to other matters, one man warned the other that they should whisper. Yeomans heard it all. They talked about obtaining guns. In the morning, Yeomans crept out of bed and informed the innkeeper, who happened to be an enthusiastic supporter of independence. In turn, he called a local militia officer, who arrested Newkerk and McDarmoth and brought them before the Kingston committee. After Yeomans told the members what she had heard, the two conspirators confessed, but this time, instead of being released, they were sent to the New York Committee for Detecting and Defeating Conspiracies.[50] What happened next is unclear. A good guess would be that Newkerk and McDarmoth were banished and spent the war assisting the British in New York City.

Throughout the country, committees charged with enforcement had a number of punishments they employed to discourage domestic enemies. As we have seen, small and inadequate prisons were not the answer. Nor was the use of torture. Confronted with people accused of possible crimes against the Revolution, they could disarm a suspect, put the person under house arrest, order an individual paroled for good behavior, or compel someone convicted of a crime to join the Continental Army. State courts rather than local committees handled charges of treason and the seizure of loyalist property.[51] The most severe punishment available to the committees was banishment, a procedure that involved sending a particularly dangerous individual to a neighboring state or occasionally to areas occupied by British forces. Banishment occurred most often in New York. Committee records show that suspects who refused to take an oath of allegiance to the state were often subject to "Transportation to the Enemies' Lines."[52] In 1777, for example, a committee in Schenectady, New York, found John Winkworth "to be an Enemy to the Country" and therefore resolved, "he should be ordered by the Chairman to leave the District with his Family and Cloaths and Provision."[53]

In Albany banishment raised a sensitive question about revolutionary justice and economic class. A group of prominent residents who had clearly thrown in their lot with the British held a loud party that revolutionaries interpreted as a "daring insult." According to depositions taken by a committee, "The morning of the 4th of June [1776] was ushered in with the firing of guns, pistols, &c. by boys, negroes, &c. A circumstance not agreeable to the inhabitants of this city, knowing the scarcity of powder." When "many of the inhabitants of this city" went to investigate, they discovered several of the wealthiest gentlemen in Albany "with a number of the lower sort of people carousing, and singing God save the King." The members of the Albany committee clearly were uneasy about calling such powerful persons to account, but they knew that the ordinary people in the city had had their fill of brazen Tory activities. The committee ordered seven men "removed out of this county," since, as its members explained, "We plainly foresaw that nothing could be done with the rabble who were influenced by them [the Tory gentry], till they were removed." After all, they continued, "Complaints were made that the most atrocious offenders were screened in Albany, while every poor, low fellow was immediately prosecuted for only lisping out things which those people uttered daily in the most daring language."[54]

Banishment represented a particularly severe punishment because it exposed a person's property to seizure by the state. But even in cases involving persons regarded as dangerous enemies, the committees—especially in New York State—made significant distinctions. When the New York assembly passed a law ordering the wives of men banished for political crimes to follow their husbands into exile, dozens of women protested. They recognized, perhaps, that by deserting their farms they would place their family's holdings in jeopardy, and so they appealed to the members of the committees. Often their petitions succeeded. In October 1780, Lucretia Woodward and Jerusha Ingraham managed to convince a committee that however their husbands might have behaved during the Revolution, the wives were in fact of "good Character and that their remaining in the Country will not be detrimental to the Freedom & Independence of this [New York] and the United States." Early the next year a group of women asked the committee for a review of their situation. They were granted permission to stay because they "have always behaved themselves in an unexceptionable Manner and that they [local authorities] do not think their remaining at their Habitations will endanger the safety of the States." Jane Moffit managed to differentiate her political views from those of her absent husband. She had been ordered to leave the community, but "notwithstanding the Political Sentiments of her Husband, the said Jane Moffit has always been esteemed a Friend to the American Cause and that they do not conceive that her remaining within the State will tend in any Manner whatsoever to the Prejudice of the Freedom or Independence of this or the United States."[55]

V

The specter of Judge Hanson hangs over our discussion of revolutionary justice. There is no question that many Americans hated and feared domestic enemies, and throughout the war, they urged authorities to administer harsh punishments whenever people accused of supporting Great Britain came before them. But as we have seen, the officials charged with enforcing the Revolution avoided as much as possible extreme measures. They repeatedly tried to find ways to reconcile suspects, even those who had said or done things that might strike us today as bordering on treason. It would seem that the members of the local committees—or in some states justices of the peace—could have used their authority as a tool of vengeance. Their reluctance to do so begs a question. Why not? Other revolutions have witnessed massive bloodshed as ever more strident calls for ideological purity have compromised the normal rule of law. Except in matters of intellectual history, Americans have seldom compared the practical aspects of their revolution with those of countries such as France. This is a failing. To do so might explain why ordinary Americans—with notable exceptions involving African American slaves and Native Americans allied with the British—favored moderation over martyrdom and terror.[56]

Even contemporaries tried to comprehend such restraint. Some explanations for moderation bordered on the conspiratorial. People charged with administering tough justice failed to do so because suspected Tories were their relatives or friends or persons with whom they carried on business dealings. In a newspaper article addressed "to the Justices Empowered by the Court to Deal with the Tories," a writer wondered why local officials were not aggressively pursuing suspected domestic enemies. Was it because the accused was "a relation to yourselves"? Or that he is "eminent in his profession and a family doctor"? Or was moderation a way of hedging one's bets on the war? Perhaps those monitoring Tory activity reasoned that if the United States lost, Tory friends "may be a means of saving you."[57]

Another theory insisted the problem resulted from potential witnesses who refused to testify because they had received favors from Tories.[58] "A Friend of Liberty" writing in the *Connecticut Gazette* added a dimension of doubt, announcing, "The committees of inspection, especially of those towns infested with Tories, are requested to remember the importance of their trust."[59] Although warnings about secret cabals did not gain much traction, a few revolutionaries blamed excessive moderation on the unwillingness of the people to elect the type of men who would take a hard line on justice. An author who identified himself in a public journal as Oliver Cromwell asked, "Are there not men in public stations who make it their study to favor the great villains and punish the small? Is it not high time to make a separation, to oblige those who favor the enemy, and will not swear allegiance to these States, immediately to depart? Can the soldier leave his wife and children with that cheerfulness which he otherwise would, when he knows there are so many snakes in the grass?"[60]

Closer to the truth is an obvious explanation. Americans not only feared that the Revolution might descend into anarchy, but also preserved a strong sense of the importance of maintaining a rule of law. Of course, during the war it was often very hard to sustain the procedures that the colonists had long associated with criminal justice. The committees insisted that the measures they took to enforce the new revolutionary regimes were temporary, accommodations made in the face of extraordinary circumstances. One person complaining that officials were too lenient in punishing Tories confessed, "The law says, 'every man is to be deemed honest till convicted by trial, and suspicion of guilt is no proof of facts.'" This kind of legal scrupulosity, he argued, only served to undermine the popular will. "Our greatest difficulty arises," continued Astrea de Coelis, "from want of sufficient evidence, and though the line between Whig and Tory is very easy to ascertain, yet the foundation of law, and the sacred regard we entertain for the liberties of the subject, are such as I am afraid will save many a scoundrel from the gallows."[61] Another Pennsylvania writer gave the enforcement committees high marks. "Since this contest commenced," he observed in the *Pennsylvania Packet*, "the inhabitants of this State, like those of other States, have often been reduced to many trying and important situations. We have seen Committees and Constitutional Bodies of men appointed by the people, who have suspended the prevailing laws of the land." The record was not a source of embarrassment. "These Committees have exercised the most sovereign authority, and such [people] as have suffered by the same will have the justice to allow that they never punished as high as the crime deserved."[62]

However important maintaining a rule of law may have been to Americans, we should not forget where our reappraisal of the Revolution originally began. We asked where it took place. As we have seen, ordinary people experienced revolution within small communities. The sense of rejection by Great Britain, the need to be assured that resistance could be justified before God, and the challenge of living with fear, all of these occurred within the context of dense social relations, within long-standing networks of friends and relatives. It was in these situations that men and women devised workable definitions for revolutionary justice; it was here that they resolved the tensions between passion and constraint. Gold Silliman knew this world. Writing about the social fabric of a Connecticut town, he reminded his wife, Mary, "A great Number of those who are at Bottom Friends to their Country among us, and who would take it excessively ill to be thought otherwise, have Brothers, Fathers, Sisters, Sons, & in short every sort of Relationship that you can mention among the Enemy." When such people saw the local committees using "vigorous Measures" to pursue family members, they gave into sentiment and engaged in "Modes of Behaviour that are altogether inconsistent with the Character of the Patriot."[63]

The unenthusiastic enforcement of a Massachusetts act passed in 1777 confirmed Silliman's observation about the difficulty of enforcing excessively vigorous measures. The statute bore the ominous title—"An Act for Securing This and Other of the United States, Against the Danger to which they are Exposed, by the *Internal Enemies* therein." A preamble explained that the legislature had discovered, "there are some within this State, who, from sordid motives, or from wicked and inveterate dispositions, are secretly endeavoring to counteract the united struggles now making for the preservation and establishment of American Liberty." The law ordered the voters in every town to elect a collector of evidence who was responsible for identifying persons "whose residence in this State is dangerous to the public peace or safety." An especially insidious provision allowed "any freeholder or other person, qualified to vote" to make a public accusation—in other words, a declaration before the town that a neighbor's support of the Revolution was in doubt. Communities drew up what were called "black lists," and when the majority agreed that this or that individual threatened the community's security, his name was submitted to a justice of the peace. If the suspicious character could not explain his behavior, his case was advanced to the Massachusetts Board of War. Those proved guilty could anticipate being transported "off the Continent, to some part of the West Indies or Europe."[64]

Many towns went through the motions of implementing the new law. Collectors of evidence were in fact elected throughout the state. But whatever the threat from Tories may have been, townspeople seem to have enforced the act as they alone saw fit. They typically gathered names of suspicious characters—perhaps five or six people—but before submitting the names to higher authorities they usually gathered a second time. On this occasion they edited the lists, often dropping most of the original names. Sometimes communities would allow neighbors who had expressed lukewarm support for independence to take a new oath of allegiance. When that happened, their names disappeared from the list.

The Worcester town records reveal how revolutionary justice became local justice. On June 16, 1777, the selectmen presented "the names of a number of persons whom they Esteemed Enemies & Dangerous to this and the other United States of America." Then, people attending the meeting added seventeen more names. A few weeks later two more names were appended to the list. But by this time some residents were having second thoughts about the whole exercise. On June 30 those at a meeting "voted that the Town-Clerk be and hereby is Directed to Suspend making the Return of the Names of all those Enemical persons (until he shall have further Directions of the Town.)" A few names still remained on the Worcester list. At the end of November the town dropped most of these. After discussion it "Voted to Receive Capt John Curtis, Nahum Willard, David Moore, Samuel Moore, and Micah Johnson Junior into the Town's favor and that further prosecution against them, as Enemies to the United State of America shall cease."[65]

Worcester sorted out its own political problems within a complex web of friendships and relations. Theirs was not a unique experience. Ordinary people throughout the country came forward, making judgments about neighbors, participating in a revolution that drew strength from an expanding web of popular participation. They experienced a new political culture firsthand, on the ground where hard decisions about allegiance were made and recorded. But the revolutionaries achieved something else. They did not allow passions to run amok. If they had not done so—indeed, if they had taken their cues from the likes of Judge Hanson—we might now be telling ourselves a very different story about how the American people made a revolution work.

CHAPTER FIVE

BETRAYAL

Betrayal is the nightmare of revolution. The word suggests the possibility of a major breach of confidence. It throws fundamental assumptions about allegiance to a common cause into question, raising the kind of doubts that one might experience upon discovering that a friend has collaborated with an oppressive regime. As with other resistance movements throughout the world, the American Revolution spawned suspicions of betrayal. After 1778, as the war dragged on with no end in sight, many people began to question the commitment of other revolutionaries. But, most important for our story, at a time when mutual trust seemed at risk, Americans did not follow the divisive script that has compromised so many revolutions throughout the world. To be sure, some denunciations of neighbors occurred. Far more common, however, was an impressive effort by ordinary people to reaffirm their revolutionary goals by working together to support the fight for independence. By sustaining revolutionary solidarity, they created a new political culture.

A new wave of doubt about the actions of other Americans had little to do with the Tories, who had actively supported Great Britain from the start. To be sure, such internal enemies remained a challenge to security, especially in contested military zones. Rather, what became an increasingly troublesome issue was a growing conviction that some people who had at first welcomed the appeal for national independence were now engaging in economic practices that threatened the well-being of other Americans who had made—and who continued to make—personal sacrifices on behalf of a revolutionary cause. As a writer in the *Pennsylvania Packet* observed, at the beginning of the war everyone proclaimed unity, pledging uncompromising support for a shared political goal, "and no one then ever dreamt, that our struggles against the common oppressor would involve us in mutual oppressions of each other, of the most pernicious and heinous nature."[1]

Americans were not naïve about the demands of war. They understood the necessity of sacrificing material comfort as long as the fight against Great Britain continued. The conflict drained scarce resources and elevated taxes. Such things were to be expected. But even so, revolutionaries believed that the burdens of war should be shared—if not equally, then at least fairly—and when it appeared that opportunists were profiting from the hardship of others, previously muted social tensions flared, exposing divisions between farmers and merchants, between residents of cities and the countryside, between people on fixed incomes and those whose wealth depended on market transactions, and most significant for our purposes, between those who championed the good of a community and the ambitions of individuals.

As difficult questions about shared economic sacrifice for the revolutionary cause arose, fundamental notions about patriotism evolved, taking on striking new meanings that Americans had not anticipated at the start of the war. Of course, it was always patriotic to resist an invading enemy. But after 1778 popular ideas of what constituted patriotism expanded. It came to involve more than heroic sacrifice on the field of battle. Love of country also implied that one would renounce private economic gain that harmed neighbors. Individual self-advancement was viewed as a threat to the community; it eroded political unity. In *A Practical Discourse Against Extortion* (1777) the Reverend Jonathan French put the point bluntly. As a culture of greed took root in America, he worried that appeals to revolutionary patriotism had become no more than a rationalization for "craft, avarice, and self-interest."[2]

During the hectic months before the signing of the Declaration of Independence, no one had given these issues much thought. But as popular enthusiasm for the rebellion waned, it soon became apparent that the "sunshine patriots," as Thomas Paine called them, were not able to sustain a revolution. Financing the war proved much more difficult than anyone had anticipated. The Congress issued huge amounts of paper currency backed by little more than a hope of obtaining foreign loans and a faith in the willingness of ordinary Americans to accept the bills at face value. It was inevitable that the flood of money would quickly depreciate, forcing people to pay ever more for household necessities. The phrase "not worth a Continental" reminds us just how serious these problems were for the entire population. Making matters worse, disruption of trans-Atlantic commerce drove up the price for vital imported goods, such as cloth and metal items.

These developments touched the lives of most Americans. It affected the well-being of families. Indeed, it would be fair to state that after 1778 economic insecurity threatened the very success of the Revolution. That is a large claim. It is a largely unfamiliar one. Most histories of the final years of the American Revolution concentrate on key battles and diplomatic negotiations with European nations.[3] The problem with this account is that it diverts attention from how Americans negotiated the ongoing demands of revolution. It also obscures the fact that it was in small agricultural communities where the resistance against Great Britain was sustained when the prospect of success seemed so uncertain.

Continuing support for the Revolution is not something we should take for granted. Popular support for revolution often wanes when supplies run short, and history certainly offers many examples of how hyper-inflation can undermine political stability. One thinks, for example, of the collapse of the Weimar Republic or the financial crises that have plagued countries such as Argentina or Venezuela. If the American people had lost faith in their cause, the defining and climatic moment would have occurred during the late 1770s when expectations of easy victory gave way to the harsh reality of paying for the cost of war.

Such a catastrophic collapse of confidence did not occur, of course. By asking why Americans did not give up on their own revolution, we recover a largely forgotten story of resilience and inventiveness on the community level. Ordinary people saved the Revolution. They do not usually receive credit for their achievement. Instead, praise goes to national leaders well versed in economic theory who put forward plans for how the government should restore fiscal stability. They counseled retiring the Continental currency as quickly as possible, chiefly through taxes. But however worthy these proposals may have been, the people responded to the challenge in ways that revealed their revolutionary aspirations. Not since the early days of organized resistance when hundreds of communities pledged to boycott tea had so many Americans taken such a passionate interest in solving a shared problem.

The precipitous fall in the value of the Continental currency met with grumbling and complaint. That was not surprising. Rising prices forced

Americans who had not participated in battle to accept a huge and unexpected level of sacrifice. How they responded to this challenge reminds us of their extraordinary commitment to fundamental revolutionary values. At the community level their resilience reaffirmed political solidarity, but with this difference. During the later years of the war people defended revolution not only as a fight for national independence, but also as a means of creating a more just society. This is a significant point. What we encounter in the effort of ordinary Americans to stabilize the nation's currency is the birth of a new political order. It was at this moment when we can state confidently that a colonial rebellion had in fact evolved into a genuine revolution. Indeed, to answer a question posed at the beginning of this book, what made the American Revolution truly revolutionary was the growing determination of newly empowered Americans to endorse a social contract based on community solidarity rather than on unbridled individualism.

To ridicule the revolutionaries' efforts to advance economic justice would be easy. After all, how much can scattered communities do to remedy economic problems that were national, even international in scope? But such concerns need not deflect the argument. However ineffective the local responses may have been in restoring the economy, they helped sustain popular resistance at a crucial moment during the war, and perhaps more significant, they brought ever-larger numbers of people into an ongoing political experiment. The experience of regulating local economies—of fighting for collective values rather than for individual liberty—gave them greater confidence in their right and ability to determine the character of political affairs. Instead of giving in to the sirens of surrender, Americans took on responsibility for shaping a revolution on their own terms.

I

Ezekiel Russell understood the issues at stake. This obscure printer helps us to reconstruct the revolutionary mentality of a people struggling with doubt and recrimination. In 1777 he was endeavoring to keep his printing business afloat. Russell had recently moved to Danvers, Massachusetts— formerly Salem Village of witchcraft notoriety—looking for new opportunities. Business sense persuaded him to locate his shop near the Bell

Tavern, a popular institution for local residents and commercial travelers. But the conflict with Great Britain exacerbated Russell's challenge. Paper was hard to obtain, and in order to maintain a supply of paper, he was forced to remind "the ladies ... to remember he still continues to pay cash for linen rags, sail-cloth, and weaver's thrums [short pieces of waste thread or yarn]." Because of such problems many other printers cut back on the number of titles they released, and during the later years of the war few were able to publish the kinds of long and learned political pamphlets that had been more common during the run up to independence.[4]

Perhaps because Russell was looking for something capable of generating substantial public interest, he took on the production of a remarkable work, *The Downfall of Justice; and the Farmer Just Return'd on Thanksgiving Day.* He described the piece as "a comedy, lately acted in Connecticut." About the origins of the play nothing is known. It might well have been Russell's own creation. In any case, *Downfall of Justice* went through at least two editions—a sign of its modest commercial success—and the second printing included not only the Thanksgiving Day comedy, but also a long poem described as "a fable, by way of an address to a countryman, on his petitioning Jupiter for an amendment of his circumstances." Why a simple New England "peasant"—Russell's word—would be praying to a Greek god for greater wealth is unclear, especially since the publication develops an ethical argument that draws principally on the teachings of the New Testament. To enhance the work's appeal, Russell adding a number of original illustrations. Woodcuts of this complexity required time and money. They depict a family celebrating a Thanksgiving meal as well as several cartoons. In one of the cartoons the Devil observes a group of selfish merchants plotting to increase profits, in another long-suffering soldiers complain about the state of the economy, and in a third an honest farmer promises to barter with his neighbors rather than become an "extortioner" by "selling the Necessities of Life."

The separate elements of the *Downfall of Justice*—the play, poem, and illustrations—blend traditional Christian morality with a condemnation of sharp dealings in the revolutionary marketplace.[5] If Russell had merely provided an account of the sudden spike in inflation or a critique of the fiscal policies of the Congress, he would most likely not have reached an audience of ordinary Americans, people who thought of economic relations in terms of fairness. The entire work rehearses long-standing demands—

some dating from the sixteenth century—for merchants and farmers selling agricultural products to observe a "just price." The key assumption was that economic exchange should not be governed solely by profit. From this perspective, everyone in a community bore responsibility for the well-being of other people. Charging poor neighbors exorbitant prices was objectionable because it was fundamentally wrong, and if we perceive the web of economic transactions as sophisticated theorists such as Adam Smith or Alexander Hamilton might have done, we will miss how much Americans experiencing revolution still viewed the marketplace from a premodern, moral perspective. In this context, it was not hard for Russell's readers to interpret their suffering in conspiratorial terms, even as evidence of betrayal.

The play opens just as the members of a well-to-do farm family return from church and are sitting down for a sumptuous Thanksgiving dinner. These are extraordinarily unattractive people, complaisant and quite candid about their contempt for poorer neighbors. The patriarch is a man of strong opinions, and throughout the celebratory meal he makes it clear that he expects his wife, who spent a long time preparing the food, and his children to endorse his self-satisfied perspective on social relations within their community. The group consumes a fat goose; everyone drinks glass after glass of cider—presumably of the hard variety. The father eats so much that he has to unbutton his "Sabbath-day coat."

During the table conversation the wife apologizes for the quality of the pudding. It apparently was not up to her normal expectations. But the mediocre result did not really matter. After all, "the town folks would jump at a bit on't poor as it is." To which her vapid daughter observes, "Why 'tis said that scornful dogs sometime jump at a dirty pudding." The mother interprets these words as a mean-spirited insult. Rounding on the daughter she exclaims: "Why *Sarah!* I'm sure my pudding isn't dirty, I was never reckoned a slut in all my life." No, no, the daughter replies. Her mother was certainly not a slovenly housekeeper. "I don't mean so," protests Sarah, "only that the town folks us'd to scorn every thing but the best, but now they'd be glad even of a crust of your pudding. I expect some of them along to-morrow or next day begging as the Indians us'd to do the day after thanksgiving. I can't but laugh to see how foolish they'l look." With this declaration of social and racial superiority the entire family has a good laugh. They take a measure of satisfaction from knowing that whatever the condition of the pudding they are better than the "town folks" and the indigent Indians.

What made this self-satisfied family especially rebarbative—at least, in Russell's eyes—was hypocrisy. After all, they had spent the morning listening to a sermon, and then, at the beginning of the thanksgiving dinner, the father offered a prayer. According to the stage directions, "The Farmer proceeds to crave a blessing; in the run of which he pities the poor and needy thro'out the world." And after the feast, he instructs his sons and daughters on how Scripture can be interpreted to justify driving hard bargains with the poor.

After witnessing such a stream of sanctimonious twaddle, Jack—the family slave—can endure no more. What about sharing? What about a sense of obligation to the less fortunate in the community? "Well Masser," Jack states, "I don't tink 'tis fair ting when poor fok canno get noting in he belly." To be sure, the farmer avoided appearing mean-spirited in public; he prayed on behalf of the poor throughout the world. But all of it was just empty rhetoric. According to Jack, "Masser got rye enuf, wheat enuf, cyder enuf, ebery ting enuf." Surplus made no difference to the greedy farmer. He refused not only to share basic necessities with his unfortunate neighbors, but also to sell these goods to other families at any price, not in Continental dollars nor in hard money. The slave found the whole situation distressing, and concluded his outburst, "*Jack* pitty poor folk."

Of course, it would have been unlikely for a slave to criticize a master's behavior so openly. That was the author's point. For a person so dependent on a white farmer—someone on the very bottom of the social hierarchy—to condemn hypocrisy and appeal for charity made the criticism all the more effective. If a slave dared to confront his master in this way, then the reader of the play could not help but wonder what the "poor town folk" were saying about the selfish farmer.

The Downfall of Justice hints at the simmering popular anger. After the farmer brags that he anticipates demanding a much higher price for cattle next spring, his son observes that the plan would only work "if the town folks don't rise and take them away, and I am bloody 'fraid they will; and if they should, I doubt but the authority would justify them in't." The threat makes no sense to the farmer. Why would people even contemplate taking goods from their rightful owner? Did they not respect his right to property? The son explained that neighbors might engage in forms of popular justice, because "the most of 'em an't able to buy at that price." The wife interjected that the people have no right to seize private property, whatever the provocation. The farmer assures her, "If they should [come] I would flail 'em."

Jack makes out better than one might have expected. To be sure, the master loses his temper over Jack's speech. "Why, you black Bastard," he exclaimed, "han't you victuals enough to stop your mouth?"[6] The problem with Jack was that he did not appreciate what a good life he enjoyed. Did the slave not realize that he ate better than did the poor white folk he pitied? "There's a hundred mechanics don't live half so well as you do," the farmer reminded the slave. The argument silenced Jack, but not before the wife declared, "I do wish our *Jack* wou'd mind his own business, and not be always a talking of things that don't concern him at all."

What Jack refused to ignore was a practice of timing the market. The master saw no reason to sell produce, whatever the demand, when he knew he could fetch a higher price in a few months. This was how the market-place worked, even during a revolution. However desperate the poor may have been, the farmer could always point out that they did not understand the logic of capitalism.[7] No doubt that was true in part, but they judged behavior by different economic rules. For them, the needs of others could not be ignored in the name of enhanced profits. To take advantage of vulnerable neighbors was not good business; it was extortion, placing individual gain above a moral obligation to care for the other members of the community. The farmer, however, defended his rights. "I have good cyder enough," he observed, "and this year intend to take care of't. . . . I have been offered five dollars a barrel, and wouldn't look at it, it will fetch me fifteen in the spring." Holding back on the sale of firewood and oxen also made good economic sense. The reader of this "comedy"—depressingly dark humor at best—is left with questions. What happens when wealthy people mock the concept of just price? What response should be given to the mother in one of Russell's illustrations whose children declare, "Mamma, I want bread," to which she replies, "My dear children my heart breaks for you. It is out of my power to relieve you"?

The author of *The Downfall of Justice* links the behavior of this fictional farm family to the Revolution subtly, almost in passing. The patriarch's son makes a reference to an article he had read recently in a Hartford, Connecticut, newspaper entitled, "A Looking Glass." The article was no invention. The piece, which would have been familiar to many of Russell's readers, condemned an epidemic of greed that had swept over the country.

The fact that it was republished in several different journals suggests that it spoke to the concerns of ordinary Americans.

According to "A Looking Glass," "oppression consists in taking advantage of the necessity of others to extort from them an unreasonable price for the necessaries of life; and is an offense against the laws of reason and morality, and inconsistent with the righteous and beneficent rules of Christianity, and resembles the infernals whose character is to devour one another." True patriots accepted Continental bills. Discounting this national currency represented "the grossest cheat." It insulted patriotism. Of course, the writer admitted, the merchant and the farmer should profit from honest work, but there were limits on acceptable rates of return. "I appeal to everyone," the writer urged, "and call upon all, to reconcile, if they can, the present enhanced prices of articles with the rules of common honesty." The Revolution itself was at risk. "I ask the question, will your army continue to defend you in the field, when their wives and their children are famishing and crying for bread at home, through your intolerable oppressions; or will they turn their arms against you, and do themselves justice?"[8]

II

During the Revolution most of the country was not involved directly in major military campaigns most of the time. This was especially true for New England after the British evacuated Boston in 1776. Among other things, this situation meant that for small communities removed from the actual fighting the demands of war only slowly began to affect the quality of everyday life, usually in the form of a sacrifice of basic material comfort. Indeed, during the early days of revolution a serious economic crisis seemed only a remote possibility. Americans came forward enthusiastically to support resistance to Great Britain, and although the paper money initially authorized by the Continental Congress lacked secure backing, it held its own.

But by late 1778, as the war continued without prospect of quick resolution, the currency suffered precipitous depreciation. The price of basic household items suddenly rose by several hundred percent. People reliant on the marketplace for food found that it required forty Continental Dollars to equal the buying power of a single silver dollar. The problem grew worse. By 1780 the currency was essentially worthless.[9] Making the situation even more disturbing was the fact that American soldiers who had enlisted for three-year terms of service found that steep depreciation made it very hard for them to maintain wives and children. The Reverend Eliphalet Wright offered a blunt assessment of the situation. "It seems as if our rich men, like so many hard millstones, had got the poor people between them, and had agreed to grind them to death. How lamentable is it to hear a poor woman, with half a dozen small children, whose husband is in the army, complaining that she cannot procure a shirt for a poor half frozen child, under five shillings per yard, nor a little salt under 18 shillings per bushel."[10]

Throughout the country, people complained bitterly about the difficulty of making ends meet. Sometimes the rhetoric became extreme. Commentators wrote of starving families. It is doubtful that the distress ever reached that point. Nevertheless, for Americans who had celebrated the Declaration of Independence, the devaluation of the paper money was deeply dispiriting. After all, for most people the Continental currency was the most physical reminder in daily affairs—other than local men joining the army—that there was a new government in place, and if a key symbol of the republic collapsed, it seemed only a matter of time before people might begin to question whether personal sacrifice was worth the effort. The alarm sounded in several different states. In July 1779 someone writing for a Massachusetts newspaper under the name A FARMER drew attention to "the sudden and rapid fall of our currency—the very soul of our political existence."[11] About the same time the *Virginia Gazette* announced, "the field of battle is changed for the field of the budget."[12] Looking back at the experience of the previous two years, a writer in the *Pennsylvania Packet* noted in 1780, "the depreciation became, at length, an object of such magnitude, and was so intimately connected with every movement, both political and military, that every eye became familiarized to it. The laws acknowledged it, and the newspapers, in successive essays, proclaimed it aloud."[13]

The Continental Congress was fully aware of the growing domestic peril. In a circular letter signed by John Jay and addressed to all Americans in 1779, it appealed to the public to support the failing currency. The representatives of the national government made a powerful, although desperate argument for economic patriotism. Had the grumblers forgotten the fundamental ideals that energized resistance in the first place, asked Jay? They had originally united to establish a government "on the generous principles of equal liberty, where the rulers of the states are the servants of the people, and not masters of those from whom they derive authority." Perhaps when the outcome of the war was still in doubt some people might have been reluctant to honor Continental currency. That was all in the past. By 1779, Congress insisted, the country's prospects had greatly improved. "The Independence of America is now fixed as Fate, and the present Efforts of Britain to break it down are as vain and fruitless as the Raging of the Waves which bear against the Cliffs."

While that assessment may have been overly optimistic, Congress used the fiscal crisis to put forward an argument about the basic relation between popular sovereignty and the public's responsibility to maintain the face value of the nation's currency. Acceptance of Continental money amounted to a pledge of allegiance. "It must be evident to every Man who reads the Journals of Congress or looks at the face of one of their Bills, that Congress have pledged the Faith of their Constituents for the Redemption of them." Whatever Congress did, it did in the name of the people. That was the point of republican government. It followed from this assertion that the people "have pledged their Faith" in the Continental currency, "not only collectively by their representatives, but individually." Americans had no excuse for refusing to accept the currency or for taking advantage of the distress of other revolutionaries. The entire republican experiment hung in the balance. "Can there be any reason to apprehend that the Divine Disposer of human events, after having separated us from the house of bondage, and led us safe through the sea of blood, toward the land of liberty and promise, will leave the work of our political redemption unfinished.... [and] Suffer us to be carried back in chains to that country of oppression?"[14]

Congress's patriotic rhetoric had little effect. The currency continued to lose value, and as the crisis deepened Americans wanted to identify the causes of their distress. They did not find abstract economic explanations persuasive. They were certain that the blame for the massive depreciation must rest with identifiable individuals.[15] Abstract arguments about the amount of unsecured currency in circulation had little traction with Americans angry about the rising prices for household goods in their communities. They wanted names. Some traced the problem to the efforts of

British agents to destabilize the currency. Others pointed to counterfeiters who turned out worthless paper. But by far the most common conclusion was that the American people had only themselves to blame. During the course of the war the revolutionaries had lost their way. At the beginning of the contest, they had demonstrated a commendable willingness to sacrifice for the common good. For complex reasons, however, revolutionary solidarity had dissolved, and a surge of selfish individualism had dramatically undermined the initial commitment to cooperation.

In private market exchanges—individuals buying and selling goods—the American people had betrayed their own cause. The evidence for moral failure was painfully obvious. Repeatedly, and in all regions of the country, commentators accused the people of putting profit before patriotism. One New Jersey writer lamented how rare it had become to encounter "a steady and firm attachment to the glorious cause of freedom." What had gone wrong? "The allurements of pleasure, and the universal rage for money have almost bereaved us of our senses."[16] A corrosive indulgence for material pleasure had taken root. Everywhere one encountered "a selfish principle of love of riches, ease, luxury, and dissipation."[17]

Recriminations of this sort echoed throughout the country. A declaration published in the name of "the CITIZENS and INHABITANTS" of Williamsburg, Virginia, lamented that "a spirit of extortion, which hatched in the obscure corners, among the selfish, the disaffected, the most despicable of human creatures, has spread like low born mist through the land."[18] The same miasma could be encountered in Massachusetts: "We are striving," one minister in Newburyport exclaimed, "who shall best improve his private interest, and make the most money, although it be to the endangering, and perhaps the destruction of our country and our invaluable liberties."[19] The Reverend Charles Chauncey, a respected Boston minister, insisted that a willingness to take advantage of one's neighbors in economic dealings "has overspread the land with such selfishness as has been destructive of that public patriotic spirit which was its glory: 'Tis this that has engaged such multitudes to 'seek their own,' to the neglect of, and in opposition to, 'the weal of others.'"[20]

For centuries Christian moralists had warned people against the dangers of luxury and avarice.[21] Obsession with the acquisition of material goods, they insisted, was potentially idolatrous, a failure that turned worldly baubles into false gods. The revolutionaries, however, pushed this traditional condemnation of greed in a specific political direction. They linked the success of the Revolution with ethical behavior in the market-place. This condemnation of selfishness might have generated fatalism. If people were really concerned only with their own economic welfare, then it would seem that there was little the country could do to restore a shared commitment to a common political cause. However, that is not how the rhetoric of self-loathing worked in practice. Commentators knew that the people might sin—they might sin all the time—but their fallen condition was no excuse for despair. Even in the darkest hour they were still capable of reform. Like the early Puritans who founded New England, revolution-aries could redeem themselves. But little time remained for genuine atone-ment, these moralists warned.

Large numbers of Americans believed that it was their responsibility— and their responsibility alone—to meet the economic challenge. As the Reverend William Gordon, another Massachusetts minister, explained in a sermon delivered on the first anniversary of the Declaration of Indepen-dence, those Americans who "once called themselves high sons of liberty" had succumbed to the temptation of quick profits. "If men in this day," Gordon declared, "will not be content with a livelihood, and will make themselves fortunes, immense fortunes, out of the distress of the people, I say, let the curse of heaven fall upon their substance, their unhallowed gains." God might punish, but the people were responsible for the restora-tion of prosperity.[22] They could save the Revolution.

This assumption energized the townsmen who attended a 1779 town meeting in Worcester, Massachusetts. "The amazing high prices of goods of all kinds, and the necessaries of life in particular demand our most serious consideration," they declared. "After we have survived a four years' war, and have been more successful than could be expected, to become prey to monopolizers, and other Devils of no principle but to raise them-selves on the ruins of the country, is intolerable. If we suffer such pro-ceedings any longer, our existence, as a people, is at an end." The mem-bers of this community felt that they had to respond to the call for action. "No time is to be lost, something must be done and that quickly."[23] As we have seen repeatedly, the focus of revolutionary experience for or-dinary Americans was in communities, where in conversations with friends and neighbors people addressed national challenges.

The popular resolve to save the Continental currency and to reduce sharp dealing in the marketplace soon exposed serious divisions within revolutionary society. The irony must have been apparent to everyone. Ever since Americans had taken up arms against Great Britain they had stressed the necessity of unity. Unless they cooperated they stood no chance of defeating an enemy that possessed superior military resources. But the economic crisis pitted revolutionaries against other revolutionaries, a situation that threatened the very sense of shared purpose that had kept the country together after George Washington retreated from New York City and endured a string of humiliating defeats. In an attack on the spreading culture of greed, the Reverend Jonathan French reminded Americans that profiteering "is exceedingly detrimental to the community, by weakening society, and endangering the state." Avariciousness eroded unity. "It creates jealousies, excites feuds, and animosities, destroys mutual confidence, and becomes the bane of that public union in which chiefly the strength of a State consists."[24]

For a demonstration of the accuracy of the Reverend French's analysis, one had only to consider how farmers and merchants accused each other of unscrupulous dealing. The merchants—generally those who resided in larger port cities—sold imported goods such as cloth and metalware. For them, the cost of doing business rose dramatically during wartime because of the risk of the British navy capturing American ships and the increased price of insurance. However valid the reasoning, they demanded larger returns on imported items, and in response to the steady rise in prices, the farmers charged more for their produce.

Mutual suspicion soon poisoned normal transactions between the larger towns and cities—reliant on a supply of meat and grain—and the countryside that demanded European manufactures. One writer in New Jersey described the growing mistrust. "Some with whom I have conversed," reported Crito, "having considerable landed property, are ever exclaiming against the rapacity of the merchant and trader. These are perpetually finding fault with the high price of provisions and the articles which they are obliged to purchase of the farmer."[25] Both groups accused the other of responsibility for undermining the flow of trade. If the merchant raised prices, then the farmer followed suit, insisting that he had no other choice. In *A Practical Discourse Against Extortion*, the Reverend Jonathan French explained how the cycle of suspicion fed on itself: "The complaints in the country are chiefly leveled against the merchants, in the maritime towns;— that they have taken advantage of the times and laid extravagant prices on almost every article, which the necessities of the people have compelled them to purchase;—The country perceiving this, and knowing the trading towns could no more subsist without the produce of the lands, than they themselves without the wares of the merchant, immoderately raised the price of almost every necessary of life ... as high as the general demand would admit."[26]

As mutual trust eroded, greed quickly spiraled out of control. People asked themselves why they should sacrifice when a few, highly visible opportunists were doing so well. "This is as much to say," observed French, "when a sin is become general, it is no sin to follow a multitude to do evil."[27] Economic survival provided an excuse for blatant self-interest. As the *Pennsylvania Gazette* explained in 1779, "The prices of foreign produce having ... risen to a monster height, the farmer and mechanic were of course led to raise the price of their labors in self-defense."[28] Members of the merchant class accused farmers of adding to the problem by withholding "small meats, hay, butter, and other articles of consumption" from "our markets."[29] Although such arguments probably made sense at the moment, the hostility between major groups in the market economy jeopardized revolutionary unity. As the Reverend Israel Evans, who served as a chaplain in the Continental Army for the entire revolution, observed in 1779, patriotism had given way to "the selfish principles of the times."[30]

Although all Americans contributed—however indirectly—to a culture driven by economic self-interest, some individuals merited special condemnation. These were men who perceived the disruptions of war largely as a means of personal advancement. Before independence these people had done little to distinguish themselves from neighbors. But however unremarkable they may have appeared in former times, they found ways during the Revolution to profit from the privations of other Americans. In the eyes of their critics they were parvenu, mere social climbers. No doubt, assessments of this sort gave voice to common snobbery; perhaps ordinary revolutionaries did not understand how the conflict with Great Britain had created unprecedented situations in which those possessing some capital and a willingness to take huge risks were able to acquire quick wealth.

Whatever the case, a surge of profiteering appeared to have muddled traditional social relations. LIBERTAS, writing in the *New-Jersey Gazette* in 1780, railed against "the avaricious hawker, who at the commencement of the war, had neither character, fortune, education or merit, and with no other capital than a few barrels of rum, has by barter, transportation, and concealment of his goods at one time, and cruel extortion from the necessitous of another, amassed a fortune."[31] When the townspeople of Worcester, Massachusetts, gathered in 1779, they observed, "many of the respectable merchants and fair-traders have retired from business." Who now controlled the local marketplace? Barely able to restrain their anger, the residents identified a "number of locusts and canker worms, in human form, who have increased, and proceeded along the road to plunder, until they have become odiously formidable, and their contagious influence dangerously prevalent." Not surprisingly, the Worcester meeting labeled the crass newcomers as the "pestilent mushrooms of trade" and resolved that they should "be subjected to the resentment and indignation of the public, whether their conduct proceeds from a general disaffection to public measures, and the independence of these states, or from private motives of sordid interests."[32]

The attack on the canker worms of commerce resonated persuasively in other regions of the country. A TRUE PATRIOT, writing in the *Pennsylvania Gazette*, blamed a rising generation of dodgy business figures not only for the growing maldistribution of wealth in society—the richer sorts obtaining an unmerited share of resources—but also for the decay in the work ethic that had allowed ordinary people time out of mind to enjoy a comfortable living. In the midst of war the rules of economic behavior had suddenly changed. "Thousands of the most honest and respectable citizens of America" who had always championed "sobriety and economy" found themselves having to "behold many men, whom they looked upon in the commencement of these troubles ... as such whose fathers they would have disdained to have set with the dogs ... raised to immense wealth, or at least carry the appearance of a haughty, supercilious and luxurious spendthrift."[33] A New Jersey newspaper shared this hostile view. A group of new men interested only in their own financial success had manipulated the market. "In this manner," the journal insisted, "has the honest and truly industrious part of the community been made the victims of the avarice and unpunished villainy of these wretches."[34]

Even though commentators seldom identified specific individuals who had engaged in unethical economic activities, they were quite certain how such miscreants went about rigging prices to their own advantage. They were masters of oppression. This practice took several different forms, but fundamentally, the enemies of market stability—those people who refused to honor Continental currency at face value or to trade goods at a just price—schemed to maximize profits without giving the slightest thought to the welfare of ordinary buyers or sellers. A widely accepted definition of such behavior explained that "oppression consists in taking advantage of the necessity of others to extort from them an unreasonable price for the necessaries of life; and it is an offense against the laws of reason and morality; and is inconsistent with the righteous and beneficent rules of Christianity, and resembles the infernals [inhabitants of hell] whose character is to devour one another."[35]

The assumption empowering rhetoric of this sort was that moral considerations had to moderate traditional rules of supply and demand. Common sense alone indicated that it was wrong to gouge a neighbor during a commercial transaction simply because one could do so. In normal times one might trust competition in the marketplace to establish a fair price, but war radically altered such mechanisms. As a tradesman from New Jersey noted: "I am well aware, and expect to hear the old trite observation, that trade will regulate itself. I know it will in ordinary cases, but we are concerned in an extraordinary one."[36] Since most states were slow in enacting laws prohibiting farmers or merchants from setting prices as they alone saw fit, it fell to the public to enforce economic justice. "The whole," rests upon the virtue and common consent of the community," declared a respected leader in Philadelphia. "I have no doubt but combinations have been formed for raising the prices of goods and provisions, and therefore the community, in their own defense, have a natural right to counteract such combinations, and to set limits to evils which affect themselves."[37]

Speculators who violated the rules of the moral economy went by different names. Revolutionaries often demonized them as forestallers or monopolizers, archaic terms that had been in common use in England and America more than a century earlier. Indeed, the belief in existence of a just price harked back to a premodern world in which commercial dealings were determined in part by obligations of social responsibility. Forestallers gained advantage by purchasing imported goods or agricultural produce in high popular demand and then refusing to sell them to those most in need until the price had risen substantially. This is exactly what the obnoxious farmer in *The Downfall of Justice* did. No matter how much his neighbors were suffering, he refused to sell them grain or cider until he could be assured of a sizeable profit. It did not matter to him if hard-pressed townspeople offered hard money or Continental currency. Moral issues had no place in this man's calculations. The goal was to create artificial scarcities by manipulating the flow of goods.

Monopolizers did much the same thing, only on a larger scale. To be sure, the economic vocabulary was imprecise, with forestalling and monopolizing frequently lumped together as closely related crimes against the community.[38] As a writer in the *New-Jersey Gazette* announced, "there is a sort of creature, with which this country has of late been infested called, by some *jobbers* or *speculators*, but whom I call by the name of *monopolizers*."[39] Whatever one called the offense, people had no problem identifying it when they saw it. According to a report in Boston's *Continental Journal* (1779), "there had been an unlimited number of monopolizers, hawkers, and such like vermin, that have for a long time way-layed every road, and are in every town buying up everything that is for market; thus they hold everything in their own hands."[40]

In practical terms it probably did not matter a great deal that the language Americans employed to describe wartime profiteers was imprecise. Their vocabulary was loose, sometimes confused, often more emotional in character than technically descriptive. About one element, however, they were in complete agreement. The most serious threat to revolutionary unity, they argued, was extortion. This deeply rooted vice was at the heart of all the country's problems. It caused merchants to monopolize imported goods. It persuaded forestallers to time the market in anticipation of obtaining higher prices. Even when they were not sure about the exact difference between jobbers and speculators, revolutionaries repeatedly insisted that those who practiced extortion valued their own economic welfare more highly than they did liberating the country from British rule. A group in Williamsburg, Virginia, appealed in 1779 to all the freemen of the state to "crush that spirit of extortion."[41] In Massachusetts the Reverend William Gordon advised Americans "if men in this day will not be content with a livelihood, and ill make themselves fortunes, immense fortunes, out of the distress of the people, I say, let the curse of heaven fall upon their substance, their unhallowed gains."[42]

Americans did their best to define extortion. In a sermon aptly entitled *Reflections on Extortion,* the Reverend Abraham Keteltas depicted extortion as a sin "whereby a person who has any thing to sell, taking the advantage of his neighbor's necessity, [and] requires more for it than a reasonable price." Like others who condemned price gouging, Keteltas recognized that establishing a reasonable price might be difficult, raising conflicting and subjective measures of fairness. He solved the problem. "Such a price as is consistent with the various duties incumbent upon us as Christians, as members of society, and as friends to LIBERTY." All one needed to calculate the just price was "conscience," an attribute that many commentators at the time thought had recently gone missing.[43] The Reverend Jonathan French tried to bring clarity to the situation by drafting for the members of his Andover congregation an imagined prayer for extortioners. A person pleased with his ill-gained profits, he thought, might greet each new day with words of praise for selfishness: "I congratulated myself at what I have already accumulated by extorting from others. May my merchandize still prosper, or my husbandry increase: but may scarcity and want still be the fate of my country, and more and more abound."[44] Another man put it more simply: extortion was "exceedingly detrimental to the community."[45]

With so many Americans—most of them supporters of national independence—willing to take advantage of their neighbors, it seemed essential and urgent to restore unity and fairness in the marketplace. Perhaps the most ingenious suggestion for how to reform the economy and save society came in 1779 from a committee "of the city and liberties of Philadelphia." The group addressed their ideas to all their "fellow citizens throughout the United States." The argument put forward recognized that in normal times the various state legislatures were fully capable of devising regulations to discourage extortion. But the country was in the midst of a war. Moreover, economic chaos had encouraged greedy merchants and farmers to come up with fresh and imaginative ways to cheat the public. Like the modern-day hackers who remain one step ahead of regulators, they constantly invented new schemes to manipulate the market. Elected assemblies, focused on the challenge of keeping an army in the field, found that they could not keep up with the ever-changing face of deception. In addition, there was always the unnerving possibility that elected officials might themselves be complicit in the very practices that had put the Revolution at risk. As the committee reported, "It is to those evils, too amphibious to be defined, and too subtle as well as too transitory to become the object of established laws, that we wish to apply a remedy."

Faced with widespread extortion, the Philadelphia group called upon self-constituted committees of concerned citizens to enforce economic fairness. These committees were not intended to replace ordinary government officials. Rather, they would complement constitutional authority, assisting it in identifying guilty parties, and because the citizen committees were not burdened with a need to observe formal, time-consuming legislative procedures, they could keep up with the changing forms of market manipulation. "The ingenuity of men in the invention of new crimes," wrote the Philadelphia committee, "the prostituted ingenuity of others in screening criminality from legal punishment; the additional opportunities which a state of war affords to the subtle, the selfish, and disaffected ... render the revival of committees, during the present war, not only a convenient but a necessary appendage to civil government."

The Philadelphia plan harked back to the country's revolutionary origins. On the eve of independence, when hundreds of extralegal committees had policed the importation of British goods, especially tea, this kind of extreme populist rhetoric might have been viewed as liberating, an appeal to the people to resist oppression. Although no one in 1779 equated regularly elected American representatives with members of Lord North's parliament, there was no question of the radical character of the Philadelphia proposal. The people were encouraged to take over a key function of government, to do so completely and on their own authority. All they had to do was establish a network of committees charged with enforcing market justice and claiming legitimacy solely on the basis of the will of the people. "We hold this maxim," the group proclaimed, "that where the offense is publically dangerous or injurious, and the laws unable to relieve or punish, the community in its own defense, and for its farther security, has a right to expel [profiteers]."

Like so many ideas associated with economic justice in a time of revolution, the guidelines for committee enforcement were vague. The people were certainly expected to do more than police "the laws of a settled and well-regulated society." What then, one might ask, were the limits of popular intervention? "We cannot construct laws that will reach all cases, and therefore, we maintain the right, as well as the necessity, of holding every man accountable to the community for such parts of his conduct by which the public welfare appears to be injured or dishonored, and for which no legal redress can be obtained." The Philadelphia writers assured readers that the formation of a parallel authority possessing enforcement power was only a temporary measure, something necessitated by the challenges of war. After all, "the exertions which are sometimes necessary to be made by the inhabitants of an invaded country, for their own preservation and defense, are frequently of such peculiar and extraordinary quality, that they ought not to become the rule of legal government in times of peace." Whenever it came, peace could restore the normal order. The people could surrender their right to punish extortion. But that moment had to be postponed. "We conceive [the remedy] can be no other than the discretionary power of the citizens organized, and acting through a committee."[46]

Some Americans who had supported the Revolution challenged the claim of the Philadelphia committee to extralegal authority. When a number of local merchants protested that the committee had no right to exercise such seemingly unlimited powers over city residents who were simply trying to avoid bankruptcy, the committee responded with an extraordinary, highly original argument about the relationship between private property and civil responsibility. In September 1779 merchants whose ships were still sailing the Atlantic despite the risks of war submitted a memorial to the committee, which declared among other things that "the limitations of prices is in principle unjust." However serious the economic crisis, the merchants insisted that commercial regulations issued in the name of the people invaded "the laws of property by compelling a person to accept less in exchange for his goods than he could otherwise obtain." The committee ridiculed the argument. What were the merchants demanding? "A right to an unlimited extortion, such as prevailed before the [price] limitations took place?" Was it not "far more unjust" for the merchants to contend that "because the foreign necessaries of life are in the hands of a few" that they alone could set the price for these goods?

The committee did not deny the logic of capitalism. The merchants, it observed, deserved a "reasonable profit," and in normal times the price for imported items would reflect the competing forces of supply and demand. But the war transformed the character of Atlantic commerce. Indeed, the risks and expenses were so great that many Philadelphia merchants had quit the business, leaving foreign trade "in the hands of a few." In a situation like this—one that invited extortion—the people had to protect their own interests. We hold, the committee announced in words that dramatically proclaimed a populist vision of economic justice, "that the social compact or state of civil society, by which men are united and incorporated, requires, that every right or power claimed or exercised by any man or set of men, should be in subordination to the common good, and that whatever is incompatible therewith, must, by some rule or regulation, be brought in subjection thereto." Whatever the costs of doing business, merchants erred in thinking that they could charge as much as they liked for household necessities. They had no right to do so, because "the principles of public justice and common good require it [the profits] to be limited."

The Philadelphia committee then spelled out in detail how the social contract worked in practice. As everyone knew, the occupation of the city by a British army and other severe military reverses had greatly reduced the number of ships engaged in international trade. According to the committee "there was not a vessel, scarcely a boat to be seen in the river." Surviving merchants desperately needed help to restore business. For this, they relied on "the accumulated assistance of the several trades and manufactures concerned in the art of building and fitting out vessels for sea." An impressive list of workers was involved. It included ship carpenters, joiners, blacksmiths, gunsmiths, rope makers, block makers, tanners, curriers, printers, and "laborers of several kinds." Without these human resources the merchants would have had little hope of survival. Why did these workers aid the merchants? What were their expectations? Wages provided part of the answer, but more to the point, they acted from a sense of the importance of reciprocal needs.

Building ships in wartime was fundamentally a community project. Therefore, although the tradesmen had no claim in the property of the vessel, "they and the state in general have a right in the service of the vessel, because it constitutes a considerable part of the advantage they hoped to derive from their labors." The workers and their employers had entered into an implicit agreement "that the property of the vessels is the immediate right of the owner and the service of it the right of the community collectively with the owner." It was that basic understanding of economic relations that gave the committee its undoubted authority to establish a just price for goods. It insisted that the merchants were not really defending the principle of "free trade." To the contrary, they were only defending a "freedom of extorting. That kind of thinking ran counter to the spirit of the Revolution. There was no justification "for every man to do what he pleases." Such arguments were "repugnant to the very principles on which society and civil government are founded."[47]

The economic crisis brought forth new ideas that even today sound extremely radical. It also invited the people to participate in an ongoing conversation about the meaning of the Revolution. Indeed, Americans were imagining a very different political culture from what they had known at the start of the war. About the *where* of the Revolution there can be little doubt. The demand for fair play in the marketplace put the focus of revolutionary resistance once again on communities. Instead of waiting for the market to right itself, the American people turned to local committees to save their revolution.

III

The prospect of restoring fairness to the marketplace electrified revolutionaries. Ordinary citizens came forward and voiced their opinions on prices and wages, showing us not only how during a major crisis people sustained a sense of solidarity, but also how a formerly monarchical political culture transformed itself on the local level into a republican society. A revolution waged in the name of the people had become the people's revolution. About this development one need not consult the texts of state constitutions or writings of republican theorists to appreciate what was happening. People in small communities enthusiastically assumed the responsibility of dealing with issues that affected their well-being.

The effort to eradicate extortion in everyday commercial transactions acquired an almost evangelical character. The challenge reinforced popular commitment to the Revolution itself. Not since the heady days of 1774 and 1775, when hundreds of towns had formed committees providing an infrastructure of resistance, had so many people reached out to other Americans to address a common problem. Once again, communities became revolutionary sites. A Connecticut committee in 1779, for example, gave its full support to other committees in other states and proclaimed its determination "by the blessing of providence and the united efforts of our Fellow Countrymen, to rescue ourselves, our country and posterity, from poverty, misery, and destruction."[48]

The stimulus for a revival of revolutionary spirit was the belief that the people—acting as responsible citizens—had every right to express their opinions about the state of the economy. Gone were the days when Americans deferred to their betters about such matters. The controversy over how to deal with extortion and the unwillingness of some people to accept Continental currency revealed a growing sense of equality—limited, of course, to adult white men—that the revolutionary experience had encouraged throughout the country. An article in the *Pennsylvania Packet* insisted that in a republican society "every right or power claimed by any man or set of men should be in subordination to the common good." To drive home his point, the writer asked readers to consider whether a single self-serving merchant had "a right to exact what prices he pleases." The answer was a resounding "no." Why? Because the people "are free to declare he has no such right." They—and they alone—had a fundamental right to limit extortion.[49] In 1779 a general meeting of the inhabitants of Boston resolved "that is the right of a free people to enquire into all the public and private grievances, and seek proper modes for redress."[50] Investigation into the collapse of the economy required complete transparency. The people would judge who was responsible. According to a piece by Crito in the *New-Jersey Gazette*, "In pursuance of this principle it will be necessary that the said committees inform themselves as minutely as possible of the current prices of all things within their respective States, and the causes of the different prices of the same articles in different places."[51]

Americans were well aware of the sudden surge in the formation of new committees throughout the country. As they had done at the start of the controversy with Great Britain, they read the newspapers, which informed them how other towns were responding to the collapse of the economy. As a writer in the *Connecticut Courant* urged, "REMEMBER that the old spirit of opposition to the Stamp Act, that first originated in Boston and sounded the alarm bell through the Continent, is not yet smothered, but shall soon burst, with unabating vengeance, on the heads of monopolizers, as it did on the odious stamp Masters. By HEAVEN IT SHALL NOT DIE. VOX POPULI."[52] Journal stories of this sort provided information and reinforced the bonds of resistance. A single community, of course, could not have saved Continental currency or stayed the flood of extortion. But if others cooperated—if national unity still meant something—then it might be possible to restore justice and patriotism in the marketplace.

The broad reach of a newly empowered press helped sustain the Revolution by assuring local committees that they were not acting on their own. An announcement of an approaching meeting of "the Committees of Inspection of the several Towns in the County of Hartford," for example, explained that it would "consider of the Doings of the Committees of Philadelphia, Boston, etc. And of the Address of the Committee of Philadelphia to all the Committees and inhabitants of the several States, respecting the lowering the Prices of Goods and the Necessaries of Life, preventing Monopolizing, and using our joint Interest to appreciate the Currency."[53] A similar gathering in New London, Connecticut, gave approval to "the rising Spirit in the City of Philadelphia, against the enormous Growth of Monopoly and Oppression, and that we will cooperate with the other Towns in this State in every Measure to remedy that growing Evil."[54]

As one might expect, some communities kept more complete records of their activities than did others. Some towns simply noted that they were trying as best they could to deal with the problem of runaway inflation and commercial practices that betrayed the common good. What is significant for understanding how people sustained the revolutionary process is the number of communities that publicly announced their support for economic patriotism. The figure—scores of towns throughout the country—provides a rough measure of revolutionary participation. Williamsburg, Virginia, left a detailed record of its efforts to restore market fairness. This community, of course, had a history of resistance dating back to Patrick Henry's celebrated seizure in 1775 of gunpowder then under control of the colony's last royal governor. By 1779 the political landscape had changed. The challenge was how best to revive the economy. On July 14 an appeal went out to area residents calling for the formation of a committee capable of dealing with a plague of "monopolizers, forestallers, and engrossers" (the latter were traders who purchased large quantities of goods in order to limit the supply and thereby to raise the price) as well as addressing "the avarice and extortion of individuals." The notice reminded the inhabitants of Williamsburg that now, more than ever, the crisis required "the timely and spirited exertions of the independent and patriotick friends to their country."

Why had a revolution that began with such high expectations gone so badly off course? In answering this question, the authors of Williamsburg's newspaper provided a summary view of the nation's recent history. At the beginning of the conflict with Great Britain, the Americans had faced not only "a very powerful and well appointed enemy," but also "traitors nursed in the bosom of their own country." The revolutionaries had performed well over four years—better than one might have anticipated—but after the nation proved that it could hold its own on the battlefield, it found that it had to deal with an even more insidious foe.

These new enemies aimed at nothing less than the destruction of the financial integrity of the United States. They had done so by encouraging a "spirit of extortion." The only hope to remedy the situation was the immediate creation of "a committee of fifteen freeholders ... chosen by the inhabitants of the city who shall be called a committee of inspection and observation, the majority of whom shall have power to act. The duty of which committee shall be to inspect the conduct of the inhabitants of this city, and enforce obedience to such resolutions as from time to time shall be agreed on by the general town meeting." The statement drew authority from an implicit association with the country's first revolutionary resistance, with committees that had initially enforced a boycott of imported goods. The organizers of the Williamsburg effort pledged that its committee would communicate with other committees and would work to expose "to the publick" anyone who violated its regulations "as inimical to the rights and liberties of America." And somewhat ominously, the members insisted that their aggressive efforts to crush extortion posed no threat to the public, since "the virtues of the people at large can easily redress what the laws cannot reach."[55]

The people of Albany, New York, joined the wave of popular enthusiasm that renewed the revolutionary spirit. On June 21, 1779—in other words, about the same time that committees met in Williamsburg and Philadelphia—"a great majority of the citizens of Albany assembled at the market house of this city." They immediately nominated men to serve on a committee of observation for the purpose of "taking into consideration and adopting measures to check the evils arising from the depreciation of the Continental currency; to prevent monopolies; to reduce the exorbitant prices exacted for the necessaries of life; and to restrain a variety of other abuses and imposition." Soon after the members of the committee held their first session to set prices, they dispatched a letter to the communities surrounding Albany to urge their cooperation. The "calamities the country labors under" were immense. The entire revolution was in peril. What had caused this dire situation was not in doubt. The list included an "infamous spirit of monopolization," the spread of extortion "which disgraces human nature, grinds the faces of the poor, the widows and the fatherless," and the many enemy agents who schemed at subjecting Americans "to the tyranny of Britain."

The challenge of regaining control over the economy seemed almost overwhelming. Like the Philadelphia committee, the Albany group concluded that the laws on the books could not possibly solve the problem. Elected officials deserved no blame. After all, "it was not possible for a virtuous and wise legislature to foresee, that evils of such fatal and destructive tendency would arise, and that therefore no adequate provision to prevent or cure them is or could be made by regular laws." Although the committee spoke in the name of the people—its source of authority—it assured the residents of the nearby communities that it did not sanction "anarchy or confusion." Still, formal law did not limit its powers. The committee declared that it had a right "to deviate from the strict line of law . . . where a close adherence would render it incapable of answering the great ends of its appointment." Perhaps a little defensive about such broad claims to extralegal authority, the men selected to serve on the Albany committee assured everyone that its efforts to establish economic justice had received "unparalleled unanimity . . . [from] the citizens of every rank."[56]

A group in Middlesex, New Jersey, responded to the spread of extortion by forming a "Society of Whigs." Claiming that the members acted out of patriotism, this body—really a committee by a different name—described themselves as "a number of gentlemen of this county, the firm friends of the present revolution in America" who could no longer endure "the embarrassment of our public affairs, through the ill state of our paper currency and the numerous attempts of our internal enemies." There was no time to wait. The situation demanded that people gravely concerned about the country's future organize "to defeat the designs of these traitors." To join the Society of Whigs one had to sign a pledge consisting of several

parts, a public procedure which if nothing else helped to distinguish genuine revolutionaries from neighbors who probably only wanted to keep
their political options open. Unlike the committees in Williamsburg and
Albany, the New Jersey gentlemen insisted that their major goal was supporting the established government. They downplayed the notion that
they possessed extralegal powers derived directly from the people. Nevertheless, members promised "to detect and prosecute such traitorous inhabitants of this State as shall openly condemn and violate its salutary laws."
Those who wanted to participate—men of "known character and sound
principles"—were also expected "to support and strengthen the executive
authority in the execution of the laws, and to assist them in calling out the
force and the supplies of the state against our enemies."[57]

Other New Jersey communities joined the expanding effort to save the
nation's economy. Burlington County selected a committee charged not
only with setting the prices for basic goods, but also with enforcing these
regulations. Soon after its creation during the summer of 1779, it warned
local residents "that if any person or persons within the jurisdiction of this
committee shall either give or receive more for their merchandize, produce,
labor, &c. than is fixed by this Committee, and being thereof duly convicted, they shall be held up to the publick in a manner adequate to their
offense." What exposure involved in practice was left unstated. There was
no doubt, however, that it would have been unwise to ignore the committee's ruling. Its members declared that they would keep "a watchful eye on
all persons within their jurisdiction" to make certain that none of their
resolutions were violated. And then, in a declaration that seemed especially menacing for an extralegal group that insisted it wanted "to support
and strengthen the civil authority," it invited "the gentlemen officers of the
militia ... [to] give their assistance."

In addition to helping the government establish fair market practices,
the Burlington committee enlarged its mandate far beyond the oversight
of local trade. "We will consider it as our duty," it announced in a newspaper, to help regularly elected officials "in detecting and bringing to deserved punishment all such as are guilty of profanity, immorality, extrava-
gance and dissipation; or extortion and oppression, and all such practices
as tend to the unjust advantage of individuals, and injury of the community."[58] Even outside New England, where Puritan traditions were still
strong, people believed that moral reform and economic justice went hand

in hand. At about the same time a committee of twelve men in Somerset, New Jersey, passed a series of resolutions designed to stop "the train of calamities which the rapid and unnatural depreciation of our currency has brought upon us."[59] The inhabitants of the North Ward of New Brunswick "unanimously agreed" that they would immediately "exert themselves to the utmost of their power" in an attempt to bring down prices and uphold the value of the Continental currency.[60]

The various committees took on a very difficult assignment, perhaps far more complex than they had initially anticipated. Still, their energy was impressive. Establishing the fair price for goods and labor required the collection of detailed information not only about the state of the current market, but also about commercial practices that had been in place before the war. A writer in a New Jersey newspaper advised revolutionaries that if they were serious about price and wage controls, they had no time to lose. "In pursuance of this principle," he observed, "it will be necessary that the said committees inform themselves as minutely as possible of the current prices of all things within their respective States, and of the causes of the different prices of the same articles in different places—whether these are owing to a real scarcity to the expense of carriage, or to a spirit of monopoly and extortion."[61] At first, no one seems to have viewed evaluating the price of "all things" in all places as a near-impossible goal.

As one might expect, communities in Massachusetts kept the fullest records of their activities. In an effort to combat "Monopoly and Oppression," the town of Newburyport published a broadside listing scores of items. These figures probably reflected long and tedious meetings in which residents argued exactly what it meant to set prices "according to the Usages and Customs which [had] been practices in said Town." No doubt, they relied on personal memory—always a problematic source of information. The members of the committee discussed the fair price for such things as cheese "manufactured in America," "Turkeys, Dunghill Fowls, and Ducks, to be sold by the pound," "Liver Oil, by the barrel," and "DINNERS at Taverns, of boiled and roast meat . . . exclusive of wine." They established the proper wages for carpenters, joiners, caulkers, barbers, masons, and "Day Labourers."[62]

The "Inhabitants of Salem" put together an even more exhaustive list. The town assigned the task of setting prices to a committee of nineteen men. The assignment strained the group's abilities to the limit. They intended to publish as soon as possible a full price and wage list that could be circulated in published form among local residents. Buyers and sellers would then know the local rules governing the market. Much like the Newburyport committee, the Salem regulators set prices for scores of items. The alphabetical list began with "Ale-Wives, and Herrings, per Barrel, the same Price as in Boston." Residents could not charge more than three dollars per week for "Boarding, and Lodging (Common)." The prices for coffee and chocolate, oats and rum, tea and turnips were published, as were the wages for carpenters, shoemakers, blacksmiths, and card makers. Few activities escaped the committee's inquiry. One curious entry stands out: "Sexton—For digging a Grave for a grown Person, usual Attendance on the Funeral, and tolling the Bell, 9 [shillings]—For the Use of the Pall, 3s.—Under-Bearers, at 3s each." At the beginning of the war, the members of this committee could not have imagined that sustaining the Revolution would involve regulating the wages of pallbearers. As was the case with the boycott of tea and other British imports in 1774 and 1775, the published lists were a declaration that the personal and private in everyday life were again becoming political, visible expressions of revolutionary commitment.

No matter how hard the Salem group worked, it quickly discovered that it could not keep up with how the local market actually worked. Prices changed too rapidly; people disagreed on what constituted a just price. The challenge was almost too much for the committee, and it understandably announced in a broadside distributed on September 6, 1779, that because "all regulations of all articles cannot [be established] with the utmost Precision, or brought into an exact Proportion with each other, Indulgence must be made." One wonders to whom this appeal was directed: to local families desperate to obtain basic household commodities? To sellers who knew that inflation would soon raise the price for goods?

However imperfect the final regulations may have been, the committee insisted that the pressing need to bring wages and prices under control excused whatever errors it may have made. It promised to listen to every complaint and avoid "all Suspicion or Surmise of general or particular Partiality." Although well intended, the price list left too much to individual prudence. What was one to do if one wanted to sell something that did not appear on the official list? The committee advised discretion. It informed people who had things to buy or sell to gauge as best they could a just price by analyzing the prices of publicly listed goods and then on their own to lower asking prices to correspond to reductions on the items appearing on the official broadside. The whole system generated uncertainty. The demands of economic patriotism remained elusive. "As it is impossible to ascertain the specific Value" of various goods, the committee concluded, "so as to bring them to an exact Proportion to other Articles more easily estimated, it is recommended that the Seller proportion his Price to the known Reduction of the Prices of other Goods, as a Means not only to preserve his Character to peaceable Times, but also to remove all Jealousies and Apprehensions of an unequal or partial Accumulation of what will be esteemed unjust wealth."[63]

Revolutionary committees soon discovered that however determined they were to save the nation's currency and bring justice to the marketplace, they could not on their own control prices and wages. Commerce recognized no boundaries, certainly not local ones.[64] Someone unhappy with regulations passed by one town such as Salem or Newburyport could simply take country produce or European imports to the next village, where people might willingly pay higher prices to obtain what they needed. Cooperation was essential to success. As the representatives to a "Convention of New England and New York" concluded, "there is great reason to apprehend that the good and salutary purposes of such a measure [setting prices] will soon prove abortive unless other States, more especially those who are contiguous to them immediately pursue similar measures."[65] It was a situation similar to what modern countries throughout the world face with the globalization of trade.

The committees responded by cooperating with other committees, usually by supporting county or statewide initiatives intended to discourage extortion. During the summer of 1779, for example, representatives from 121 Massachusetts towns gathered at Concord to devise more effective ways to halt the continuous rise in prices. The delegates immediately went to work setting prices on items such as salt, sugar, and coffee. These figures, the convention noted, should "be considered as the highest prices, at which produce and merchandize, of the best quality, are to be sold." Anyone demanding more money for these goods "shall be held and deemed as enemies to this country, and treated as such." The first Concord meeting apparently did not yield the positive results the delegates had hoped for.[66] A second meeting in October endorsed many of the same re-solves that had passed during the earlier convention, a sign that for one reason or another, economic conditions in the state were not improving.[67] Similar meetings occurred in Plymouth, Suffolk, and Middlesex. The Plymouth convention condemned the "extraordinary lust for gain," which the delegates claimed would "astonish all future generations, and give a vi-cious cast to [our] noblest achievements."[68] A convention of towns in Worcester County condemned "monopoly and oppression" and declared that they would expose the enemies of the United States "whose diabolical business it is to destroy the peace and unity of the people."[69] There were calls for regional meetings of town committees in New Hampshire, Rhode Island, Connecticut, and New York.[70]

No community effort to revive the Continental currency or to eradi-cate the desire to maximize profits—even if it came at the expense of vul-nerable neighbors—seems to have made the slightest difference in how Americans behaved in the marketplace. The problem was not that they had lost faith in independence nor that they endorsed the idea that one should be allowed to maximize profits. The major problem in achieving universal compliance was basic human nature. With families to clothe and feed, people made compromises, torn as they were between their public obligation to support price and wage controls and their need to survive the war. At the start of the conflict with Great Britain forgoing drinking tea was a relatively small sacrifice to make in the name of revolutionary soli-darity. But after 1778, the Revolution demanded more from the people. Local appeals for a thoroughly radical reformation of economic behav-ior—the total condemnation of avarice—were as unrealistic as were earlier Puritan attempts to eliminate sin. People bought and sold what they needed, perhaps embarrassed and hoping to avoid exposure, and grumbled that some Americans continued to see the Revolution as an opportunity to increase their personal wealth.

The committees suffered from another serious disadvantage. However strident their rhetoric, they lacked the resources that broader enforcement would have required. Because of their ambivalent claims to authority—on the one hand, they spoke as the legitimate voice of popular resistance, while on the other, they insisted that they only intended to provide addi-tional support to regular state officials—they had few ways to punish oppressors and extorters. Placing offenders in jail was not an option. Instead, the committees threatened to shame fellow citizens who had driven hard bargains by publishing their names in newspapers.[71] The inhabitants of Roxbury, Massachusetts, declared that anyone ignoring the prices set by committee "shall receive the severest of all temporal punishments, the displeasure and contempt of the people—and upon conviction of a second offense before said committee shall have his name published in the several Boston newspapers ... as a pest of society, and unworthy [of] the confidence and esteem of all mankind."[72] Other revolutionary groups argued that known extortioners should be shunned, and thereby "be cut off from all intercourse and dealings with the other inhabitants of the town for such a term of time as the committee of inspection should appoint."[73]

At no time did any community, even those frustrated by the economic situation, turn to physical coercion. Committees exercised remarkable constraint. The newspapers of the period contain only a handful of cases in which the people accused of economic crimes were named, and these were ordinary traders, not major merchants or members of leading families.[74] What, then, was the enforcement role of these committees? A piece in the *Connecticut Journal* entitled "The Honest Farmer's Political Creed, and Resolution" saw no need for committee intervention. Voluntary good behavior in the marketplace, he thought, would be sufficient to discourage selfish practices. "If any of our neighbors," explained this writer, hold back the goods "which they have to sell in order to raise the price, [so] as to force the laws to give way, and so to become of none effect," counter measures would be devised. By publicly advertising other sources of goods for sale at a lower price, honest traders would assure buyers "that a pretended scarcity may not be made use of, to set aside the law, and let in high prices and ruin upon the country like a flood."[75] In clearer prose the Concord Convention simply recommended "Christian equity and benevolence."[76]

Why, revolutionaries asked, did such a widespread appeal for economic reform achieve so little? Had Americans failed to understand the relation between commercial justice and patriotism? No doubt, some merchants cheated, moving goods from place to place in order to avoid local regulations.[77] There was more to the question. A meeting of "the Committees of Safety, &c., from a great majority of the towns in the county of Worcester" provided a candid answer. Not surprisingly, people were reluctant to inform on their neighbors. The Revolution counted for a lot, to be sure, but their network of friends and relatives—those they dealt with every day—counted for more. Unlike the Tories, who had posed a possible physical threat, the people who ignored price and wage guidelines did not reject the American cause, or at least, they would have denied doing so. As the Worcester committees explained, "The well disposed people have desired and wished for a reformation [of selfish economic behavior] from a conviction of the offender's own conscience, and were loth to expose his name, for the first offense." There was something more going on than faith in the ability of good people to change their ways. Even though they were urged to watch closely the dealings of other residents of their communities, they refused to come forward because "the offender is an acquaintance, an intimate friend, a neighbor, a relation, or a gentleman, whom they are loth to offend."[78]

The young republic's great fiscal crisis—a threat to the Revolution that dominated public attention for at least three years—ended with a whimper. Congress decided to stop printing money, thus addressing, albeit belatedly, the flood of unsecured paper currency that had sparked double-digit inflation. The states took over the obligation of paying for their own war debts. Some were more responsible than others, but taxation at the state level began to remove a lot of worthless Continental currency from circulation. Prosperity did not return, nor would it for many years.

IV

How Americans addressed the currency crisis raises a larger point. It is a story that invites us to re-evaluate what we think we know about our political origins. Indeed, it challenges us to revise basic assumptions about the character of revolutionary experience. By focusing on community mobilization, rather than on battles and congressional acts, we encounter an unfamiliar cast of characters. These are ordinary Americans who at a critical moment in our country's history sustained a common cause and energized a new political culture. They were the true founders. That claim does not mean that we should discount the accomplishments of celebrated generals and statesmen. Nevertheless, by awarding the people an expanded role in the revolutionary story we transform the history of revolution. Although the people have usually been assigned relatively minor parts—as spectators of events rather than as significant actors—they now speak to us with an independent voice.

No doubt, some persons at the time viewed the collection of price and wage data and discussion of commercial regulations not only as a misguided effort, but also as a colossal waste of time. Critics insisted that the market would eventually take care of itself. They said that meddling with the imperatives of supply and demand—however severely the public may have suffered—would only serve to deprive hard-working farmers and risk-taking merchants of their rightful returns. Moral considerations played no part in the calculus of gains and losses.

However persuasive such arguments may have been, they are largely irrelevant to our interpretation of how Americans actually confronted a problem that threatened revolutionary solidarity. Faced with economic collapse, they revived a committee system that had initially sparked popular resistance to Great Britain. After 1778 a huge number of people unexpectedly spoke up, protested special privilege, and served on committees that gathered information. They may have been unable to control inflation or save the Continental currency, but their activism—their confidence that their own efforts mattered—helped greatly to sustain the Revolution at a moment when the prospect of military victory seemed uncertain. Participation of this sort should not be taken for granted. Civil society demands that citizens give public voice to their most pressing concerns. That is exactly what Americans did at a key moment in the development of a new republican political culture.

It is also significant that Americans perceived their communities as the appropriate sites for revolutionary conversations. Rising wages and prices were not abstract or theoretical issues. They were topics that involved neighbors, in other words people with names and histories who happened to be carpenters, or joiners, or gravediggers. Self-serving economic behavior—or misbehavior—mattered only insomuch as it affected the fabric of daily life. It was on this level that the state of the local economy became political. It was here as well that an economic crisis merged with assumptions about a moral order. People condemned extortion not simply because it brought suffering to vulnerable Americans, but also because it was fundamentally unjust. Extreme self-interest violated assumptions about mutual trust and responsibility. Laws that excused or encouraged avarice had no legitimacy in this revolutionary environment. As a writer in a Pennsylvania newspaper explained, "There are crimes at this time actually existing, which are not declared so by any other laws than those of Heaven, necessity and justice. Laws which are antecedent to all social laws, eternal and immutable in themselves, and of course, superior to all others in their moral obligation."[79] This author might have cited John Locke's *Second Treatise* to bolster his point. But there was no need. The people understood the relation between rights and responsibility.

A chronicle of committee experience reminds us that however enthusiastically these groups defended the right of the people to intervene directly in political affairs, they expressed uneasiness about going too far, about inviting anarchy or mob rule when the fundamental goal was persuading honest people to accept a just price for their goods and services. As we have seen in the discussion of other stages of revolution—in the administration of revolutionary justice, for example—communities struggled to establish a balance between compliance and mercy, between rules and punishment. Some people whose privileges were called into question probably resented the actions of local committees and wished that constitutionally elected or appointed leaders would find ways to curb popular attempts to regulate the economy. The complacent farmer in *The Downfall of Justice* would have taken that position. But such things are matters of personal judgment. It has always been tempting to label calls for social justice as extreme or irresponsible.

Sacrifice for the common cause was not an obligation reserved only for the poor, or for those on fixed salaries, or for soldiers on contract, or for those Americans who relied on farmers and merchants to supply household goods at a just price. As the author of "The Honest Farmer's Political Creed" insisted, "In every instance in which the laws of the land do not provide effectually to prevent injustice, we will with more care, of our own accord, do the thing that is right, that no man may be wronged, by the prices of labor and country produce being higher than they used to be before the present war."[80] Fairness was the goal. Revolutionaries called it patriotism.

CHAPTER SIX

REVENGE

Revolutions generally end badly. Whatever their original goals, people who have endured years of sacrifice for a cause that promised liberation from an oppressive regime often discover that armistice introduces chronic political instability. In these situations appeals for unity give way to coups and countercoups, and constitutions are rewritten to support the agenda of whoever happens to hold power.

The American Revolution provides an exception to this dreary narrative. This is not something we should take for granted. It was a close call. The achievement goes missing from our accounts of the Revolution largely because we commonly focus attention on the early days of rebellion—especially on the dramatic events leading up to the Declaration of Independence—while failing to give much thought to what may have been an even more impressive accomplishment: the peaceful return of thousands of former domestic enemies—known at the time as refugees—into the very communities that they had terrorized only a few years before. What made the revolutionary settlement all the more remarkable was that a desire for retaliation ran very deep, potentially poisoning postwar society at the moment of triumph. There is no question that if ordinary Americans had given license to anger and hate, the Founders could not have saved the Revolution.

We do not often think of the American Revolution in these terms. We celebrate abstract principles—freedom and liberty—while ignoring how men and women perceived a war in which they lost friends and relatives as well as property. But revenge was always part of the story. At the beginning of the contest with Great Britain, Thomas Paine observed how the experience of violence encouraged deep resentment. It festered. *Common Sense* assured Americans that they had every right to be angry, very angry, so angry in fact that they need not have second thoughts about the desire to get even. Before trying to forgive a cruel enemy, he wrote, revolutionaries should "examine the passions and feelings of mankind." "Hath your property been destroyed before your face?" Paine asked. "Are your wife and children destitute of a bed to lie on, or bread to live on? Have you lost a parent or a child by their hands, and yourself the ruined and wretched survivor?" If a person could endure this and still counsel reconciliation, "then, you are unworthy the name of husband, father, friend, or lover, and whatever may be your rank and title in life, you have the heart of a coward."[1]

A demand for revenge swept through the country during the last days of the Revolution. As early as the Battle of Yorktown, people began discussing the fate of the refugees, the thousands of loyalists who had fled their homes during the war to areas under the control of the British Army. Revolutionaries wondered how these enemies could possibly return to their former communities. The refugee crisis came to a head in 1783, when details of the peace treaty first circulated throughout the country. The agreement contained specific provisions, protecting most Tories from prosecution by the government of the United States for what many Americans saw as war crimes.

Although national leaders praised the treaty, people in large numbers throughout the country insisted that the refugees could not—indeed, should not—ever expect former neighbors who had sacrificed so much during the conflict to allow them to return. This was a moment when Americans clearly and strongly disagreed with congressional and state political leaders whose writings have long dominated our understanding of the Revolution. The outpouring of public hostility was unprecedented. On the refugee question compromise seemed impossible.

The bloodbath that one might have predicted did not occur. The American Revolution could have ended—as most revolutions have done—with spasms of political instability or with irreconcilables sponsoring continued violence. At the time—especially during 1783—informed commentators were certain that peaceful settlement between the refugees and those who had fought for independence was an unlikely prospect. Sir Guy Carleton, commander of British forces, warned that the Tories still living in New York City should expect retaliation. "Civil dissentions have been so heightened by the blood that has been shed in the contest," he observed, "that the parties can never be reconciled."[2]

Carleton misread the political landscape. Achieving a genuine peace on the ground—however bitter the memories may have been—was a remarkable occurrence. Comparisons come to mind. After more than a century

Americans are still arguing about issues that brought on the Civil War. The French and Irish Revolutions—just to cite two well-known examples— ended violently. None of this happened in the newly independent United States. Cries for revenge quickly died away, and people who had suffered severely during the war focused on rebuilding their lives.

The great refugee debate stirred the greatest passion at the community level. It was here—as we have seen before—where Americans gave voice to their pain and then, after long discussions with neighbors and family members in town meetings, arrived at their own understanding of how best to end a long war and address the future of a new republic. At a time when political hostilities again threaten to destroy the fabric of civil society, the revolutionaries remind us how to resolve even the most divisive issues.

I

Although the Revolutionaries had reportedly tried to restrain violence on the community level throughout the war, they found the final reconciliation with former domestic enemies very difficult. To appreciate more fully the widespread temptation to seek revenge, we might examine an extraordinary incident when things really did go bad. The story involves a South Carolina judge and a thoroughly objectionable person with the unlikely name of Matthew Love. It is important to reconstruct the local context. The Revolution came late to the South. After failing to destroy George Washington's army in the middle states, British leaders in London welcomed intelligence that suggested that loyalist support for the Crown was much greater in the South than in any other region.[3] Although the accuracy of the information was suspect, the British organized an entire southern campaign based on the belief that once a large military force was in place, the loyalists would rise up and sweep the revolutionaries from the area.

Like so many military plans that sound much better in distant capitals than they do on the ground where the fighting takes place, the southern strategy did not work. Local loyalists attacked revolutionaries with a ferocity that shocked both American and British commanders. Instead of helping to pacify South Carolina and Georgia, loosely organized groups of Tories looted and killed, introducing mayhem throughout the countryside.

These actions provided justification for the revolutionaries to use the same tactics. The level of violence—neighbors attacking neighbors—horrified General Nathaniel Greene, the commanding officer of the Continental Army in the area. He lamented that the "Whigs and Tories pursue each other with as much relentless fury as beasts of prey." The prospect of plunder, he concluded, had "so corrupted the Principles of the People that they think of nothing but plundering one another."[4]

In a society riven by murder and destruction Matthew Love gained a reputation for extreme cruelty. At some moment during the war, he joined a gang of Tories organized by the infamous William "Blood Bill" Cunningham. At the start of the conflict Cunningham backed the revolutionaries, but when he failed to receive a promotion he felt he deserved, he changed allegiance. By 1780 he had recruited a number of Tories who carried out guerrilla operations along the border between South Carolina and Georgia. When Cunningham learned that a group of revolutionaries had tortured and killed a relative, he raised the level of violence by killing large numbers of men who tried to surrender. He was responsible for several massacres that took place in 1781. South Carolinians who fought for independence considered Cunningham the most despicable figure in the state.

Love may have met Cunningham in Ninety Six, a small upland community that was the scene of several battles during the Revolution. Love was born in Ireland, but little else about his early life is known. What is certain, however, is that he participated enthusiastically in atrocities carried out by Cunningham's followers, described as a group comprising "about 150 white men & Negroes." According to a letter written in 1784 by Aedanus Burke, a prominent political figure in South Carolina and immigrant from Galway, Ireland, Love had taken a major part in several massacres of American revolutionaries. "A man by the name of Love, who had dwelt in the district before & since the war & married there, was one of Cunningham's party, & a principle actors in this tragical business," Burke reported. Witnesses claimed that Love personally killed wounded revolutionaries.[5]

The victims were undoubtedly people Love had known in Ninety Six. Burke learned that after one engagement, "Love traversed the ground, where lay the dead and dying, his former neighbors and acquaintances, and as he saw signs of life in any of them, he ran his sword through and dispatched them. Those already dead, he stabbed again." With good reason Burke concluded that Love "was thenceforth held in universal execration."

What happened next must have surprised everyone. When the war ended, instead of taking refuge in Florida—as Cunningham had done—Love returned to Ninety Six, assuming that the community would forgive him. He brazenly announced that however he had behaved during the conflict, the peace treaty with Great Britain prohibited authorities from prosecuting him. Worried that Love's argument might have validity, local officials immediately locked him in jail and waited for a state judge to determine the prisoner's fate.[6]

The responsibility fell to Burke, then riding circuit for the newly re-established South Carolina court. Anyone familiar with state politics would have known that Burke was favorably disposed to allowing former loyalists to return to civil society. But, of course, Love presented a special case. Few Tories had committed such horrific war crimes. As was the custom at the time, Burke addressed potential grand jurors from the bench. He felt obliged to explain in terms the public could understand the legal basis for Love's appeal. An audience of townspeople closely followed the proceedings. Burke observed that the spectators included "fathers, sons, brothers, and friends of the slain prisoners."[7]

In an impressive statement Burke worked out the logic of the situation. He began by comparing the United States at the end of a long and difficult war to European nations where genuine peace was much harder to achieve. "In Europe," Burke explained, "after a war, foreign or domestic, and peace restored; the contending parties, the offended and offending live in vicinity; and this not only keeps alive the memory of old wrongs, but gives occasion for new ones: so that a treaty of peace does not always produce real peace and tranquility." American conditions were different. After all, the old enemy—Great Britain—was three thousand miles away from South Carolina and "nearer we have no foes, unless we ourselves should make them by our internal dissentions." Burke conveniently overlooked the fact that while the British Army had departed, many hateful characters such as Love remained. Deeply disturbing memories lingered in Ninety Six.[8]

As Burke reminded the jurors, a dangerous "spirit of revenge" had spread throughout the region. It eroded trust. It retarded the establishment of a genuine civil society. The war had to end. Although the violence seemed to have stopped, Burke warned that at any moment a retaliatory act could spark a fresh round of murder and destruction. Drawing upon his considerable rhetorical skill, Burke explained that "although that boisterous tempest of the passions is now repressed, and everything round us seems tranquil and quiet, yet we fear that without a very forceful exertion of the judicial authority, the high temper of men will for some time, like the waves of the sea, after the storm has ceased, continue to move with mischievous tumult and impetuosity."

Raw emotion was the problem. Unless tempered by "the whole power of government," people would give in to anger and hate. In words as relevant throughout the modern world as they were for Ninety Six, Burke depicted a contagion of violence: "Our citizens from a habit of putting enemies to death, have reconciled their minds to the killing of each other; and it is too true, I fear, that many by custom, may be so brutalized, as to relish human blood the more he has shed of it." Even more strongly, he insisted, "Private revenge may be truly called the demon of civil discord, and should be banished from the land as if were a pestilence."[9]

Burke then declared that although Love behaved wickedly during the war, the prisoner could not be punished under current South Carolina law. The peace treaty prohibited state courts or individuals from retaliating for wrongs occurring before 1783. The people of Ninety Six may not have wanted to hear this decision, but however disappointed, they had to realize that Congress had addressed the refugee problem. The law was the law. Burke worried that the people attending the court proceedings might not accept his ruling. But in fact they seemed remarkably calm. As he recalled, "there was no appearance, no look of disapprobation directed against a man so generally detested: all seemed reconciled, & the Court immediately adjourned." A group of respected community leaders attended the judge, making sure that he arrived safely at his lodgings.

After they had wished Burke a good night, a party of citizens described "as respectable for Services & good Character as any in the district" returned to the jail. Taking care to avoid making noise that might disturb the judge, they released Love, forced him to mount a horse, and rode to a nearby woods. The group halted "under the limb of a tree, to which they tied one end of a rope, with the other round his neck, & bid him prepare to die; he urging them in vain the injustice of killing a man without trial, & they reminding him, that he should have thought of that, when he was slaughtering their kinsmen."

The point of the story is that Love's fate was unusual. It shows us that the American Revolution could have ended on a bloodier note. It was certainly possible for Love's death to have provoked a new round of violence in South Carolina. Nothing of that sort occurred. The people of Ninety Six re-established normal routines without visible signs of anger. Burke seemed surprised how quickly citizens of "good character" were able to overcome unpleasant memories. In a report to the governor of South Carolina written a year later, he noted, "The people of Ninety Six wish ardently to forget the injuries of the War, provided those do not return among them, that have committed wanton acts of barbarity. Many plunderers and other mischievous people now set down among them without molestation; nor can I learn that there exists resentment against any man who acted like a Soldier & fought them in fair open action." Burke blamed Love for what had taken place. After all, he had provoked the fury of the community by returning home. The lynching could have been avoided if only he had moved away.[10] Although this may have been a case of blaming the victim, the entire episode reflected what was occurring in less dramatic fashion in other regions throughout the country.

II

Historians have long known that a large number of loyalists left the United States at the end of the war. How many Americans actually moved to Canada, England, or the Caribbean Islands cannot be ascertained with precision. The figure was probably about 60,000, an impressive total since in comparative terms it was greater than the number of people who left France during a much more violent revolution.[11] What often escapes notice is that a much bigger group of British supporters elected to remain in the country. Again, the records are problematic, but a reasonable estimate suggests that the number may have been as high as 400,000. Since the total population of the United States was about 2,500,000—a number that includes about 250,000 African American slaves—we can begin to understand why the refugee crisis seemed so threatening to the stability of the new republic.

Although a group of loyalists moved to England early in the war, far more moved to occupied cities such as New York, Charleston, or Newport.[12]

One can only speculate why so many disaffected people decided to stay. Some may have reasoned that since they had not taken up arms during the conflict or provided military intelligence to the enemy, they had no need to fear retaliation for their allegiance to the Crown. Other domestic exiles had engaged in wartime commerce—smuggling goods into occupied zones, for example—and may have thought that their actions would be forgiven or perhaps just overlooked. Some, of course, had sincerely believed in the superiority of the imperial system, but with the prospect of peace, they accommodated to the new government. On the personal level motivation in such matters remains a mystery.

The possibility that so many refugees might remain became a slowly increasing concern for revolutionaries. Although General Cornwallis's surrender at Yorktown in 1781 signaled that the war would soon be over, Americans had no idea how long it would take to negotiate a final treaty guaranteeing independence. Only after military operations had been suspended—after people began to look forward to the restoration of peace—did revolutionaries appreciate fully that the refugees posed a serious obstacle to the stability of postwar society. Initially, newspaper writers did not speak of revenge. A few writers grumbled about disloyalty and desertion, but in these pages one encounters little evidence before the summer of 1783 that the issue had the capacity to spark a major political crisis, one that could put at risk the entire revolutionary settlement. When the wave of discontent broke, Americans once again redefined patriotism, this time in terms of rejecting the refugees.

Murmuring apprehension exploded into open hostility as soon as the nation's journals published the full text of the peace treaty. The main points were not in dispute. The country's leaders celebrated the moment as a great diplomatic success. They were correct. Benjamin Franklin and his colleagues persuaded the British not only to guarantee the sovereignty of the United States but also to cede to the United States most of the land east of the Mississippi River.[13]

While people welcomed these concessions, they expressed utter shock at provisions in the treaty that seemed to protect from punishment those Americans who had supported the Crown during the war. Articles 5 and 6, in particular, triggered a huge negative reaction.

ARTICLE 5th. It is agreed that the Congress shall earnestly recommend to the Legislatures of the respective States to provide for the Restitution of all Estates, Rights and Properties ... of Persons resident in Districts in the Possession of his Majesty's Arms, and who have not borne Arms against the said United States. And that Persons of any other Description shall have free Liberty to go to any Part or Parts of any of the thirteen United States and therein remain twelve Months unmolested in their Endeavours to obtain the Restitution of such of their Estates, Rights, & Properties as may have been confiscated ...

ARTICLE 6th. That there shall be no future Confiscations made, nor any Prosecutions commenced against any Person or Persons for or by Reason of the Part which he or they may have taken in the present War and that no Person shall on that Account suffer any future Loss or Damage either in his Person, Liberty or Property; and that those who may be in Confinement on such Charges at the Time of the Ratification of the Treaty in America shall be immediately set at Liberty, and the Prosecutions so commenc'd be discontinued.[14]

It is no wonder that enemies of the Revolution such as Matthew Love concluded that they could resume their former lives without penalty. The negotiators appeared to allow the return of confiscated loyalist property. It seemed as if those Americans who had deserted their own country in a time of need might at worst experience the insults of former neighbors, but they could now claim that the law was on their side.

The two surprising articles provoked an immediate and angry response. It is significant that the most vituperative rhetoric came not from leading state and national figures—men who sat in legislatures, for example—but from people who had sacrificed so much to secure independence. National leaders tended to be accommodating. The discontent boiled up from communities. It was here that revolutionaries interpreted the peace through the lens of local experience, a perspective on events that members of elite groups at the time often labeled as parochial, even counterproductive to political and social progress. But at this moment the opinions of the leaders carried only marginal weight. With memories of wartime sacrifice still fresh in their minds, Americans reasoned about political matters within an intense emotional web of neighbors and family.

This point is significant, because the refugee crisis strained communication between local communities and national leaders who claimed to speak for them. New Yorkers who attended "a large and respectable Meeting of the freeholders and freemen of the county of Westchester," for example, expressed annoyance at what they saw as the inconsistent directions they received from state and national leaders. While the fighting had raged, their leaders had advised against ever trusting "any of those under the name and description of Tories" with a share in government. But now, with peace in the offing, the same elite officials suddenly changed their tune. They urged the people to accept the refugees "as fellow-citizens, without a single exception." What could account for such a radical shift? The Westchester group suspected that the enemies of revolution had managed to worm their way into positions of influence. The process had to stop.[15]

Although people throughout the country refused openly to challenge the authority of the federal government, they took solace in the wording of the treaty that instructed Congress to recommend that the separate states accept the return of the refugees without further impediment. After all, to recommend something was not an order. There still seemed to be time to address the issue. Several national leaders—John and Samuel Adams, for example—recognized how volatile the situation had become. Samuel feared that the return of the refugees could occasion "perpetual Quarrels" and "perhaps frequent Bloodshed."[16]

Many newspapers agreed. Articles encouraged popular resistance, claiming that the resettlement of these people could jeopardize the entire revolution. The *South Carolina Gazette* republished a strong protest that had originally appeared in a Virginia journal. A colonel who had served in the Continental Army reportedly explained to "the Board of officers of the Virginia Line" that even if the state legislature urged citizens to receive the refugees, the people should ignore the law. "I cannot conceive that we shall, as individuals, become bound thereby, to suppress our just resentment, or the abhorrence we much feel for such base characters. I must confess, sir, and I trust that I do not stand alone in this house when I say so, that the idea of ever associating with those detestable scoundrels, can never be made reconcilable to my feelings." Could responsible Virginians, he asked, not see the danger of being overrun by "these monsters of dissimulation and perjury" whose chief goal was the destruction of republican institutions that had "taken eight years to defend"?[17]

Newspapers in other states carried similar declarations, which serve as a rough but reliable index to the intensity of popular feeling. The leading journal in New Hampshire, for example, warned readers that the peace treaty had persuaded some Americans to consider seriously accepting the refugees back into free society. The author admitted that the situation of these former enemies was "truly deplorable." Some might pity them and even be tempted to overlook past behavior. That would be a terrible decision, he insisted. Return was unthinkable. "Self-preservation," he explained, "nature's first law, requires us to keep their crimes in view, and by the remembrance of their guilt, to cherish our resentment. It is impossible that persons so uniformly opposed to the revolutionaries, should on a sudden be cordially reconciled to it." If they did come back, they "might destroy the basis of our liberty."[18]

An Old Whig from Rhode Island also counseled resistance. Peace did not call for generosity or forgiveness. Was there the slightest chance, he asked, that someone "who, urged on by pride and high-flying monarchical principles, left his country in the hour of danger and distress, [could] become a good citizen"? The possibility was highly unlikely. Such deserters, concluded the Old Whig, were "utterly unfit to participate with us [in] the blessings of freedom and independence." What then should the refugees do? Leave the country?[19]

Some commentators wondered why the American negotiators had accepted articles five and six. Ignorance about the details of the conversations that had taken place in France invited speculation about why the refugees had been treated so well. One popular theory argued that the British representatives were responsible. Although they were eager to be done with the whole conflict, they apparently felt that they had to show compassion for those who supported the king during the Revolution. The options were limited. No one, of course, wanted to resume fighting over a seemingly marginal issue. And so, according to this explanation, British agents salved their conscience about deserting former defenders by ceding the entire problem to the United States Congress. Recommending a policy of settlement to the states was preferable to admitting openly that the refugees were on their own.[20]

However the peace negotiators had reasoned, Americans made it clear that the situation on the ground called for revenge rather than generosity. The burden of enforcement fell—as it had during earlier stages of the Revolution—to the people or to groups claiming to act in the name of the people. In New York City the Sons of Liberty experienced a revival. Not since 1775 had they voiced opposition to policies with which they disagreed. The goal of this reconstituted association was to put pressure on the state legislature to control the return of the Tories. Although the Sons did not advocate vigilante justice, they did remind the public that throughout the war the enemies of independence had been driven by "rancor, malice, and cruelty, which disgraces human nature." No genuine revolutionary could afford at this late date to welcome back dangerous ideological enemies. "The security of those inestimable and sacred rights, which you have suffered so much to obtain, and which it is your honor and interest to preserve, require your firmest support," they announced.[21]

The resurgence of self-constituted groups such as the New York Sons of Liberty exposed once again an unresolved political tension between community associations and higher state and national authorities. Throughout the Revolution ordinary people had turned to committees to address troublesome local issues—how to mobilize resistance to Great Britain at the start of the conflict, the policing of Tories during the early years of the war, and the campaign against economic extortion—and although these committees often could claim little more than extralegal standing—the voice of the people—they insisted that their activities were intended only to complement the work of regularly elected officials. The goal of the committees was assisting government in its effort to advance revolutionary justice and fair play. But, of course, the popular demand to punish neighbors perceived to be British sympathizers or wartime profiteers always threatened to devolve into the coercive settling of private disputes.

No one endorsed vigilantes, however welcome they may have seemed from time to time. For revolutionaries, anarchy had no more appeal than did tyranny. The balance between the two extremes was hard to establish, especially when the call to resist the return of the refugees generated such passion. As a writer identified as "Half a Million" explained in the *Boston Gazette*, "We have no scruple to declare, that although we disapprove of violence from the hands of individuals, yet we never can consent to their [the refugees'] return, and we never can think of our liberty safe while persons black with every political and almost every moral crimes are allowed to reside among us."[22]

Like many other revolutionaries eager to exclude the refugees, "the freeholders and other inhabitants" of Marblehead, Massachusetts, ignored the tension between constitutional authority and popular justice. While the country waited to discover whether the articles of the treaty would in fact become the law of the land, these people pushed forward, setting the local rules of return on their own. The sudden arrival in Marblehead of a particularly troublesome refugee—Stephen Blaney—forced the community to address the larger question of who would be welcome to live in the town at the end of the war. It resolved on April 24, 1783: "That a Committee of Inspection and Correspondence be appointed with full powers to correspond with similar committees of other towns—to examine into the characters of all persons who have or may come to this town, and appear to have been Refugees from this or any of the United States, and to warn all such persons to leave the town within six hours after notice is given." The town also authorized the committee to take suspicious persons into custody and if found to be potential enemies, ship them "to the nearest port of Britain." The people who attended the Marblehead meeting knew that their committee would exercise extralegal powers, but that presented no problem. The members of the committee had no reason to fear possible repercussions for their actions, since the town pledged "at all events, [to] indemnify and support them, until the sense of Congress and of the [Massachusetts] legislature be known."[23]

Other towns interpreted the wording of the treaty—a recommendation from Congress to the states—as an invitation to deal with the refugee crisis on their own terms. The results of these local discussions were inscribed in scores of still extant official town records. They provide evidence of broad and heated popular participation in the debate over resettlement. It was an extraordinary although often overlooked moment in the history of the Revolution. People in large number turned out for these meetings; they demanded a voice in defining a political future. Although driven initially by anger, they came in time to appreciate the emotional limits of revenge and to imagine a new society in which they could simply get on with their lives without violence. But first they had to negotiate the transition from war to peace, something that proved difficult after eight years of fighting. Thomas Paine understood the challenge. As he observed in "The Last Crisis" (1783), "'The times that tried men's souls' are over,—and the greatest and compleatest [sic] revolution the world ever knew, is gloriously and happily accomplished." Americans now faced the final crisis. "To pass from the extremes of danger to safety," Paine noted, "from the tumult of war to the tranquility of peace, though sweet in contemplation, requires a gradual composure of the senses to receive it."[24]

Perhaps no community had a more difficult transition from war to peace than did Lexington, Massachusetts, a place to which George Washington would later pay moving tribute as where "the first blood in the dispute with G. Britain was drawn."[25] In 1783 the Reverend Jonas Clark, pastor of the Third Church of Christ, headed a committee of citizens charged with providing the town's representative to the Massachusetts legislature with instructions. Members of his congregation had died on Lexington Green in 1775; memories of loss ran deep. Selected specifically by his neighbors to voice their concerns, Clark opened his statement praising Americans for their brave resistance to oppression throughout the war. "We have been happily carried through a Contest, in which all that we held dear as a Free People was at Stake: and . . . effected a REVOLUTION great in itself, and Glorious in the Eyes of the astonished World!"

But the people of Lexington still had much to accomplish. "Perhaps there was never a Time (not even in the Height of the Contest, or Depth of our Distress) when Attention, Firmness, Penetration, Wisdom, and Integrity were more necessary than the Present," Clark observed. The last great challenge for the community was prohibiting the return of anyone who had deserted it and supported the British. Clark recognized that Articles 5 and 6 seemed to allow refugees to return, but in his view, the state still had time to take a much harder line. Once more, the people had to resist. After all, the men who had deserted Lexington during its time of need were "Conspirators, Traitors or Rebels" who "have left the Society— they have left the Country under which they held—by which they were protected in—and to which, they owed Liberty, Property & Life—and they have joined the Enemy." Their behavior deprived them of "all Claim to Privilege, Property or Protection, in the Society, State, or States, they have left." They were "one and ALL, ALIENS from the COMMONWEALTH."

One might have predicted that after venting such anger Clark would have sanctioned some form of rough justice. Instead, at the moment of decision, he insisted only that the community's elected representative argue the case against the refugees in the state legislature.[26] As we shall discover in many other communities—although certainly not all—the heated rhetoric of revenge functioned almost as an end in itself. Condemning traitors and rebels was one thing; taking extralegal means to get even quite another.

The "freeholders and other inhabitants" of Worcester, Massachusetts, took a more aggressive stand. The community's resolutions passed in May 1783 must have resonated persuasively with revolutionaries in other states, since newspapers in New Jersey and Pennsylvania republished the full text of the Worcester decisions. Much like the people of Lexington, the men who attended the Worcester meeting justified their rejection of the refugees within a larger account of their fight for independence. They constructed a narrative of heroic resistance in the name of rights and freedom. "This country more than eight year since, was invaded, and been scourged by a war, which for the purpose of reducing it to the servile subjection of foreign domination had been, by sea and by land, wasted." The bitter contest "has desolated and burned whole towns, and rendered wretched, and turned out thousands of virtuous Americans." The Loyalists not only had turned their backs on this destruction, they had actually prolonged the conflict. After all, it had been "a war promoted, encouraged, and invited by those, who the moment the bloody banners were displayed, abandoned their native land, turned parricides, and conspired to involve their country in ruin, tumult, and in blood." Worcester declared that such treasonous behavior justified "a forfeiture of the conspirator's civil and political relation to their injured and betrayed country." And now the deserters could never come back. Indeed, they had lost "our *confidence, friendship, or society.*" To guarantee that they would not attempt to creep back into Worcester, the patriotic inhabitants formed a Committee of Correspondence, Inspection and Safety—an echo of the original revolutionary mobilization of 1775—to identify and remove enemies who tried to return. There were constraints on revenge. The town specifically restricted the committee's powers of surveillance to such time as Worcester received "further order of government."[27]

Woburn, Massachusetts, a small community north of Lexington, held a general town meeting in May 1783. The inhabitants put forth a passionate argument for excluding refugees that drew on the Old Testament as well as personal experience. They instructed their representative to the state assembly to resist any attempt to facilitate the return of hated enemies. They reminded him that Woburn "has unanimously voted against the re-settlement in this State of all such men, as have, in our glorious contest for liberty, proved inimical to their country, let them be of whatever denomina-tion: whether stigmatized by the name of Tory, Refugee, Conspirator, or Ab-sentee." It was a moment of revolutionary reaffirmation. Rejection of the refugees reinforced a strong positive sense within the community of how Woburn's sacrifice—its martyrdom for independence—justified rejection of friends and neighbors who had not supported the Revolution when it was most needed. The refugee crisis encouraged the community to give voice to what the war meant to them. "When the British King (like Re-hoboam of old) answered our Petitions with threats of whipping with scorpions, and the alarm was sounded, 'To your tents, O Israel: what por-tion have we in David? Neither have we Inheritance in the Son of Jesse (or George):' The Whigs obey'd, but the Tories shrank from danger." The people of ancient Israel had rebelled against an oppressive king; so too had those of Woburn. Great hardship resulted from that patriotic decision. "Our burned town, and the wanton destruction of property, the loss of our blood and treasure, must ever prove an insuperable barrier against such men [the Tories] being reinstated." They could not imagine living again with the "devotees to the shrine of royalty." The residents of Woburn warned against making a signal compromise—even one exception—since according to the maxim *principiis obsta* (resist the beginnings) sanctioned by theologians and physicians, one should always demand "the early sup-pression of morbidic qualities." It followed logically that "the same maxim is applicable in political injuries to the Commonwealth."[28]

In late May 1783 "the good people" of Rombout—a community in Dutchess County, New York—decided how they would handle the refugee crisis. That their anger ran deep was not surprising. This area had witnessed extreme partisan violence throughout the war. Although Rombout—officially known as a precinct—was very small, its decision and subsequent declaration seemed to reflect the thoughts of many other Americans. Newspapers in Pennsylvania and South Carolina carried the complete text. Indeed, those present at the Rombout meeting seemed aware that they were addressing a larger audience. "Being justly alarmed at the critical situation of public affairs," the residents announced, "[the people of

Rombout] have deemed it necessary to assemble for the purpose of declaring to their friends in other precincts, as well as the states at large, their resolutions respecting the conduct to be observed by the Whigs, in regard to those abandoned miscreants who deserted the country in its glorious struggle for independence."

The community advised all revolutionaries never to forget that the king's supporters were responsible for the conflict with Great Britain. In this narrative the entire conflict resulted solely from the "ambition, avarice, and perfidy" of the Tories. The American forces had eventually emerged victorious, but the crimes of the Tories remained fresh in popular memory. "From the beginning of the war to this day," the revolutionaries explained, "they have been guilty of the most horrid and inhuman murders that ever disgraced the records of any country." A second resolve warned that if persons who had aided the British dared remain in Rombout after seven days, they could expect to receive "the just punishment due to such infamous parricides." The final resolutions called for residents to expel immediately enemies who tried to return to their homes. Even more menacing, the community denounced all individuals who attempted to assist someone on the run. The town announced, "we will not associate with any person who may harbor or entertain Tory fugitives; but on the contrary we will deem them enemies to the independence and peace of the states, and treat them accordingly."[29]

III

Americans who expressed the greatest hostility to the return of the refugees soon discovered that calls for revenge needed to be buttressed by reasoned argument. Their raw emotion could mobilize individuals for a cause, at least temporarily, but the energy driving anger and hate dissipated quickly. No doubt, there were people living in their own communities whose enthusiasm in pursuing former enemies had ebbed, and now, after the announcement of a peace treaty, most were prepared to let bygones be bygones. These local conversations exploring the pros and cons of reconciliation are significant for our purposes because they expose strands of revolutionary thought—about perceptions of open and fair elections, for example—that often escape notice in the established narratives of the drafting and ratification of the Constitution.

The arguments advanced for excluding loyalists from postwar society drew upon common-sense equity as well as procedural claims. Many Americans could not understand why the peace negotiators had entertained the possibility that Tory exiles could demand a return of property seized by revolutionary governments when ordinary people—especially soldiers—had suffered such severe economic losses during the war. It seemed only fair that people who had actively supported independence should receive the compensation that they deserved.[30] Other Americans pointed out that since the treaty stipulated only that Congress should "recommend" allowing the return of the loyalists, and since the federal government could in fact do little more than attempt to persuade the various states to accept articles 5 and 6, it fell to the states to regulate the return of the refugees. If the states were sovereign in such matters—internal security, for example—then they had complete authority to exclude or punish whomever they pleased.[31] The whole thrust of the procedural argument was to put pressure on state legislatures to take a hard line on the refugee question.

More revealing in reconstructing how ordinary Americans envisioned a future political culture were repeated claims that the return of the refugees threatened the success of the Revolution. The nub of the problem was the assumption that individuals could not change their political ideology. Fundamental beliefs about the character of government authority were like the leopard's spots. If one believed in monarchy and accepted the idea that aristocrats deserved privilege simply because of birth, then one could never become a genuine citizen. There could be no compromise. The notion that the war experience might have moderated the principles of some loyalists was at best naïve. According to New York's Sons of Liberty, "It is impossible that Whigs and Tories can ever associate, or mingle together, or that government can be considered completely established, while so great a number of Tories, both of wealth and influence remain in this metropolis."[32] The *New Hampshire Gazette* insisted that the return of too many refugees "might destroy the basis of our liberty."[33] In an even more striking call to resistance, a Pennsylvania journal advised readers, "The spirit of 75 still beats high, and *must* beat high, or American freedom is no more."[34] Revolutionaries in New York announced that they "conceive there would be a glaring inconsistency at the moment of planting the empire of freedom, to suffer the seed of sedition to be scattered in and grown up with it."[35]

In this uneasy political context a re-energized defense of liberty focused on free and open elections. To be sure, throughout the United States the franchise had long been limited to adult white men. Eligible voters usually had to own property, but the amount needed to fulfill the law was seldom very demanding. Compared to contemporary England, for example, the American electorate was impressively large. Many people who assumed it was their right to participate in elections—and in New England states to instruct representatives on specific issues pending before the legislature— had come of age insisting that there could be "No Taxes Without Representation," and at the moment the country achieved independence, they were unwilling to surrender a meaningful voice in the selection of government officials.

Participation was the bone of contention. Returning refugees seemed to threaten the integrity of the democratic process, which many Americans regarded as a fundamental goal of their revolution. They reasoned not only that former enemies would never adopt new political principles— once a Tory, always a Tory—but also that resolute fugitives would use personal wealth and social standing to pervert elections. If the refugees were allowed back, the nation that had waged a war in part to eradicate aristocratic privilege would find itself burdened with a class of self-empowered individuals of a monarchical turn of mind. In April 1784 the New York Sons of Liberty announced: "We have not observed a single instance to justify the hopes that a Tory may be redeemed—they indeed have given us most emphatic evidence to the contrary—and an indifferent observer would conceive, by their confidence and assuming manner, that they were the *victors*, and we the *vanquished*: This then bears the presumptive evidence that they have the fond expectation of being the ready instruments in restoring their King's government."[36] The *New Jersey Gazette* echoed the complaint. "Is it not evident," the paper asked, "to every judicious observer that the Tories, the Tory-affected, the neutral, the mongrels, the political speculators" are coming forward to compete for political offices that properly should go only to men who risked their lives during the Revolution?[37] People in Massachusetts voiced fears that the refugees might actually win offices in the state.[38]

The source of the problem was the exceptional personal wealth that revolutionaries believed the returnees would use to gain or regain political influence. If they were allowed to return, it seemed inevitable that former enemies would use their money to pervert the will of the people. Ordinary Americans who had sacrificed their own prosperity during the war did not now have the resources required to compete against such well-funded opponents. The Reverend Nathaniel Whitaker, a respected Salem minister, explained exactly how the refugees could plausibly go about undermining the principles of freedom and equality that were at the heart of the fight for independence. In a passionate sermon entitled *The Reward of Toryism* (1783), Whitaker celebrated the country's military victory. "AMERICA is FREE!," he proclaimed. "Those who lorded it over us, who threatened to bring us to their feet, are constrained to acknowledge us free and independent, and relinquish all claim to our obedience and submission." Even at the moment of victory, however, a daunting challenge remained. "Our Independence is gained," Whitaker observed, "but our danger is not over, nor is our work done." Americans would be extraordinarily naïve not to realize that returning Tories "will probably soon engross the chief wealth of these states; and, as wealth begets power, they will easily possess themselves of the chief seats of government, pervert our counsels, and reduce us, by their acts, to that subjugation to Great Britain which the power of their arms could not accomplish."

No doubt, drawing on his knowledge of international trade—in ports such as Newburyport, Salem, and Boston—Whitaker noted that throughout the war Tory exiles had been busy forging favorable contracts with leading English merchants. They had schemed to build up "a large supply of goods," items that patriotic American firms could not easily obtain. It followed from this that because of their competitive advantage rich Tories will "be able to influence our elections." After years of resistance to British arms, Americans risked losing the cause for which they had fought. "We are so intoxicated with the joy of peace," Whitaker insisted, "so bewitched with the love of gain; so enamored with the cheapness of their goods, (which is the very bait to their barbed hook, that is designed for our ruin) that there is reason to fear that no warning will move us."[39]

Whitaker was not a crank. He gave voice to the concerns of many other people about the return of the refugees. Brutus, for example, alerted the readers of Philadelphia's *Independent Gazetteer* to a Tory plan to undermine the freedom of ordinary Americans. The Tories wanted above all else for the state assemblies to excuse their failure to support independence. The chances of legislative success, Brutus argued, could be gauged "in proportion to their money and influence." Because the contest promised to be a close call, revolutionaries had to expose the power of wealth in postwar elections. If they did not do so, they would "become the abject tools of the party who favors and procures them a pardon." Counting ballots would determine the meaning of independence. "There is no alternative," Brutus concluded: "either Whigs or Tories must be expelled, and it ultimately rests with you, my fellow citizens, to determine which."[40]

A rival Philadelphia newspaper worried that it might already be too late to turn the ideological tide. "It is hardly safe any longer to speak disrespectfully of Tories," wrote Numa. "To what is this owing? To the wealth, the weight, the boldness of this society . . . We see the cause of Whiggism sliding away from us: We see Toryism rising in triumph; and we are afraid to exert ourselves to stop the mischief."[41] This commentator was surely guilty of hyperbole. But even as he exaggerated the danger, he played on a widespread anxiety that too much money in too few hands—especially if those were the hands of former enemies—would undermine the rough sense of social equality that made the country's new government worth defending. It was that kind of thinking that persuaded a group resisting the return of the refugees in New York to declare, "The doctrine of Toryism contains in it an irreconcilable hatred to free governments—it is the bane of our political existence, and there is no other antidote but banishment."[42]

Uncertainty about the nation's political future encouraged conspiratorial thinking about how a group of Tories were secretly organizing to take control of the United States. Like most theories that raise the specter of dark plots, those associated with the refugees had only a tenuous relation to facts. The number of actual potential conspirators was quite small, as everyone at the time understood. Most Americans who expressed hostility to the return of the Tories were fully aware that some of them had just made unfortunate choices and were not particularly threatening. They had tried as best they could throughout the war to anticipate which way the ideological winds were blowing. Other Tories were responsible for the destruction of physical property, perhaps even for killing revolutionaries. As the conflict with Great Britain came to an end, however, suspicion fell not on possible war criminals but rather on wealthy returnees allegedly determined to seize political power in the new republic.

Writing in a Hartford newspaper, "A Connecticut Tory" found a clever means to warn revolutionaries of the new Tory danger. Pretending to be an enemy agent, he laid out the complete strategy for undermining independent government. For people inclined to believe such things the piece confirmed their worst fears. Here was a returnee revealing the details of a complex plot. "Attached as we are to arbitrary government," he explained to his co-conspirators, "we can never be happy under the present democracy; still less can our friends expect any favors, while the Congress and the army, our greatest enemies, retain a share either in power or influence." The challenge was formidable, since "many steps are yet to be taken before we can wholly overthrow the Congress and the Legislatures, and establish an aristocracy of our own creation." Unless unnamed Tory operatives could bring about "the destruction of the present government," there was no hope of guaranteeing the safe return of the refugees.

A Connecticut Tory reminded supporters—in words that made sense to conspiracy theorists—"We have always succeeded best in laboring in the dark, fomenting the prejudices of the people and venting falsehoods without danger and detection." In this imagined scenario it seemed possible to mislead ordinary Americans some of the time. But there were limits to their gullibility. It was always possible that they would suddenly wake up and realize that they were the victims of false news. The Tory plot would achieve nothing "should the people once be provoked to open their eyes, and recollect how many of their present popular leaders have been notorious through the course of their lives, as attached to the British government, encouragers of illicit trade, leaders of faction and dissention, enemies to all establishments civil and religious, bankrupts in property, or persons wholly destitute of every principle of honor and honesty."[43]

The rising crescendo of fear and censure soon provoked other Americans to enter the conversation over the future of the refugees. They dismissed the whole episode as the result of ignorance. Far from being a threat to democracy, they argued that wealthy Tories could assist the recovery of the national economy. Writing under the penname Phocion—a legendary statesman of ancient Greece—Alexander Hamilton reminded revolutionaries in a widely republished commentary that fear and disappointment often encourage people to do things that they later regret. It was not the refugees who represented a danger to the country's future. Rather, the problem was the irresponsible circulation of conspiracy theories. "Nothing," Hamilton wrote, "is more common than for a free people, in times of heat and violence, to gratify momentary passions, by letting into the government, principles and precedents which afterward prove fatal to themselves."

Hamilton boldly condemned the misguided efforts to persuade the various state legislatures to curtail the rights of the refugees. If Americans targeted an entire group—in this case all former Tories—then they might at some future date decide to exclude or punish other groups solely on the grounds that they were associated with a despised category of people. Using the law to punish persons simply because they may have made bad choices in the past ran counter to common sense and distributive justice. Hamilton reminded his anxious countrymen, "The people at large, are sure to be the losers in the event whenever they suffer a departure from the rules of general and equal justice, or from the true principles of universal liberty." It was true that many revolutionaries found articles 5 and 6 of the peace treaty objectionable. But, he asked, what was the alternative? Banishing all refugees? Private revenge? The law of the land—and that now included the formal treaty—prohibited such arbitrary punishment. According to Hamilton, "No citizen can be deprived of any right which the citizens in general are entitled to, unless forfeited by some offence. It has been seen that the regular and constitutional mode of ascertaining whether this forfeiture has been incurred, is by legal process, trial and conviction," and however angry the people may be, consistent with the treaty "there can be no future prosecution for anything done on account of the war."[44]

In a brilliant turnabout Hamilton argued that the refugees represented no danger whatsoever either to the nation's economy or its political culture. He recognized that some Americans claimed that suffering "those wealthy disaffected men to remain among us, will be dangerous to our liberties; enemies to our government . . . endeavoring to undermine it and bring us back to the subjection of Great Britain." But he then asked what continued hostility would achieve. After all, what makes a person a good citizen is self-interest. The regime that offers opportunities to aspiring entrepreneurs, Hamilton explained, need not worry about ideology. Prosperity in the new nation would tame ideology and render monarchy irrelevant. "Make it the interest of those citizens, who, during the revolution, were opposed to us to be friends to the new government, by affording them not only protection, but a participation in its privileges, and they will undoubtedly become its friends."[45]

Some cities that had fallen on hard times, such as New Haven and New London, Connecticut, found the economic logic persuasive. They invited scores of known Tories—many of them merchants who had spent the war in New York City—to become residents. There were some exceptions. Refugees who had "committed unauthorized and lawless plundering and murder" were not welcome.[46] Those possessing trade goods and capital, however, could be forgiven past sins. A piece that ran in several newspapers entitled "A Dialogue Between a County Justice and a Committee Man, concerning the LOYALISTS, &c" drove home the same point. The county justice insisted that wealthy Tories were a tonic for depressed trade. Indeed, "Some trading towns begin to open their eyes; if I am informed right, New-London has reconsidered the matter, and open their town, and given free liberty for all people of fair character, let their principles have been what they might, to come and rent, buy and settle amongst them." He added that he hoped the United States would be known as a nation that could "fight and forgive.[47] "A Patriot" from South Carolina agreed. He was certain that "if PRIVATE RESENTMENT can distract the Tranquility of Government, Trade will forsake our shores, and Contempt and Reproach must of consequence take place."[48]

Although it is difficult to estimate the impact that Hamilton's piece made on public opinion, his pragmatic take on the return of the refugees gained traction with each passing month. Indeed, by early 1784 the storm had passed. Americans who had sustained the war for independence did not suddenly welcome former enemies, but they soon discovered there was not much they could do to punish them. Newspapers reported a few incidents of violence—nothing as violent as the hanging of Matthew Love—but even if these events actually occurred, they did not incite people living in other communities to behave likewise.[49] No doubt, revolutionaries shunned returning Tories; perhaps insults were exchanged. But as Americans turned their attention to restoring civil society after a long war, they lost interest in a continuing vendetta.

The rhetorical bark—calls for exclusion or disenfranchisement—soon exceeded the danger of the bite. The worst threat directed at the refugees was a reminder that ordinary American people would not forget who had failed to support the fight for independence. In a widely circulated piece entitled "A Last Advice to the Tories and Refugees in New-York," a writer warned that Tories who "have done nothing, and said nothing" might possibly escape the wrath of former neighbors, but "depend upon it, they will ever be treated as underling wretches, and held in abhorrence and contempt." And, he added, be "assured, every action you have done, and every word you have spoken against your country, will be remembered against you, and [you] will be infallibly executed, or perpetually banished, or you will be so harassed that you will be obliged to make your escape or exile yourselves."[50] It is true that such censure may have intimidated some refugees, perhaps persuading them to move to Canada. But most of them stayed in the United States.

The sudden end of the great refugee crisis was remarkable.[51] Some state legislatures made tepid attempts to marginalize returning Tories. These initiatives generally came to nothing. Statutes allowing local authorities to seize the property of known enemies who had left the country during the war failed to generate much income for governments desperate to reduce debts incurred during the war. And, in fact, many Americans who had taken the British side successfully reinvented themselves in the new republic.[52] A few even served in elected positions.[53] One can understand the Reverend Israel Evans's amazed sense of accomplishment at the end of 1783. From his perspective the war had concluded on a note of generosity and forgiveness, free from a call for revenge. "This war," he argued, "is now closed with greater honor, if possible, than it was begun and persecuted. Of all our glorious days, none have been more pleasing to the dignified and generous mind, than those, which have followed the departure of our enemies from this city [New York]."[54]

Why Americans willingly reabsorbed so many people who had supported the British remains something of a mystery. One possibility should be quickly dismissed. No evidence survives to indicate that the revolutionaries were exceptionally tolerant and generous. They gave voice to the same destructive emotions as have revolutionaries living in other regions time out of mind. Although they allowed refugees to rejoin civil society, they turned a blind eye to the suffering of slaves—20 percent of the nation's population—and they seldom criticized the killing of Native Americans, who had aided the British and who continued to resist colonists' western expansion.[55] We would be on more solid interpretive ground if we noted that ideological differences at the end of the war were not so great as they may have appeared at the start. Conditions changed. Many Tories felt that George III had abandoned them during the peace negotiations. They easily accommodated themselves to a new republican society that was not radically different from the monarchical order they had known in colonial times. They still could appeal to the common law. They spoke the same language their neighbors spoke. They were overwhelmingly Protestants. The public culture—arts and literature—remained profoundly British.

There may have been a more prosaic reason for accommodation. Relatively few Tories had ever been die-hard enemies of independence. Throughout the contest with Great Britain these people strove simply to survive, a pragmatic goal achieved by adopting fluid political identities. Former neighbors and relatives understood that while some Tories had committed terrible crimes, most had merely kept their heads down.[56] As "A Patriot" in South Carolina explained, "I feel an honest indignation with others against those miscreants, but their disappointment is their sufficient punishment.... It is really unworthy the dignity of our superior standing to betray marks of fear either of their power or influence, and to promote mobs for their extermination, is like a man's taking a dose of poison because he is afraid of dying."[57] Hated refugees often turned out to be cousins or brothers. In these circumstances such behavior could be forgiven. And finally, in a country as large as the United States in 1784, even the most notorious enemies could easily reinvent themselves in a new community.

William Moultrie offered as good an explanation as did any contemporary for the rejection of revenge. A celebrated Continental Army officer and political leader in South Carolina, Moultrie reflected on why local legislators had shown so little enthusiasm for punishing the refugees—this in a state where Americans had killed other Americans with abandon. "When it comes to be considered," Moultrie wrote, that many men sitting in the South Carolina assembly in 1783 "had been fighting during the whole war; and some of them perhaps with their wounds still bleeding; and others just returned from captivity and banishment, it is not to be wondered at, that they should be in an ill humor, and displeased with their countrymen" who had helped the British. Yet, these same revolutionaries "when they had got possession of their country again, and peace restored, they were softened by pity, and had compassion for their fellow citizens."[58]

IV

The path from rejection to reconciliation varied from place to place, from person to person. Everyone had a story about the end of the war. Linus Parker, a stout supporter of independence, recounted his own experience in Pittsfield, a small community in western Massachusetts. During the long conflict the town had been on constant alert because of Tory activities in the area. In May 1777 a British officer who had been captured and held in a Hartford jail escaped, and with the help of loyalists who maintained a chain of safe houses, he tried to reach Canada. The local committee of safety learned that Captain McKay and his servant might be hiding near Pittsfield, and more, that a dubious character, John Graves, had assisted in the plan. Committee members immediately informed the Massachusetts Board of War that Graves was a dangerous enemy. He certainly seemed "to be a low-spirited, insidious fellow . . . [who entertained] strong prejudices against the liberties of America."

When committee members interrogated Graves they discovered that other Tory conspirators were involved. They posed a serious threat to the security of the community. One suspect, Gideon Smith, lived in nearby Stockbridge, and an order went out immediately for his arrest. Smith must have received a warning, because just as a group of Pittsfield militiamen arrived at his house, he made a desperate bid for freedom. But, as the story went, when Smith suddenly realized that Linus Parker, reputed to be the best sharpshooter in the region, had him in his sights, he surrendered.

Years later, Parker and Smith discussed the incident at Stockbridge. Smith could not resist asking whether Parker would have actually shot him. Without hesitation Parker responded, "As quick as I ever shot a deer!" After a moment's reflection, Smith concluded, "Then it would have been all over with me." With peace assured, the two old men could reminisce about a time when few Americans could imagine reconciliation with despised enemies.[59]

Parker and Smith knew that story of independence could have taken a very different turn. After all, American revolutionaries—like other revolutionaries throughout the world—were subject to almost irresistible passions. They heard the sirens of revenge. They experienced hate. And they would have expressed no remorse had their former enemies chosen exile over resettlement. But in this political culture other considerations came into play. Americans managed to reconcile potentially destructive conflict within their communities. The contest with Great Britain did not end badly because ordinary people restrained raw emotion and stood up for a rule of law. They respected the peace treaty even though they thoroughly disliked key articles of it. If they had not done so—if they had preferred private revenge to accommodation—we would now be telling a story about a failed revolution.

CHAPTER SEVEN

REFLECTIONS

For Americans in search of original political meanings, a history of independence holds obvious appeal. It seems self-evident that the generation responsible for creating a new republic understood the fundamental ideals that have energized the shared political culture of the United States. The effort to recover original meanings usually involves an exhaustive analysis of the writings of the Founders. Such an approach has merit.[1] It focuses attention on a small group of revolutionary leaders who boldly encouraged Americans to overthrow monarchy and aristocracy and then, after 1776, to establish a new government based solely on the will of the people. But, as we have seen, there is something missing from this familiar story: the story of those people whose will the republican system was meant to reflect. Ordinary Americans—a founding people rather than a few Founders— also had a voice in defining the values that distinguish our political system from tyrannical regimes throughout the world. We might consider one such contribution. How exactly, we might ask, did ordinary Americans define *liberty?*

The Founders have long dominated our understanding of liberty. During the run-up to independence, they repeatedly declared that its preservation provided sufficient justification for taking up arms against Great Britain. Without liberty, they insisted, ordinary people lost their freedom, which meant in practice that they had to obey legislation passed by Parliament without their consent. That was intolerable. The highly visible experience of African American slaves reminded revolutionaries of what their lives might be like if they found themselves subject to whims of despotic masters. After all, without liberty Americans could be stripped of the fruits of their own labor; their property would be at risk. But if the Americans managed to win the war—indeed, if they protected liberty—they could look forward to unprecedented freedom. Every citizen would be free to pursue his or her own definition of happiness. From this perspective liberty was something that individuals rather than communities enjoyed. One either possessed liberty or not. Compromise was not acceptable.[2]

The ordinary people who sustained the revolution in small communities throughout America developed a different understanding of liberty, one that is now more than ever worth recovering. It was not that they rejected the insights of the leading Founders. Rather, as they seized control of the Revolution, they crafted a more nuanced sense of the meaning of liberty. About the extreme dangers associated with the loss of liberty they thoroughly agreed with the learned political essayists of the day. It seemed axiomatic that if ordinary people could not exercise independent political judgment—if neither they nor their representatives had a voice in legislation—then they became the slaves of tyrannical masters. As the Reverend Gad Hitchcock explained to a congregation in Plymouth, Massachusetts, when men are "deprived of liberty, oppressed, and enslaved, [they] . . . sink below the primitive standard of humanity."[3]

But for ordinary revolutionaries—and the ministers who gave meaning on the community level to a new political culture—the threat of slavery was only part of the discussion. They did not treat liberty as an all or nothing proposition. To be sure, slavery was to be avoided at all costs. At the same time, however, Americans who served on revolutionary committees believed that too much liberty presented an equally worrisome threat to civil society. Excess of freedom invited anarchy and licentiousness—in other words, it promoted a kind of selfish individualism deemed corrosive to community solidarity. True liberty required constant attention to balancing order and freedom. As the members of the various local committees repeatedly discovered—in their control of domestic enemies, in establishing revolutionary justice, in discouraging profiteering, and in dealing with refugees—constraint was as important as passion in sustaining the fight for independence. The preservation of liberty on the local level, they discovered, required negotiation and compromise, understanding and determination.

Establishing a healthy balance between crushing slavery and irresponsible freedom proved difficult. As they had done in calling for an appeal to heaven, ministers offered guidance. In a sermon entitled *Liberty Described and Recommended* (1775), Levi Hart, a highly respected Connecticut minister, praised liberty as a positive good. He immediately qualified his enthusiasm, however. Some people always gave in to excess. "Liberty is frequently used to denote a power of *doing as we please.*" That kind of self-indulgence—an expression of individualism—posed a serious danger to civil society. Hart's lesson was clear. "Civil liberty doth not consist in a freedom from all law and government,—but in a freedom from unjust law and tyrannical government." Liberty could only flourish in stable communities. According to Hart, "Liberty may be considered and defined with reference to society:—Mankind in a state of nature, or considered as individuals . . . are not the subjects of *this freedom.*"[4]

In *America's Appeal to the Impartial World* the Reverend Moses Mather, an outspoken defender of revolution who was briefly imprisoned for his political views, opened his sermon with an observation that none of his listeners found controversial. "It is evident," Mather stated, "that man hath the clearest right, by the most indefeasible title, to personal security, liberty, and private property." That claim immediately raised in his mind a need to define liberty more precisely. It surely did not enjoin Americans to regard freedom as a right enjoyed as individuals. "Liberty consists in a power of acting under the guidance and control of reason," Mather insisted. "Licentiousness [is] in acting under the influence of sensual passions, contrary to the dictates of reason." In his own community this advice meant that while "we point out arguments against the errors and abuses of government, we ought cautiously to distinguish between government and its abuses . . . lest we raise an army of rebel spirits more dangerous and difficult to reduce, than all the legions of Britain."[5]

The Reverend Samuel West, who wrote a moving account of the fighting at Lexington and Concord, insisted that liberty meant little when divorced from the mutual social responsibilities associated with community life. "We need the assistance of others," West stated in 1776, "which if not afforded, we should very soon perish; hence the law of nature requires, that we should endeavor to help one another, to the utmost of our power in all cases, where our assistance is necessary." Advancing an argument that resonated throughout revolutionary America, West continued, "When a man goes beyond, or contrary to the law of nature and reason, he becomes the slave of base passions, and vile lusts; he introduces confusion and disorder into society. . . . Hence we conclude that where licentiousness begins, liberty ends."[6]

We should attend closely to such sentiments. They are the views of a people locked in a long, uncertain, and costly struggle to attain a liberty for which they knowingly risked everything. If our search for original meanings stops with the Founders, we have done a grave disservice to the many, many thousands more ordinary Americans to whom at least as great a debt is owed, if not a greater debt for what Americans have achieved together as a nation.

Throughout the long struggle for independence, the committees tried as best they could to sustain a rule of law. Of course, fear and zealousness occasionally combined to undermine a commitment to fair and open procedure. But on the whole the committees restrained themselves when partisan anger invited punitive actions that could have permanently divided communities. It was a process of ongoing negotiation that involved ever-larger numbers of ordinary Americans. The participation of so many new men in public life transformed theoretical arguments for a government based on the will of the people into revolutionary reality. Americans did not set out at the beginning of the contest with Great Britain to turn a colonial rebellion into a genuine revolution, but that is exactly what happened. As the war continued, local committees communicated with other committees—in neighboring towns and other states—and in the process they powerfully reinforced at the national level a revolutionary mentality that affirmed the people's commitment to balanced liberty. And even more important in understanding the creation of a new national identity, an expanding awareness of revolutionary solidarity gave legitimacy to a locally grounded political culture that defended freedom and order in the name of liberty.

In our attempt to recover revolutionary meanings we should remember that whatever their failures may have been, the American people at the end of the war gave voice to the possibility of an open, more tolerant society that they believed would provide a beacon of freedom for men and women in other nations. Deep-seated racial bias limited the appeal. But the original vision has echoed through the generations. It continues to be a powerful source of pride and guilt, a reminder of what America could be if modern communities overcome fear and promote justice.

As the Reverend Levi Frisbie observed in his *Oration on the Peace*, "Happy indeed would be the effects of the American Revolution, should it be the means of communicating liberty and happiness to millions of mankind."[7] Zabdiel Adams, a minister who gave the Lexington anniversary sermon in 1783, encouraged the members of the families who had lost loved ones to look ahead, to imagine the possibilities that their sacrifice had created. "Independency and freedom are the wish of all men," Adams explained. It was also true that "Freedom ... may be abused to purposes of licentiousness." The revolutionaries understood the dangers of extremes. The goal was worth the price, for as Adams reminded them, "if it be not our own fault, we may *now* be the happiest people on the face of the globe."[8] The key words here are "not our own fault." If Americans choose to encourage intolerance or close their borders to those seeking freedom and liberty, if they allow people of great wealth and assumed privilege to erode the bonds of civil society or fail to learn how to live with others who hold very different political views, the fault lies not with the original revolutionaries, but rather with us.

NOTES

Most archival sources such as sermons can be found in Early American Imprint Series I (1639–1800) by Readex.

INTRODUCTION: REVOLUTIONARY VOICES

1. A model of this type of analysis can be found in R. F. Foster's *Vivid Faces: The Revolutionary Generation in Ireland 1890–1923* (2014).

2. Major titles include Bernard Bailyn, *The Ideological Origins of the American Revolution* (1967); Gordon S. Wood, *Radicalism of the American Revolution* (1993); J. G. A. Pocock, *The Machiavellian Moment: Florentine Political Thought and the Atlantic Republican Tradition* (2003); Edmund S. Morgan, *Birth of the Republic, 1763–89* (2012); and Jack P. Greene, *The Constitutional Origins of the American Revolution* (2010). Also helpful in understanding the debate over the character of republican ideas during this period is Daniel Rodgers, "Republicanism: The Career of a Concept," *Journal of American History*, 79 (1992): 11–38.

3. See, for example, Clifford Geertz, *Local Knowledge: Further Essays in Interpretive Anthropology* (1985).

4. The American Revolution has generated an immense historical literature. Listed here are some recent titles that have had a significant impact on my own thinking. A useful survey of recent developments in the field can be found in Michael A. McDonnell and David Waldstreicher, "Revolution in the Quarterly? A Historical Analysis," *William and Mary Quarterly*, 3rd ser., 74 (2017): 633–666. Valuable treatments reflecting quite different interpretive perspectives are Alan Taylor, *American Revolutions: A Continental History, 1750–1804* (2017); Gordon S. Wood, *Revolutionary Characters: What Made the Founders Different* (2007); Jack Rakove, *Revolutionaries: A New History of the Invention of America* (2010); Patrick Griffin, *America's Revolution* (2012); Joseph J. Ellis, *Founding Brothers: The Revolutionary Generation* (2002); Edmund S. Morgan, *The Meaning of Independence: John Adams, George Washington, and Thomas Jefferson* (2005); Gary B. Nash, *The Unknown American Revolution: The Unruly Birth of Democracy and the Struggle to Create America* (2006); and Andrew Jackson O'Shaughnessy, *The Men Who Lost America: British Leadership, the American Revolution, and the Fate of the Empire* (2014).

5. Enoch Barlett quoted in Robert McClure Calhoon, *Loyalists in Revolutionary America 1760–1781* (1973), 288. See Richard L. Bushman, *The American Farmer in the Eighteenth Century: A Social and Cultural History* (2018), ch. 9.

6. A. K. Teele, ed., *History of Milton, Massachusetts* (1887), 422–23.

7. F. Alan Potter, *Matthew Potter, His Tavern and the Plain Dealer* (n.d.), 6–30; *Pennsylvania Journal*, 28 August 1776; and William Nelson, ed., *Plain Dealer: The First Newspaper in New Jersey* (1894), 7–30.

8. See Colin G. Calloway, *Scratch of a Pen: 1763 and the Transformation of North America* (2007); Holger Hoock, *Scars of Independence: America's Violent Birth* (2017); Patrick Griffin, *American Leviathan: Empire, Nation, and Revolutionary Frontier* (2008); David Brion Davis, *Inhuman Bondage: The Rise and Fall of Slavery in the New World* (2006), ch. 7.

9. A broader comparative perspective provides a fuller sense of how revolutions actually worked on the ground. Some provocative works are Colin Jones, *The Great Nation: France from Louis XV to Napoleon* (2002); Timothy Tackett, *The Coming of the Terror in the French Revolution* (2015); Fearghal McGarry, *The Rising, Ireland: Easter 1916* (2010); Robert Kee, *The Green Flag: A History of Irish Nationalism* (1972); Orlando Figes, *A People's Tragedy: The Russian Revolution: 1891–1924* (1998); Sheila Fitzpatrick, *The Russian Revolution* (2017); and Sugata Bose, *His Majesty's Opponent: Subhas Chandra Bose and India's Struggle against Empire* (2011).

10. Joseph T. Glatthaar and Kirby Martin, *Forgotten Allies: The Oneida Indians and the American Revolution* (2007); Gary B. Nash, *The Forgotten Fifth: African Americans in the Age of Revolution* (2006); Alan Gilbert, *Black Patriots and Loyalists: Fighting for Emancipation in the War for Independence* (2012); Douglas R. Egerton, *Death or Liberty: African Americans and Revolutionary America* (2009); Jim Piecuch, *Three Peoples, One King: Loyalists, Indians, and Slaves in the American Revolutionary South, 1775–1782* (2013); and Judith L. Van Buskirk, *Standing in Their Own Light: African American Patriots in the American Revolution* (2017).

11. Winthrop D. Jordan, *White Over Black: American Attitudes toward the Negro 1550–1812* (1969); Edmund S. Morgan, *American Slavery, American Freedom* (2013); Taylor, *American Revolutions*; and Robert G. Parkinson, *The Common Cause: Creating Race and Nation in the American Revolution* (2016).

12. David Ramsay, *The History of the American Revolution*, 2 vols. (1990), 2:629–30. Also see Jackson Turner Main, *The Sovereign States, 1775–1783* (1973), chs. 1–3.

13. Ramsay, *History*, I, 315.

14. Henry Cumings, *A Sermon Preached at Lexington* (1781), 27–28.

15. Jacques LeGoff, *Must We Divide History into Periods?* (2015).

16. Barbara Clark Smith, *Freedoms We Lost: Consent and Resistance in Revolutionary America* (2010); and Woody Holton, *Unruly Americans and the Origins of the Constitution* (2008).

I. REJECTION

1. The most provocative analysis of these tensions remains Frantz Fanon, *Wretched of the Earth* (1961). A useful discussion of colonial identity within the eighteenth-century British Empire is Brendan McConville, *The King's Three Faces: The Rise and Fall of Royal America, 1688–1776* (2006); also see T. H. Breen, "Ideology and Nationalism on the Eve of the American Revolution: Revisions Once More in Need of Revising," *Journal of American History*, 84 (1997); 13–39.

2. *The Papers of Thomas Jefferson*, ed. Julian P. Boyd (1950), 1:427.

3. P. D. G. Thomas, *Lord North* (1976); H. T. Dickinson, "Britain's Imperial Sovereignty: The Ideological Case Against the American Colonies," in *Britain and the American Revolution*, ed. H. T. Dickinson, 64–96 (1998).

4. T. H. Breen, "Empire and Resistance: Reflections on the American and Irish Revolutions," in *Imperial Ireland and America: Congruities and Incongruities, Convergences and Divergences*, ed. Frank Cogliano and Patrick Griffin (2019).

5. Although much research needs to be done on the committee system in all the states during the Revolution, several studies suggest the richness of the topic: David Ammerman, *In the Common Cause: American Response to the Coercive Acts of 1774* (1974); Hermann Wellenreuther, *Revolution of the People: Thoughts and Documents on the Revolutionary Process in North America, 1774–1776* (2006); and Richard D. Brown, *Revolutionary Politics in Massachusetts: The Boston Committee of Correspondence and the Towns, 1772–1774* (1976).

6. The forging of political solidarity through newspaper coverage is explored in T. H. Breen, *American Insurgents, American Patriots: The Revolution of the People* (2010), ch. 4. A valuable analysis of newspapers during the Revolution can be found in Robert G. Parkinson, *The Common Cause: Creating Race and Nation in the American Revolution* (2016), ch. 1.

7. K. G. Davies, ed., *Documents of the American Revolution, 1770–1783, Colonial Office Series, Transcripts 1774*, 21 vols. (1972–81), 8:187–90; Peter Force, ed., *American Archives: Consisting of a Collection of Authentik [sic] Records, State Papers, Debates And Letters . . .*, 4th Series, 6 vols. (1837–53), 1:763–84; *Pennsylvania Packet*, 19 September 1774; and *Boston Post-Boy*, 12 September 1774.

8. *Connecticut Gazette and Universal Intelligencer* (New London), 3 June 1774. Bernard Bailyn explains why Hutchinson's attempt simultaneously to negotiate colonial and imperial interests failed in *The Ordeal of Thomas Hutchinson* (1974).

9. *Diary and Autobiography of John Adams* (August 1765), ed. L. H. Butterfield (1961), 1:260.

10. Elias Nason, *Sir Charles Henry Frankland, Baronet: Or Boston in the Colonial Times* (1865); F. Marshall Bauer, *Marblehead's Pygmalion: Finding the Real Agnes Surriage* (2010); Anonymous, *Watertown's Military History* (1807); *Journals of the Provincial Congress of Massachusetts in 1774 and 1775* (1838), 238; Massachusetts Archives, vol. 154 (Revolutionary Loyalists), 10 May 1775. For a similar case, see William Lincoln, *History of Worcester, Massachusetts* (1837), 111.

11. T. H. Breen, *American Insurgents*, ch. 10.

12. A valuable analysis of revolutionary causation can be found in Lawrence Stone, *Causes of the English Revolution 1529–1642* (1972).

13. Paul Langford, *A Polite and Commercial People: England, 1727–1738* (1994); John Brewer and John Styles, *An Ungovernable People: The English and Their Law in the Seventeenth and Eighteenth Centuries* (1980); R. F. Foster, *Modern Ireland, 1600–1972* (1989); Eliga H. Gould, *The Persistence of Empire: British Political Culture in the Age of the American Revolution* (2000); Nick Bunker, *An Empire on the Edge: How Britain Came to Fight America* (2015); and H. T. Dickinson, *The Politics of the People in Eighteenth-Century Britain* (1994).

14. T. H. Breen, *The Marketplace of Revolution: How Consumer Politics Shaped American Independence* (2004), ch. 7; and John C. Miller, *Sam Adams: Pioneer in Propaganda* (1936), chs. 8 and 9.

15. Breen, *Marketplace*, ch. 7.

16. Foster, *Modern Ireland*, chs. 8–10.

17. Edmund S. Morgan and Helen M. Morgan, *The Stamp Act Crisis: Prologue to Revolution* (1953).

18. Linda Colley, *Britons: Forging the Nation, 1707–1837* (2009).

19. Foster, *Modern Ireland*, ch. 8; Jim Smyth, *Making of the United Kingdom* (2001), chs. 6–7.

20. Thomas R. Adams, *American Controversy: A Bibliographic Study of the British Pamphlets About the American Disputes, 1764–1783* (1980); and specifically on the periodic essay collection *The Crisis*, see Breen, *American Insurgents*, 262–75.

21. Paul K. Longmore, *Invention of George Washington* (1999), 21–34; for Adams, *Boston Gazette*, 14 October 1765; James Otis Jr., *A Vindication of the British Colonies* (1765), in *Pamphlets of the American Revolution*, ed. Bernard Bailyn (1965), 1:568; and Gordon S. Wood, *The Americanization of Benjamin Franklin* (2004), ch. 5.

22. Colin Nicolson, ed., *The Papers of Francis Bernard, Governor of Colonial Massachusetts 1760–69* (2015), 5:187; Morgan and Morgan, *Stamp Act Crisis*, 83. Also see Nancy L. Rhoden, "The American Revolution: The Paradox of Atlantic Integration," in *British North America in the Seventeenth and Eighteenth Centuries*, ed. Stephen Foster, 255–88 (2013); and John Clive and Bernard Bailyn, "England's Cultural Provinces: Scotland and America," *William and Mary Quarterly*, 3rd ser., 11 (1954):200–213.

23. Jeremy Belknap, *The History of New Hampshire* (1792), 2:246.

24. Charles Patrick Neimeyer, *America Goes to War: A Social History of the Continental Army* (1996), ch. 5; and T. H. Breen, "An Irish Rebellion in America?" *Field Day Review* 2 (2006): 275–85.

25. David Ramsay, *The History of the American Revolution*, ed. Lester H. Cohen (1990), 1:88, 317.

26. Jonas Clark, *Fate of Blood-Thirsty Oppressors* (1776), 29–30.

27. Davies, ed., *Documents*, 8:164–66.

28. Davies, ed., *Documents*, 8:182–84; Breen, *American Insurgents*, 91–93; *Essex Gazette*, 2 September 1774.

29. *Essex Gazette*, 23–30 August 1774.

30. Force, ed., *American Archives*, 1:42–46; Thomas, *Lord North*, 32–76; Bernard Donoughue, *British Politics and the American Revolution: The Path to War, 1773–1775* (1964), 63–86. For an assessment of the acts by an angry American contemporary, see Samuel Williams, *A Discourse on the Love of Our Country; Delivered on a Day of Thanksgiving, December 15, 1774* (1775).

31. Force, ed., *American Archives*, 1:40–41, 49, 54.

32. Merrill Jensen, ed., *English Historical Documents: American Colonial Documents to 1776* (1969), 9:779–85.

33. *Essex Gazette*, 31 January–7 February 1775.

34. *NEW-YORK. The Following DIALOGUE being conceived, in Some Measure, calculated to advance the Cause of FREEDOM* . . . [21 May 1774] (1774).

35. Quoted in Donoughue, *British Politics*, 49.

36. John Shy, *Toward Lexington: The Role of the British Army in the Coming of the American Revolution* (1965).

37. Jacqueline Barbara Carr, *After the Siege: A Social History of Boston 1775–1800* (2005), ch. 1.

38. *Boston Gazette*, 1 August 1774.

39. The organization of the charity for the relief of Boston is examined in detail in Breen, *American Insurgents*, 110–27.

40. *Connecticut Courant*, 14 June 1774.

41. Quoted in Anne M. Ousterhout, *A State Divided: Opposition in Pennsylvania to the American Revolution* (1987), 58.

42. *Boston Gazette*, 5 September 1774; *Essex Gazette*, 19 July 1774; and Massachusetts Historical Society *Collections* 4 (1858), 64, 110.

43. *Boston Gazette*, 10 April 1775.

44. The impact of human sympathy on political culture is the subject of Michael Ignatieff, *The Needs of Strangers* (1984).

45. *Connecticut Courant*, 26 June 1775.

46. *Connecticut Courant*, 5 August 1774.

47. *Connecticut Gazette*, 29 July 1774.

48. Quoted in Richard Anson Wheeler, *History of the Town of Stonington, County of New London, Connecticut* (1900), 36–37.

49. For an account of a rumor that sparked a huge popular mobilization in 1774, see Breen, *American Insurgents*, ch. 5.

50. Ammerman, *In the Common Cause*, ch. 6; Jack Rakove, *Beginnings of National Politics: An Interpretive History of the Continental Congress* (1979), 49–59.

51. The full text of the Association can be found in Jensen, ed., *English Historical Documents*, 9:813–16.

52. Gordon S. Wood, "Conspiracy and the Paranoid Style: Causality and Deceit in the Eighteenth Century," *William and Mary Quarterly* 39 (1982): 401–41.

53. A comparative analysis with other major revolutions would include Sheila Fitzpatrick, *Russian Revolution* (1982); Orlando Figes, *A People's Tragedy: The Russian Revolution: 1891–1924* (1998); Sean McMeekin, *The Russian Revolution: A New History* (2017); Colin Jones, *The Great Nation: France from Louis XV to Napoleon* (2002); Timothy Tackett, *The Coming of the Terror in the French Revolution* (2015); and Howard G. Brown, *Ending the French Revolution: Violence, Justice, and Repression from the Terror to Napoleon* (2006).

54. Quoted in Hugh T. Lefler and William Powell, *Colonial North Carolina: A History* (1973), 266–68. See Merrill Jensen, *The Founding of a Nation: A History of the American Revolution 1763–1776* (1968), ch. 18.

55. Leora McEachen et al., eds., *Wilmington-New Hanover Safety Committee Minutes 1774–1775* (1974), 1–24; also Alfred Moore Waddell, *A History of New Hanover County and the Lower Cape Fear Region* (1909), 77–78.

56. Belknap, *History of New Hampshire*, 2:306.

57. Robert M. Calhoon, Timothy Barnes, and Robert S. Davis, *Tory Insurgents: The Loyalist Perception and Other Essays* (1989), 350–51; Richard Alan Ryerson, *The Revolution Is Now Begun: The Radical Committees of Philadelphia, 1765–1776* (1978), 254–55; Larry R. Gerlach, *Prologue to Independence: New Jersey in the Coming of the American Revolution* (1976), 232–50; Jensen, *Founding*, 516–30; Ousterhout, *State Divided*, 216; Jack D. Marietta and G. S. Rowe, *Troubled Experiment: Crime and Justice in Pennsylvania, 1682–1800* (2006), 181–84; and John L. Brooke, *Columbia Rising: Civil Life on the Upper Hudson from the Revolution to the Age of Jackson* (2010), 22–27.

58. Isaac Mansfield, *A Sermon, Preached in the Camp at Roxbury, November 23, 1775* (1776), 20–21.

59. See the lists in Albert Stillman Batchellor, ed., *Miscellaneous Revolutionary Documents of New Hampshire* (1910). For Maryland, see "Journal of the Committee of Observation of the Middle District of Frederick County, Maryland," *Maryland Historical Magazine* 10 (1915), 305.

60. Quoted in Gerlach, *Prologue*, 262.

61. Records in Edward M. Ruttenber, *History of the Town of New Windsor [New York]* (1911), 58–60.

62. Quoted in Gerlach, *Prologue*, 234.

63. William Edwin Hemphill, ed., *Extracts from the Journals of the Provincial Congresses of South Carolina, 1775–1776* (1960), 59.

64. Quoted in Gerlach, *Prologue*, 269, 275.

65. William L. Saunders, ed., *Colonial Records of North Carolina* (1890), 10:134.

66. Quoted in Ousterhout, *State Divided*, 108.

67. Quoted in Ousterhout, *State Divided*, 79.

68. Quoted in Gerlach, *Prologue*, 232.

69. Quoted in Jensen, *Founding*, 626.

70. Thomas Anburey, *Travels through the Interior Parts of America* (1791), 2:329–30, quoted in Edmund S. Morgan, *American Slavery, American Freedom: The Ordeal of Colonial Virginia* (1974), 378–79.

71. Mercy Otis Warren, *History of the Rise, Progress, and Termination of the American Revolution* [1805], ed. Lester H. Cohen (1999), 1:63.

2. ASSURANCE

Most of the sermons cited in this chapter can be found in Early American Imprint Series I (1639–1800) by Readex.

1. Bernard Bailyn, *Ideological Origins of the American Revolution* (1967).

2. Valuable studies of the intellectual origins of the American Revolution include Bailyn, *Ideological Origins of the American Revolution*; Gordon S. Wood, *Radicalism of the American Revolution* (1991); J. G. A. Pocock, *The Machiavellian Moment: Florentine Political Thought and the Atlantic Republican Tradition* (1975); John Phillip Reid, *Constitutional History of the American Revolution: The Authority of Rights* (1987); Reid, *Constitutional History of the American Revolution: The Authority to*

Legislate (1991); Jack P. Greene, *Constitutional Origins of the American Revolution* (2010); Edmund S. Morgan, *Birth of the Republic* (1956); and Daniel T. Rodgers, "Republicanism: The Career of a Concept," *Journal of American History* 79 (1992): 11–38.

3. See Michael Walzer's provocative analysis of the tensions between religious and secular revolutionary goals in *The Paradox of Liberation: Secular Revolutions and Religious Counterrevolutions* (2015), 134–46.

4. H. T. Dickinson, *Liberty and Property: Political Ideology in Eighteenth-Century Britain* (1979).

5. Works that have been especially helpful are Mark A. Noll, *The Rise of Evangelicalism: The Age of Edwards, Whitefield and the Wesleys* (2018); Noll, *America's God: From Jonathan Edwards to Abraham Lincoln* (2002); Nathan O. Hatch, *Democratization of American Christianity* (1976); Rhys Isaac, "Preachers and Patriots: Popular Culture and the Revolution in Virginia," in *The American Revolution: Explorations in the History of American Radicalism*, ed. Alfred F. Young (1976); Thomas S. Kidd, *God of Liberty: A Religious History of the American Revolution* (2010); Ronald Hoffman and Peter J. Albert, eds., *Religion in a Revolutionary Age* (1974); Susan Juster, *Disorderly Women: Sexual Politics and Evangelicalism in Revolutionary New England* (1996); Catherine A. Brekus, *Sarah Osborn's World: The Rise of Evangelical Christianity in Early America* (2013); Patricia U. Bonomi and Peter R. Eisenstadt, "Church Attendance in the Eighteenth-Century British Colonies," *William and Mary Quarterly*, 3rd ser., 39 (1982): 245–86; Stephen A. Marini, *Radical Sects of Revolutionary New England* (1982); and Christine L. Heyrman, *Southern Cross: The Beginnings of the Bible Belt* (1998); Douglas L. Winiarski, *Darkness Falls on the Land of Light: Experiencing Religious Awakenings in Eighteenth-Century New England* (2017).

6. See Harry S. Stout, *New England Soul: Preaching and Religious Culture in Colonial New England* (1986), Pt. 4.

7. Peter McPhee, *Liberty or Death: The French Revolution* (2016).

8. Eran Shalev, *American Zion: The Old Testament as a Political Text from the Revolution to the Civil War* (2014); James P. Byrd, *Sacred Scripture, Sacred War: The Bible and the American Revolution* (2013).

9. Dan Foster, *On Civil Government, The Substance of Six Sermons, Preached in WINDSOR*. . . . (1775), 33.

10. See Thomas R. Adams, *American Controversy: A Bibliographical Study of the British Pamphlets About the American Disputes, 1764–1783*, 2 vols. (1980); and T. H. Breen, *American Insurgents, American Patriots: The Revolution of the People* (2010), 262–74.

11. Frank Lambert, *Inventing the "Great Awakening"* (2001); and Jon Butler, *Becoming America: The Revolution before 1776* (2000), ch. 5.

12. Quotations in this section from Foster, *On Civil Government*, preface, 73, 4, 25, 26, 29, 33, 31, 59, 58, 57, 70–71, 71, 72.

13. T. H. Breen, *The Lockean Moment: The Language of Rights on the Eve of the American Revolution* (2000). See Dan Edelstein, *On the Spirit of Rights* (2018), part 3.

14. *A Prayer Composed for the Soldiery* . . . (1775), 3. This section of my book builds on ideas first discussed in Breen, *American Insurgents*, ch. 9.

15. *New-England Chronicle or Essex Gazette*, 13–14 July 1775.

16. Cited in Henry Belcher, *The First American Civil War: First Period, 1775–1778*, 2 vols. (1911), 1:208.

17. John Locke, *Two Treatises of Government*, ed. Peter Laslett (1960), 445; also 300, 397–98, 404.

18. Locke, *Two Treatises*, 445. For context see Peter Laslett, "The English Revolution and Locke's Two Treatises of Government," *Cambridge Historical Journal* 12 (1956): 40–55; and John Marshall, *John Locke: Resistance, Religion and Responsibility* (1994).

19. Linda Colley, *Britons: Forging the Nation, 1707–1837* (1992); Paul Langford, *A Polite and Commercial People: England 1727–1783* (1989); Kathleen Wilson, *The Sense of the People: Politics, Culture, and Imperialism in England, 1715–1785* (1995); John Dunn, "The Politics of Locke in England and America in the Eighteenth Century," in *John Locke: Problems and Perspectives*, ed. John W. Yolton, 45–80 (1969). A different view of Locke's importance in America can be found in Isaac Kramnick, *Republicanism and Bourgeois Radicalism: Political Ideology in Late Eighteenth-Century England and America* (1990).

20. *Boston Gazette*, 1 March 1773.

21. Cited in Roger Bruns, ed., *Am I Not a Man and a Brother: The Antislavery Crusade of Revolutionary America, 1688–1788* (1977), 338, also 428, 452–3. Also see Sidney Kaplan, *The Black Presence in the Era of the American Revolution, 1770–1800* (1973), 13. *Boston Gazette and Country Journal*, 23 August 1773.

22. Andrew Lee, *Sin Destructive of Temporal and Eternal Happiness Repentance, Trust in God, and a Vigorous, Harmonious, and persevering Opposition, the Duty of a People When Wicked and Unreasonable Men are Attempting to Enslave Them* (1776), preface.

23. Samuel Baldwin, *A Sermon, Preached at Plymouth, December 22, 1775* (1776), preface.

24. Nathan Perkins, *A Sermon Preached to the Soldiers, Who Went from West-Hartford, in Defense of their Country* (1775), 9.

25. Jonas Clark, *The Fate of Blood-Thirsty Oppressors, and God's Tender Care of his Distressed People* (1776), 15–19.

26. Other ministers developed the theme of making an appeal to heaven: William Gordon, *A Discourse Preached December 15, 1774* (1775), 12; Elisha Fish, *A Discourse Delivered at Worcester, March 28th, 1775* (1775), 22; *America's Appeal to the Impartial World* (1775), 4; John Carmichael, *A Self-Defensive War Lawful, Proved in A Sermon . . . Before Captain Ross's Company of Militia* (1775), 7; Nathan Fiske, *Remarkable Provinces to be Gratefully Recollected* (1776), 29.

27. Ezra Sampson, *A Sermon Preached at Roxbury Camp, Before Col. Cotton's Regiment* (1775), 5.

28. Clark, *Blood-Thirsty Oppressors*, 18–19.

29. Samuel Cooke, *The Violent Destroyed and Oppressed Delivered* (1777), 7.

30. Enoch Huntington, *A Sermon Delivered at Middletown July 20, 1775* (1775), 17.

31. David Jones, *Defensive War in a Just Cause Sinless* (1775), 6.

32. Joseph Montgomery, *A Sermon, Preached at Christiana Bridge and Newcastle* (1775), 12.

33. Samuel Webster, *Rabshaken's Proposals Considered* (1775), 24.

34. Montgomery, *Sermon*, 20.

35. Jones, *Defensive War* 13.

36. Zabdiel Adams, *Grounds of Confidence and Success in War* (1775), 10.

37. [John Allen], *An Oration, Upon the Beauties of Liberty* [1775, originally 1773], iii.

38. One example of many is Jacob Duche, *Duty of Standing Fast in Our Spiritual and Temporal Liberties* (1775), 14.

39. Jones, *Defensive War*, 26.

40. Montgomery, *Sermon*, 10–11.

41. Adams, *Grounds of Confidence*, 26.

42. Duche, *Standing Fast*, 14.

43. Webster, *Rabshaken's Proposals*, 22.

44. Fish, *Discourse*, 22.

45. *Strictures on a Pamphlet Entitled a "Friendly Address to all Reasonable Americans"* (1775), 18.

46. *The American Crisis* (1775), 1.

47. Jones, *Defensive War*, 6. Also Cooke, *Violent Destroyed*, 12.

48. Perkins, *Sermon*, 9.

49. Montgomery, *Sermon*, 29.

50. See the discussion of the *Crisis*, a virulent critique of George III that circulated widely throughout America in 1774 and 1775 both as a separate essay and a newspaper piece in Breen, *American Insurgents*, 262–75.

51. Allen, *An Oration*, 14–18.

52. *Strictures on a Pamphlet*, 15.

53. Clark, *Blood-Thirsty Oppressors*, 21.

54. Lee, *Sin Destructive*, 12, 16, and 19.

55. Adams, *Grounds of Confidence*, 16.

56. Fish, *A Discourse*, 24.

57. Thomas Coombe, *A Sermon Preached Before the Congregation . . . Philadelphia On Thursday, July 20, 1775* (1775). On the significance of boycotting consumer goods as a highly visible form of political protest, see Breen, *Marketplace of Revolution: How Consumer Politics Shaped American Independence* (2004), Pt. 2.

58. Lee, *Sin Destructive*, 26.

59. Enoch Huntington, *The Happy Effects of Union, and the Fatal Tendency of Divisions. Shewn in a Sermon, preached Before the Freemen of the Town of Middleton* (1776), 12.

60. Robert Ross, *A Sermon, in Which the Union of the Colonies is Considered and Recommended* (1776), 20.

61. See David Brion Davis, *The Problem of Slavery in Western Culture* (1966), ch. 12; and Winthrop D. Jordan, *White Over Black: American Attitudes Toward the Negro, 1550–1812* (1968), ch. 7.

62. *A Discourse on the Times* (1776), 4.

63. Levi Hart, *Liberty Described and Recommended* (1775), 16–21.

64. Eliphalet Wright, *A People Ripe for An Harvest. A Sermon, Delivered . . . On a Day of Public Thanksgiving* (1776), 9–10.

65. Joseph Perry, *A Sermon* (1775), 12.

66. Carmichael, *Self-Defensive War Lawful*, 23.

67. Huntington, *Happy Effects*, 20.

68. Perkins, *A Sermon Preached to the Soldiers*, 9.

69. Webster, *Rabshaken's Proposal*, 28.

70. Perkins, *A Sermon Preached to the Soldiers*, 13–14.

71. Gordon, *A Discourse*, 32.

3. FEAR

1. Valuable studies include Timothy Tackett, *The Coming of the Terror in the French Revolution* (2015), ch. 5; Sheila Fitzpatrick, *Everyday Stalinism: Ordinary Life in Extraordinary Times: Soviet Russia in the 1930s* (2000); and Wendy Z. Goldman, *Inventing the Enemy: Denunciation and Terror in Stalin's Russia* (2011).

2. Edmund S. Morgan, *American Slavery, American Freedom: The Ordeal of Colonial Virginia* (1975).

3. Holger Hoock, *Scars of Independence: America's Violent Birth* (2017); Patrick Griffin, *American Leviathan: Empire, Nation, and Revolutionary Frontier* (2008).

4. *Selected Papers of John Jay, vol. 1, 1760–1779*, ed. Elizabeth M. Nuxoll (2010), 251.

5. *Maryland Journal*, 22 July 1777.

6. Gordon Wood, "Rhetoric and Reality in the American Revolution," *William and Mary Quarterly*, 3rd ser., 23 (1966): 3–32.

7. Winthrop Jordan provides brilliant insight into the exclusionary aspects of political identity in *White Over Black: American Attitudes Toward the Negro, 1550–1812* (1968), ch. 8.

8. Robert G. Parkinson, *The Common Cause: Creating Race and Nation in the American Revolution* (2017); and T. H. Breen, "Ideology and Nationalism on the Eve of the American Revolution: Revisions Once More in Need of Revising," *Journal of American History* 84 (1997): 13–39.

9. *New York Packet, and American Advertiser*, 4 December 1777.

10. Nicholas Collin, *The Journal and Biography of Nicholas Collin, 1746–1831*, trans. and ed. Amandus Johnson (1936); and Richard Waldron, "'A True Servant of the Lord': Nils Collin, the Church of Sweden, and the American Revolution in Gloucester County," *New Jersey History* 126 (2011): 96–103.

11. Collin, *Journal*, 236–237.

12. Collin, *Journal*, 245.

13. Collin, *Journal*, 237–238.

14. Collin, *Journal*, 244.

15. Collin, *Journal*, 246.

16. Collin, *Journal*, 249.

17. Quotation in Robert Bolton, *A History of the County of Westchester, From its First Settlement to the Present Time* (1848), xvi–xvii.

18. Most helpful for an analysis of Tory sympathizers are Robert M. Calhoon, *The Loyalists in Revolutionary America, 1760–1781* (1973); Thomas B. Allen, *Tories: Fighting for King in America's First Civil War* (2010); Wallace Brown, *Good Americans: The Loyalists in the American Revolution* (1969); Paul H. Smith, *Loyalists and Redcoats: A Study in British Revolutionary Policy* (1964); and Ruma Chopra, *Unnatural Rebellion: Loyalists in New York City during the Revolution* (2013).

19. Donald Johnson, "Ambiguous Allegiances: Urban Loyalties during the American Revolution," *Journal of American History* 104 (2017): 610–31.

20. "The Art of Toryism and the Dignity of Whiggism," *Independent Chronicle*, 21 January 1777.

21. *Maryland Journal*, 22 July 1777.

22. *Maryland Journal*, 22 July 1777.

23. See, for example, David J. Fowler, "Egregious Villains, Wood Rangers, and London Raiders: The Pine Robber Phenomenon in New Jersey During the Revolutionary War" (PhD diss., Rutgers University, 1987); Adele Hast, *Loyalism in Revolutionary Virginia: The Norfolk Area and the Eastern Shore* (1982); Howard Pashman, *Building a Revolutionary State: The Legal Transformation of New York, 1776–1783* (2018); and Ronald Hoffman, Thad W. Tate, and Peter J. Albert, eds., *An Uncivil War: The Southern Backcountry during the American Revolution* (1985).

24. *Boston Gazette*, 14 October 1776; also *Pennsylvania Evening-Post*, 20 August 1776.

25. *Archives of Maryland. Journal and Correspondence of the Council of Safety January 1– March 20, 1777,* ed. William Hand Browne (1897), 87.

26. *Journals of the Provincial Congress, Provincial Convention, and Committee of Safety and Council of Safety of the State of New-York 1775–1776–1777* (1842), 1:687.

27. *Independent Chronicle*, 13 February and 29 May 1777; *Norwich Packet*, 9 September 1776; *Pennsylvania Evening Post*, 18 July 1778; *New-Hampshire Gazette*, 5 July 1783; *Boston Gazette*, 28 April and 12 May, 1777; *Connecticut Gazette*, 7 June 1776; and Hast, *Loyalism*, 133.

28. *Constitutional Gazette*, 5 June 1776.

29. *Connecticut Gazette*, 19 September 1777.

30. *Independent Chronicle*, 21 January 1777.

31. *Maryland Journal*, 18 September 1776.

32. See the "Rules for the Government of the [Baltimore] Whig Club." Prospective members eager to ferret out "secret and disguised enemies" swore on oath "that I will, as far in me lies, detect all traitors (and discover all traitorous conspiracies against this State as established by the authority of the people) without favor or affection." *Maryland Journal*, 11 February 1777.

33. *Connecticut Gazette*, 23 May 1777.

34. *Connecticut Journal*, 9 February 1778.

35. *Boston Gazette*, 12 May 1777. See Alfred F. Young's discussion of "Joyce, Junior" in "Tar and Feathers and the Ghost of Oliver Cromwell," *Liberty Tree: Ordinary People and the American Revolution* (2006), ch. 3.

36. *Freeman's Journal, or New-Hampshire Gazette*, 14 January 1777; also *Boston Gazette*, 12 May 1777.

37. *Connecticut Gazette*, 7 June 1776.

38. *Independent Chronicle*, 8 May 1777.

39. *Pennsylvania Packet*, 11 April 1777.

40. *Journals of the [NY] Provincial Congress*, 2:454.

41. *Independent Chronicle*, 9 January 1777.

42. *Independent Chronicle*, 29 May 1777.

43. *Norwich Packet*, 9 September 1776.

44. Samuel Adams to John Pitts, 15 February 1777, in *Letters of Delegates to Congress, 1774–1789*, ed. Paul H. Smith (1980), 6:278–79.

45. *Maryland Journal*, 22 July 1777.

46. *New-Hampshire Gazette*, 21 September 1776.

47. *Freeman's Journal*, 14 September 1776.

48. *Connecticut Gazette*, 25 April 1777.

49. *Continental Journal*, 15 August 1776.

50. "Norwalk Memorial," 25 October 1776, in Royal R. Hinman, comp., *Historical Collections from Official Records . . . Connecticut During the Revolution* (1842), 565.

51. *Journals of the Provincial Congress* [Albany: 15 October 1776], 687. Also *Boston Gazette*, 9 June 1777.

52. *Minutes of the Commissioners for Detecting and Defeating Conspiracies in the State of New York (Albany County Sessions)* (1909), 2:445, 448.

53. Massachusetts Archives, Vol. 183 (Revolutionary Petitions), 21 October 1777, for Charles Callahan investigation. I want to thank James Hrdlicka for bringing this material to my attention.

54. *In Council of Safety, Philadelphia, December 7, 1776* [Broadside] (1776).

55. Cornelia Dayton presentation ("Revolutionary Law") at the Huntington Library Conference, Revolutionary America, May 15–16, 2015. I want to thank Linda Hocking of the Litchfield Historical Society (Connecticut) for providing relevant materials from the Litchfield archives.

56. *Archives of Maryland*, ed. Browne, 11:309–10. Also see Aubrey C. Land, *Colonial Maryland: A History* (1981), 311–12; and Patrick K. O'Donnell, *Washington's Immortals* (2016), ch. 4.

57. *Archives of Maryland*, ed. Browne, 11:416.

58. *Calendar of Historical Manuscripts Relating to the War of the Revolution* (1868), 1:328–29. Joseph Cord was censured by the Sussex County [Delaware] Committee of Inspection for "unfriendly speeches." *Pennsylvania Packet*, 29 January 1776.

59. *Minutes of the Committee and Of the First Commission for Detecting and Defeating Conspiracies* (1924), 1:130. Also *Minutes of the Commissioners*, 2:442.

60. *Minutes of the Commissioners*, 1:349.

61. *Calendar of Historical Manuscripts*, 2:116.

62. *Maryland Journal*, 10 June 1777.

63. Quotations in Freeman Hansford Hart, *The Valley of Virginia in the American Revolution* (1942), 102–4.

64. *Minutes of the Commissioners*, 1:355.

65. *Maryland Journal*, 10 June 1777.

66. Massachusetts Archives, Vol. 182 (Revolutionary Petitions), 182–91.

67. *Connecticut Courant*, 22 July 1776.

68. *Freeman's Journal*, 14 September 1776.

69. Charles James Taylor, *History of Great Barrington* (1882), 246.

70. *Minutes of the Commissioners*, 2:443–44, 448, 451.

71. See Andrew O'Shaughnessy, *The Men Who Lost America: British Command during the Revolutionary War and the Preservation of the Empire* (2013), chs. 3 and 4; and Don Higginbotham, *The War of American Independence* (1983).

72. Cited in Robert F. Oaks, "Philadelphians in Exile: The Problem of Loyalty during the American Revolution," *Pennsylvania Magazine of History and Biography* 96 (1972): 298–325.

73. "Diary of James Allen, Esq., of Philadelphia," *Pennsylvania Magazine of History and Biography* 9 (1885), 193.

74. About the North Carolina group almost nothing is known. These were civilian prisoners, not British prisoners of war. Other states also relocated suspects.

75. *An Address to the Inhabitants of Pennsylvania* (1777).

76. Jack D. Marietta, *The Reformation of American Quakerism, 1748–1783* (1984), ch. 11; Oaks, "Exile," 208–303; and Thomas Gilpin, *Exiles in Virginia: With Observations on the Conduct of the Society of Friends During the Revolutionary War* (1848), 87–93. I want to thank Jack Marietta for his generous advice about law and religion in revolutionary Pennsylvania.

77. Books that provide historical context for the contagion of fear that swept through New York include George C. Daughan, *Revolution on the Hudson: New York City and the Hudson River Valley in the War of Independence* (2017); Burnet Schecter, *The Battle for New York: The City at the Heart of the American Revolution* (2003); Todd W. Braisted, *Grand Forage 1778: The Battleground around New York City* (2016); Judith L. Van Buskirk, *Generous Enemies: Patriots and Loyalists in Revolutionary New York* (2002); the essays in *Key to the Northern Country: The Hudson Valley in the American Revolution*, ed. James M. Johnson, Andrew Villani, and Christopher Pryslopski (2013); and *The Other New York: The American Revolution Beyond New York City, 1763–1787*, ed. Joseph S. Tiedermann and Eugene R. Fingerhut (2005).

78. *Minutes of the Committee*, 1:xii–xiii.

79. *Minutes of the Committee*, 1:13.

80. Peter Force, ed., *American Archives: Consisting of a Collection of Authentick* [*sic*] *Records, State Papers, Debates and Letters* . . . , 5th ser., 3 vols. (1837–53), 1:467–68.

81. *Journals of the Provincial Congress*, 876.

82. *American Archives*, 5th ser., 2:1314.

83. John Jay to the General Court of New Hampshire, [31 October 1776], in *Papers of John Jay*, 1:306.

84. *Minutes of the Committee*, 2:416–17.

85. Charles H. Bell, *History of the Town of Exeter, New Hampshire* (1888), 90; *Papers of Josiah Bartlett*, ed. Frank C. Mevers (1979), 134–35.

86. Quoted in Albertus T. Dudley, "Tory Prisoners in Exeter," unpublished paper, Exeter Historical Society, 9; Otis Grant Hammond, *Tories of New Hampshire in the War of the Revolution* (1917), 31.

87. *Papers of John Jay*, 134.

88. Dudley, "Tory Prisoners," 11–12.

89. *Provincial and State Papers of New Hampshire*, vol. 8, ed. Nathaniel Bouton (1894), 394.

90. *Provincial and State Papers of New Hampshire*, 394–95.

91. *Provincial and State Papers of New Hampshire*, 394.

92. *Minutes of the Committee*, 2:418, 434.

93. *Provincial and State Papers of New Hampshire*, 498.

4. JUSTICE

1. For a good account of how initial enthusiasm rapidly fell off as the war continued, see Charles Royster, *A Revolutionary People at War: The Continental Army and American Character* (1996).

2. *Archives of Maryland*, ed. Bernard C. Steiner (1927), 45:467. Also see Dorothy M. Quynn, "The Loyalist Plot in Frederick," *Maryland Historical Magazine* 40 (1945): 201–10; and Ken Miller, *Dangerous Guests: Enemy Captives and Revolutionary Communities during the War for Independence* (2014), ch. 6.

3. The judge's charge to the jury in *Pennsylvania Packet*, 12 September 1781.

4. Quotations in Thomas John Chew Williams, *History of Frederick County, Maryland, From the Earliest Settlements to the Beginning of the War Between the States*, 2 vols. (1910), 1:96–97.

5. See Michel Foucault, *Discipline and Punishment: The Birth of the Prison*, trans. Alan Sheridan (1995), ch. 1.

6. *Freeman's Journal*, 14 August 1781.

7. Williams, *Frederick County*, 1:96.

8. On prerevolutionary law, William Nelson, *Americanization of the Common Law: The Impact of Legal Change on Massachusetts Society, 1760–1830* (1994). Few legal scholars have investigated legal institutions and practices during the Revolution. Howard Pashman has provided a persuasive model of how the project might be carried out in *Building a Revolutionary State: Legal Transformation of New York, 1776–1783* (2018).

9. Jack D. Marietta and G. S. Rowe, *Troubled Experiment: Crime and Justice in Pennsylvania, 1682–1800* (2006), 181–84.

10. For example, *Calendar of Manuscripts Relating to the War of the Revolution* (1868), 2:179–82.

11. Agnew Hunt, *The Provincial Committees of Safety of the American Revolution* (1904).

12. "The Tory Act," *Connecticut Gazette*, 26 January 1776.

13. In some states legislative assemblies or executive councils appointed committee members.

14. "Journal and Correspondence of the Maryland Council of Safety July 7–December 31, 1776," *Archives of Maryland*, ed. William Hand Browne (1893), 12:281.

15. *Maryland Journal*, 18 February 1777.

16. *Pennsylvania Packet*, 8 June 1779.

17. Quotation in William Jay, *Life of John Jay* (1833), 1:49–50.

18. "An Act for Taking Up, Imprisoning or Otherwise Restraining Persons Dangerous to this State," 18 June 1777, *State Papers, Documents and Reports*, ed. Nathaniel Bolton (1874), 8:592–93.

19. "An Ordinance for the Establishment of a Mode of Punishment for the Enemies to America in this Colony [Virginia]," *Maryland Journal*, 7 February 1776.

20. *General Assembly of Connecticut, October 1776* (1776), 1.

21. *Maryland Journal*, 17 March 1777.

22. Hugh M. Flick, "The Rise of the Revolutionary Committee System," in *The History of the State of New York*, ed. Alexander C. Flick (1933), 3:209–254. Also see *Minutes of the Committee of Observation and Inspection of Northampton County, Pennsylvania 1774–1777*, ed. Michael J. Symons (1966); and Francis S. Fox, *Sweet Land of Liberty: The Ordeal of the American Revolution in Northampton County, Pennsylvania* (2000). A comparison from the French Revolution is instructive: Lynn Hunt, "Committees and Communes: Local Politics and National Revolution in 1789," *Comparative Studies in Society and History* 18 (1976): 321–46.

23. Merrill Jensen, *The Founding of a Nation: A History of the American* Revolution (1968), 634–35; Don Higginbotham, *The War of American Independence: Military Attitudes, Policies, and Practice, 1763–1789* (1983), 103–04; and Robert Middlekauff, *Washington's Revolution: The Making of America's First Leader* (2015), 124, 234–35.

24. John Shy, "Armed Loyalism: The Case of the Lower Hudson Valley" and "The Military Conflict Considered as a Revolutionary War," in Shy, *A People Numerous and Armed: Reflections on the Military Struggle for American Independence* (1976), 21–34, 181–92.

25. *Papers of William Livingston*, ed. Carl E. Prince (1979), 323. Also see *Selected Papers of John Jay*, ed. Elizabeth M. Nuxoll (2010), 1:254–55; and Clyde R. Ferguson, "Carolina and Georgia Patriot and Loyalist Militia in Action, 1778–1783," in *The Southern Experience in the American Revolution*, ed. Jeffrey J. Crow and Larry E. Tise (1978), 175.

26. James H. Kettner, *Development of American Citizenship* (1978), 179–180.

27. *Maryland Journal*, 15 July 1777; *Maryland Gazette*, 10 July 1777.

28. *Colony of Massachusetts-Bay, 1776* [broadside] (1776). And *Connecticut Courant*, 18 November 1776.

29. *Maryland Gazette*, 10 July 1777.

30. Otis Grant Hammond, *Tories of New Hampshire in the War of Revolution* (1917), 6–9.

31. "Petition from Portsmouth," 10 June 1777, *State Papers, Documents and Reports*, ed. Bouton, 8:581.

32. *Connecticut Gazette*, 2 January 1781.

33. *Minutes of the Commissioners for Detecting and Defeating Conspiracies in the State of New York*, ed. Victor Hugo Paltsits (1909), 1:10–13.

34. *Papers of Livingston*, 1:274.

35. *State Papers*, ed. Bouton, 8:592–93.
36. *State Papers*, ed. Bouton, 8:593–97.
37. *Connecticut Journal*, 9 February 1778.
38. *Maryland Journal*, 13 May 1777.
39. *Constitutional Gazette*, 5 June 1776.
40. *New-England Chronicle*, 18 July 1776. See also *Journals of the Provincial Congress, Provincial Convention, and Committee of Safety and Council of Safety of the State of New-York 1775–1777* (1842), 1:891.
41. *Journals of the Provincial Congress* (1842), 1:899; *Minutes of the Commissioners*, ed. Paltsits, 247–48.
42. Quotations from Henry C. Van Schaack, *Life of Peter Van Schaack* (1842), 67–80, 112–22, 132, 302–303.
43. *Minutes of the Committee of Observation and Inspection of Northampton County, PA. 1774–1777*, 56.
44. *Minutes of the Committee of Observation and Inspection*, 63–66. Also *Minutes of the Albany Committee of Correspondence 1775–1778* (1925), 1113–1114, 1137.
45. *Journals of the Provincial Congress*, 855–56.
46. *Pennsylvania Packet*, 29 January 1776.
47. J. E. A. Smith, *History of Pittsfield* (1869), 251.
48. *Historical Collections From Official Records, Files . . .* , comp. by Royal R. Hinman (1842), 574–75.
49. *Archives of Maryland*, ed. Browne, 16:87–99.
50. "At a Meeting of the Committee of Safety & Observation of the Town of Kingston in the County of Ulster," [9 April 1777], in *Calendar of Manuscripts*, 72–74.
51. State courts discovered that juries were reluctant to convict people of treason, a crime that mandated capital punishment. Aware of such scruples, revolutionary prosecutors reduced the charges to crimes that involved fines. Many states seized the property of notorious loyalists—usually those who had departed from their communities—but while revolutionary authorities anticipated that funds from the sale of this property would help pay for the costs of the war, they discovered that seizure of loyalist property seldom produced much money. Laws required that all liens against the property—primarily outstanding debts—be paid, leaving little money for the state. See Harry M. Ward, *The War for Independence and the Transformation of American Society* (1999), 38–40; Jack D. Marietta and G. S. Rowe, *Troubled Experiment: Crime and Justice in Pennsylvania 1682–1800* (2006), 188–90; [Massachusetts] *Acts and Resolves for 1777* (1867), 612–19; David E. Maas, *Divided Hearts: Massachusetts Loyalists 1765–1790* (1980), xi–xii; and Pashman, *Building a Revolutionary State*.
52. *Minutes of the Commissioners*, 190–94.
53. *Minutes of the Albany Committee*, 2:1131.
54. *Journals of the Provincial Congress*, 284–85.
55. *Minutes of the Commissioners for Detecting*, 2:613–19. For other New York cases involving suspects who were women, see 522–23, 525, 696.

56. Ronald Hoffman, Thad W. Tate, and Peter J. Albert, *An Uncivil War: The Southern Backcountry during the American Revolution* (1985).

57. *Newport Mercury*, 18 July 1776.

58. *Pennsylvania Evening Post*, 18 July 1778.

59. *Connecticut Gazette*, 11 April 1777.

60. *Boston Gazette*, 28 April 1777.

61. *Pennsylvania Evening Post*, 18 July 1778.

62. *Pennsylvania Packet*, 8 June 1779.

63. Quotation in Joy Day Buel and Richard Buel, Jr., *The Way of Duty: A Woman and Her Family in Revolutionary America* (1984), 133–34.

64. *Independent Chronicle*, 15 May 1777.

65. Franklin P. Price, ed., *Worcester Town Records From 1753 to 1783* (1882), 301–02, 308–09. For other towns, see Sidney Perley, *History of Boxford, Essex County, Massachusetts* (1880), 238; Charles James Taylor, *History of Great Barrington* (1882), 244–45; and William Addison Benedict, *History of the Town of Sutton* (1878), 105.

5. BETRAYAL

1. *Pennsylvania Packet*, 24 December 1777, originally published in the *Connecticut Courant*.

2. Jonathan French, *A Practical Discourse Against Extortion* (Boston, 1777). The sermon was delivered in Andover, Massachusetts, on 1 January 1777.

3. John J. McCusker and Russell R. Menard, *The Economy of British America, 1607–1789* (1985), 358–59.

4. The quotations in this section come from *The Downfall of Justice; and the Farmer Just Return'd From Meeting on Thanksgiving Day. A Comedy Lately Acted in Connecticut* (1777). I want to thank Barbara Clark Smith for bringing this play to my attention. See her analysis of the "Patriot Economy" in *The Freedoms We Lost: Consent and Resistance in Revolutionary America* (2010), ch. 4.

5. R. H. Tawney, *Religion and the Rise of Capitalism* (1998 edition), chs. 1 and 3.

6. On the slaves of revolutionary Danvers, see Harriet S. Tapley, *Chronicles of Danvers (Old Salem Village) Massachusetts 1632–1923* (1923), 50–54.

7. On the moral tensions within capitalism, see Michael Ignatieff, *The Needs of Strangers* (2001).

8. Republished in *New-Jersey Gazette*, 21 January 1778.

9. Ralph V. Harlow, "Economic Conditions in Massachusetts during the American Revolution," *Colonial Society of Massachusetts* 20 (1918), 163–90; Steven Rosswurm, *Arms, Country, and Class: The Philadelphia Militia and "Lower Sort" during the American Revolution* (1987), 170–97; and Jackson Turner Main, *Sovereign States, 1775–1783* (1973), 232–63.

10. Eliphalet Wright, *A People Ripe for An Harvest. A Sermon, Delivered . . . On a Day of Public Thanksgiving* (1776), 9–10.

11. *Massachusetts Spy*, 7 July 1779.

12. *Virginia Gazette*, 1 April 1780.

13. *Pennsylvania Packet*, 20 January 1780.

14. *Norwich Packet*, 12 October 1779; also *Connecticut Gazette*, 20 October 1779.

15. Gordon S. Wood, "Rhetoric and Reality in the American Revolution," *William and Mary Quarterly*, 3rd ser., 23 (1966): 3–32.

16. *New-Jersey Gazette*, 27 April 1780.

17. *New-Jersey Gazette*, 17 March 1779. Also *Connecticut Courant*, 8 June 1779.

18. *Virginia Gazette*, 24 July 1779.

19. Abraham Keteltas, *Reflections on Extortion* (1778) [Sermon delivered in Newburyport, 5 February 1778], 25.

20. Charles Chauncey, *The Accursed Thing Must be Taken Away from among a People, if They would Reasonably hope to stand Before Their Enemies* (1778), 23.

21. T. H. Breen, *The Marketplace of Revolution: How Consumer Politics Shaped American Independence* (2004), 184–87.

22. William Gordon, *The Separation of the Jewish Tribes, After the Death of Solomon* (1777), 31.

23. *New-Jersey Gazette*, 30 June 1779.

24. Jonathan French, *A Practical Discourse Against Extortion* (1777), 13.

25. *New-Jersey Gazette*, 16 June 1779.

26. French, *A Practical Discourse*, 13–17.

27. French, *A Practical Discourse*, 30.

28. *Pennsylvania Gazette*, 14 April 1779.

29. *Massachusetts Spy*, 2 September 1779.

30. Israel Evans, *A Discourse Delivered at Easton* [Pennsylvania] (1779), 25.

31. *New-Jersey Gazette*, 19 January 1780.

32. Town Resolves quoted in William Lincoln, *History of Worcester, Massachusetts: From Its Earliest Settlement to September, 1836* (1837), 108.

33. *Pennsylvania Gazette*, 31 March 1779. Also published in *New-Jersey Gazette*, 17 March 1779.

34. *New-Jersey Gazette*, 10 March 1779.

35. *Pennsylvania Packet*, 24 December 1777, republished from the *Connecticut Courant*.

36. *New-Jersey Gazette*, 26 May 1779.

37. *Connecticut Courant*, 15 June 1779.

38. *New-Jersey Gazette*, 26 May 1779, and *Pennsylvania Gazette*, 31 March 1779.

39. *New-Jersey Gazette*, 10 May 1779.

40. *Continental Journal*, 16 September 1779.

41. *Virginia Gazette*, 24 July 1779.

42. Gordon, *The Separation*, 31.

43. Keteltas, *Reflections on Extortion*, 6.

44. French, *A Practical Discourse*, 24–25.

45. French, *A Practical Discourse*, 13.

46. *Pennsylvania Evening Post*, 29 June 1779; and *Connecticut Courant*, 15 June 1779.

47. *Pennsylvania Packet*, 10 September 1779.

48. *Connecticut Courant*, 6 July 1779.

49. *Pennsylvania Packet*, 10 September 1779. Emma Hart, "Smith's *Wealth of Nations* and Popular Economic Ideology in 1776," paper at Global 1776 conference, Kylemore Abbey, Ireland, 7–10 January 2019.

50. *Connecticut Courant*, 6 July 1779.

51. *New-Jersey Gazette*, 16 June 1779.

52. *Connecticut Courant*, 15 June 1779.

53. *Norwich Packet*, 10 August 1779.

54. *Connecticut Gazette*, 1 July 1779.

55. *Wednesday, July 14, 1779. Williamsburg to Wit: Ever Attentive to the Interests of Their Country* (1779) [Broadside]; *Virginia Gazette*, 17 July and 24 July, 1779.

56. *New York Journal, or, General Advertiser*, 21 June 1779.

57. *New-Jersey Gazette*, 17 January 1781.

58. *New-Jersey Gazette*, 4 August 1779.

59. *New-Jersey Gazette*, 1 September 1779.

60. *New-Jersey Gazette*.

61. *New-Jersey Gazette*, 16 June 1779.

62. *In Pursuance of an Act from the great and General Court, of the State of Massachusetts-Bay, Entitled an "Act to Prevent Monopoly and Oppression"*. . . . (Newburyport, 1777).

63. *List of Prices for the Town of Salem*. . . . (1779). And *The Price Act or, the List of Prices now in Force in the Town of Ipswich, for the Prevention of Monopoly and Oppression*. . . . (1779).

64. *Connecticut Gazette*, 20 October 1779. Also see *Norwich Packet*, 19 October 1779; and Jackson Turner Main, *The Sovereign States, 1775–1783* (1973), 232–52.

65. *New York Gazette and Weekly Mercury*, 3 January 1780.

66. *Massachusetts Spy*, 5 November 1779.

67. *Massachusetts Spy*, 5 November 1779.

68. *Boston Gazette*, 16 June 1777; *Independent Ledger*, 6 September 1779.

69. *Independent Chronicle*, 24 April 1777.

70. *Pennsylvania Journal*, 27 October 1779; *Connecticut Gazette*, 15 September 1779; and *Proceedings of a Convention of Delegates from Eighteen Towns in the County of Essex*. . . . (1779) [Broadside].

71. *Massachusetts Spy*, 12 August 1779.

72. *Independent Ledger*, 19 July 1779.

73. Samuel Sewall, *History of Woburn, Middlesex County, Massachusetts* (1868), 382.

74. *Independent Chronicle*, 2 September and 14 October, 1779; *Independent Ledger*, 19 July 1779; and *Pennsylvania Packet*, 22 July 1779.

75. *Connecticut Journal*, 1 April 1778.

76. *Massachusetts Spy*, 5 November 1779.

77. *New-Jersey Gazette*, 29 September 1779.

78. *Independent Chronicle*, 24 April 1777.

79. *Pennsylvania Packet*, 8 June 1779.

80. *Connecticut Journal*, 1 April 1778.

6. REVENGE

1. Thomas Paine, *Common Sense*, in *Complete Writings*, ed. Philip Foner (1945), 1:22–23.

2. Quoted in Ruma Chopra, *Unnatural Rebellion: Loyalists in New York City during the Revolution* (2011), 211–12. See Maya Jasanoff, *Liberty's Exiles: American Loyalists in the Revolutionary World* (2012), ch. 1.

3. Piers Mackesy, *The War for America 1775–1783* (1993), ch. 14; and Paul H. Smith, *Loyalists and Redcoats: A Study in British Revolutionary Policy* (1964), 139–42.

4. Quoted in Rebecca Brannon, *From Revolution to Reunion: The Reintegration of the South Carolina Loyalists* (2016), 27; and the essays in Brannon and Joseph S. Moore, eds., *The Consequences of Loyalism: Essays in Honor of Robert M. Calhoon* (2019). For a fuller understanding of the character of irregular warfare in the South, see Ronald Hoffman, Thad W. Tate, and Peter J. Albert, eds., *An Uncivil War: The Southern Backcountry during the America Revolution* (1985); and Leslie Hall, *Land and Allegiance in Revolutionary Georgia* (2001).

5. Quotation in Michael E. Stevens, "The Hanging of Matthew Love," *South Carolina Historical Magazine*, 88 (1987), 60–61.

6. Brannon, *From Revolution*, ch. 2; and *South Carolina Gazette and General Advertiser*, 10 June 1783.

7. Quoted in Rebecca Brannon, "Reconciling the Revolution" (PhD diss., University of Michigan, 2007), 319.

8. *South Carolina Gazette*, 10 June 1783.

9. *South Carolina Gazette*, 10 June 1783.

10. Burke letter dated 14 December 1784, in Stevens, "The Hanging of Matthew Love," 55–58. Also Robert S. Lambert, *South Carolina Loyalists in the American Revolution* (1987), ch. 17.

11. Paul H. Smith, "The American Loyalists: Notes on Their Organization and Numerical Strength," *William and Mary Quarterly*, 3rd ser., 25 (1968): 258–77.

12. Jasanoff, *Liberty's Exiles*, Introduction and ch. 1; Judith L. Van Buskirk, *Generous Enemies: Patriots and Loyalists in Revolutionary New York* (2002); Robert M. Calhoon, "The Reintegration of the Loyalists and the Disaffected," in *The American Revolution: Its Character and Limits*, ed. Jack P. Greene (1987), 51–74; Chopra, *Unnatural Rebellion*, 136–58; and Don Johnson, "Ambiguous Allegiances: Urban Loyalties during the American Revolution," *Journal of American History* 104 (2017): 610–31.

13. See Richard B. Morris, *The Peacemakers: The Great Powers and American Independence* (1965).

14. Morris, *The Peacemakers*, 461–65.

15. *New York Journal*, 29 April 1784.

16. Samuel Adams to John Adams, 4 November 1783, *Founders Online*, National Archives, Washington, DC.

17. *South Carolina Gazette and General Advertiser*, 22 July 1783. Also *Boston Evening Post and General Advertiser*, 19 April 1783; *Boston Gazette*, 5 May 1783.

18. *New Hampshire Gazette*, 26 July 1783. Also *South Carolina Gazette and General Advertiser*, 22 July 1783; *Boston Gazette*, 14 April 1783; *South Carolina Weekly Gazette*, 21 June 1783.

19. *Newport Mercury*, 11 October 1783.

20. *Boston Evening Post and General Advertiser*, 19 April 1783.

21. *New York Journal*, 8 April 1783.

22. *Boston Gazette*, 5 May 1783.

23. Report of meeting held on 24 April 1783, *Boston Gazette*, 5 May 1783. See Oscar Zeichner, "The Rehabilitation of Loyalists in Connecticut," *New England Quarterly* 11 (1938):308–30.

24. *Boston Gazette*, 19 May 1783.

25. *Diaries of George Washington*, ed. Donald Jackson and Dorothy Twohig (1979), 5:477.

26. Charles Hudson, *History of the Town of Lexington, Middlesex County, Massachusetts* (1868), 1:244–47.

27. *Pennsylvania Journal*, 4 June 1783. Reprinted in *New Jersey Gazette*, 11 June 1783. William Lincoln, *History of Worcester, Massachusetts* (1836), 114–15; and Franklin P. Rice, ed., *Worcester Town Records From 1753 to 1783* (1882), 440–45.

28. Samuel Sewall, *History of Woburn, Middlesex County, Massachusetts* (1868), 404–405. Similar resolutions from other towns can be found in *Boston Gazette*, 5 May 1783; Ithamar B. Sawtelle, *History of the Town of Townshend, Middlesex County, Massachusetts* (1878), 192–97; *Connecticut Journal*, 17 April 1783; George and Henry Wheeler, *History of Brunswick, Topsham, and Harpswell, Maine* (1878), 689; and *Boston Gazette and County Journal*, 5 May 1783.

29. *South Carolina Gazette and General Advertiser*, 22 July 1783. Also published in *Pennsylvania Journal*, 4 June 1783.

30. *New York Journal*, 8 April 1784.

31. *Independent Chronicle*, 29 December 1785; and *Boston Gazette*, 5 May 1783.

32. *New York Journal*, 8 April 1784.

33. *New Hampshire Gazette*, 26 July 1783.

34. *Pennsylvania Journal*, 4 June 1783.

35. *New York Journal*, 8 April 1784.

36. *New York Journal*, 8 April 1784.

37. *New Jersey Gazette*, 2 October 1782.

38. *Boston Gazette*, 5 May 1783.

39. Nathaniel Whitaker, *The Reward of Toryism* (1783), 6–7, 24–29.

40. *Independent Gazetteer*, 10 May 1783.

41. *Pennsylvania Gazette*, 2 October 1782.

42. *New York Journal*, 8 April 1784.

43. *Connecticut Courant*, 20 January 1784.

44. *Maryland Journal*, 24 February 1784.

45. *Maryland Journal*, 24 February 1784.

46. New Haven, Connecticut, Committee resolve 8 March 1784, in Zeichner, "Rehabilitation," 328.

47. "A dialogue Between a Country Justice and a Committee Man, Concerning the Loyalists, &c.," *Massachusetts Gazette*, 2 November 1783.

48. *South Carolina Gazette*, 15 July 1783.

49. Oscar Zeichner, "The Loyalist Problem in New York after the Revolution," *New York History* 21 (1940): 296–99; *New Jersey Gazette*, 5 July 1784; *Continental Journal*, 13 November 1783.

50. *Pennsylvania Packet or the General Advertiser*, 19 April 1783, from the *New Jersey Gazette* 16 April 1783. Reprinted in *Boston Gazette*, 5 May 1783, and *Independent Chronicle*, 1 August 1782.

51. John Shy, "Looking Backward, Looking Forward: War and Society in Revolutionary America," in *War and Society in the American Revolution*, ed. John Resch and Walter Sargent (2007), 7–17.

52. Zeichner, "Rehabilitation," 323–24; John Shy, "Force, Order, and Democracy in the American Revolution," in *The American Revolution: Its Character and Limits*, ed. Jack P. Greene (1987), 75–79.

53. Zeichner, "Loyalist Problem," 296–98; David E. Maas, *Divided Hearts: Massachusetts Loyalists 1765–1790* (1980), xi; Emory G. Evans, "Trouble in the Backcountry: Disaffection in Southwest Virginia During the American Revolution," in *An Uncivil War: The Southern Backcountry during the American Revolution*, ed. Ronald Hoffman, 179–212 (1994).

54. Israel Evans, *A Discourse . . . On the 11th December 1783* (1783), 17.

55. For a finely nuanced account of the deep racial tensions within the revolutionary culture, see Alan Taylor, *American Revolutions: A Continental History, 1750–1804* (2016), chs. 5, 6, and 12.

56. Donald F. Johnson, "Occupied America: Everyday Experience and the Failure of Imperial Authority in Revolutionary Cities under British Rule, 1775–1783" (PhD diss., Northwestern University, 2015); Brannon, *From Revolution to Reunion*; and Adele Hast, *Loyalism in Revolutionary Virginia* (1979), 149–51.

57. *South Carolina Gazette and General Advertiser*, 15 July 1783.

58. Quoted in Robert M. Weir, "'The Violent Spirit,' The Reestablishment of Order, and the Continuity of Leadership in Post-Revolutionary South Carolina," in Hoffman, ed., *An Uncivil War*, 70–98.

59. J. E. A. Smith, *The History of Pittsfield, Massachusetts From the Year 1734 to the Year 1800* (1869), 247–49.

7. REFLECTIONS

1. See, for example, Joseph J. Ellis, *American Dialogue: The Founders and Us* (2018); Gordon S. Wood, *Friends Divided: John Adams and Thomas Jefferson* (2017); Bernard Bailyn, *To Begin the World Anew: The Genius and Ambiguities of the American Founders* (2003); and Jack N. Rakove, *Revolutionaries: A New History of the Invention of America* (2010).

2. Bernard Bailyn, *The Ideological Origins of the American Revolution* (1967).

3. Gad Hitchcock, *A Sermon Preached at Plymouth December 22d, 1774* (1775), 17.

4. Levi Hart, *Liberty Described and Recommended . . .* (1775), quotations on 10, 13, 10.

5. Moses Mather, *America's Appeal to The Impartial World*, appendix (1775).

6. Samuel West, *A Sermon Preached Before the Honorable Council* (1776), 13.

7. Levi Frisbie, *An Oration on the Peace* (1783), 16.

8. Zabdiel Adams, *The Evil Designs of Men Made Subservient by God to the Public Good* . . . (1783), 25.

Acknowledgments

While researching and writing this book, I received generous support from a large number of people. No one was more important than Susan C. Breen, whose trenchant criticism—she would call it common sense—forced me to push the analysis of the American Revolution in fresh and exciting ways. It has been a privilege as well as a pleasure to live with such a gifted editor. Patrick Griffin, a talented historian of the British Empire, explained how the experience of the Irish people during their own revolution was relevant to the American Revolution, and during long walks in Dublin, he helped me to appreciate more fully the passions and frustrations that continue to drive popular resistance to political oppression. To Thomas LeBien, my editor at Harvard University Press, I owe a special debt. With unfailing patience and creative insight he encouraged me to put forward an interpretation of the American Revolution that gave ordinary people a major voice in the formation of a new political culture.

Several research institutions made it possible for me to work in congenial environments surrounded by splendid colleagues. I greatly appreciate how Annette Meyer and Isabella Schopp welcomed me at the Ludwig Maximilians University, Munich, Center for Advanced Studies. Michael Hochgenschwender sponsored my residency in Munich. I also enjoyed conversations with Christof Mauch, director of the Rachel Carson Center for Environment and Society, Munich. For several months I was able to use the impressive resources of the Rockefeller Library, Colonial Williamsburg. For access to these materials I thank Ted Maris-Wolf and Carl Childs. Northwestern University allowed me to use key digital resources. Jack Marietta instructed me about the complexities of the legal system in revolutionary Pennsylvania. I am especially indebted to James Hrdlicka, who provided invaluable notes he had taken in the Massachusetts Archives. My appointment as the John W. Kluge Professor of American Law and Governance at the Library of Congress allowed me to carry out research in a community of generous and helpful scholars.

At various times friends offered advice and corrected errors: Michael Lammert, Larry Hewes, James Hostetler, Eliga Gould, Joyce Chaplin, Andrew O'Shaughnessy, Peter Onuf, Max Edelson, Hermann Wellenreuther, Andrew Wylie, Mark McGarvie, Howard Pashman, Donald Johnson, Walter Woodward, and Harvey Whitfield. Two people working at Harvard University Press deserve special praise: Kate Brick and Sonya Bonczek.

Index